'All things are poison and nothing is without poison.
It is the dose that makes a thing poisonous.'

PARACELSUS, FATHER OF MODERN TOXICOLOGY (1493-1541)

STANLEY FELDMAN & VINCENT MARKS

PANIC NATION

EXPOSING THE MYTHS WE'RE TOLD ABOUT FOOD AND HEALTH

JOHN BLAKE

Published by John Blake Publishing Ltd,
3 Bramber Court, 2 Bramber Road,
London W14 9PB, England

www.blake.co.uk

This edition first published in paperback in 2006

ISBN 1 84454 271 8
ISBN 978 1 84454 271 0

British Library Cataloguing-in-Publication Data:

A catalogue record for this book is available from the British Library.

Design by www.envydesign.co.uk

Printed and bound in Great Britain by Bookmarque

1 3 5 7 9 10 8 6 4 2

© Text copyright Stanley Feldman and Vincent Marks

Frontispiece © Wellcome

Every attempt has been made to contact the relevant copyright-holders,
but some were unobtainable. We would be grateful if the appropriate people
could contact us.

Sketches by Mike Mosedale

Papers used by John Blake Publishing are natural, recyclable products made from
wood grown in sustainable forests. The manufacturing processes conform to the
environmental regulations of the country of origin.

Dedicated to Carole and Averil for their patience, understanding and love.

PRAISE FOR THE FIRST EDITION

'A bold book... thought provoking – *Panic Nation* sets out to demonstrate that, when it comes to food, we are collectively the victims of an incredible amount of hogwash... It is hard not to concede that they have a point... the arguments are sensible and even-handed. The authors do not deny that the food we eat affects us, or that it is important to eat healthily. What they do say is that our ability to look rationally at the issues is hampered by the prevalence of all sorts of myths.'

New Statesman

'This book should be read – and then recommended by word of mouth – because it deals with matters that no free press, motivated by mass circulation profits, can afford to tolerate. Truly impressive.'

Catholic Herald

'Could the ban on the pesticide DDT have been responsible for as many deaths as Hitler and Stalin? Could a new generation of children be plagued by measles because of hysteria against immunisation? *Panic Nation* makes for fascinating and provocative reading.'

Irish Independent

'This unique collection of essays debunks the scare mongering that bombards us about the safety of our food and its effects on our health. Written by experts on each topic covered, it presents some surprising facts, such as that salt does not raise your blood pressure and food does not affect the amount of cholesterol in your blood. A good read for anyone looking for the truth among the panicked headlines that determine what goes on our plates. Controversial, but Feldman and Marks do have the facts at hand.'

The Good Book Guide

'After reading Marks and Feldman's look at health scares, you will learn to ignore those news items based on "scientific evidence", outlawing yet another basic food. Moderation and good sense will be all that's needed, together with Marks and Feldman's guide to separate the truth from the lies.'

Publishing News

'*Panic Nation* provides an interesting insight into the way that tabloid fascination with scare stories can spiral out of control, and gives readers an idea of how they can avoid putting themselves at risk without believing everything that they hear.'

Farmers Guardian

ACKNOWLEDGEMENTS

A glance at the list of distinguished contributors will reveal that this book is very much a joint effort; indeed, without the enthusiastic support of these experts the work would not carry as much authority as it does. We are indebted to the members of the Millennium Society who have helped us in identifying topics that they felt needed to be covered in the book.

Scientists are used to communicating with each other in a genre that is often difficult for those outside their circle to understand. We are indebted to Jennie Bristow for her careful editing of the manuscripts so as to reduce any technical jargon to a minimum and to ensure that all the contributions are presented in a uniform, readily understandable style.

We are grateful for the assistance and encouragement of our publisher, John Blake, and to his staff, who have helped nurse the book through to this new edition. We would like to acknowledge the help of our wives, for the guidance provided by their suggestions and criticisms, and the assistance of Michaela Bergman, one of our 'guinea pig' readers, who, together with those on board the yacht *Holiday VII*, helped shape the way in which the various contributions have been presented in the book.

EDITORS

Stanley Feldman gave up his biochemistry thesis on the metabolism of the woodlouse to study medicine in 1950. Qualified (hons) Westminster Medical School 1955. He trained as an anaesthetist at Westminster Hospital, Research Fellow at University Washington USA 1957–58. Senior Lecturer Postgraduate Medical School, 1962. Adviser in Post Studies Faculty Anaesthetist 1965–70. Visiting Professor Stanford University USA 1967–68. Higginbotham Lecturer Dallas, Frederickson Orator Emory. Member Senate University London, Chair of Anaesthesia University London at Charing Cross and Westminster Medical Schools (later Imperial College School Medicine). Research adviser Royal National Orthopaedic Hospital 1994–97. Examiner in physiology for Faculty Anaesthetists, College of Surgeons and Dental Faculty.

Author/Editor of 12 textbooks on anaesthesia, including *Scientific Foundations of Anaesthesia*, *Mechanism of Action of Drugs* and *Drugs in Anaesthesia*. Editor *Journal Anaesthetic Pharmacology Review*. Contributor to the *Encyclopaedia Britannica*.

He has published over 100 peer-reviewed papers on

molecular mechanisms of drug action and post-graduate education. His most recent publication is *Poison Arrows* (Metro Publishing, 2005).

The author of several textbooks, **Vincent Marks** went from Tottenham County School on a State Scholarship in 1948 to read medicine at Oxford. Since 1970, he has been Professor, now Emeritus, of Clinical Biochemistry at the University of Surrey in Guildford. Known internationally for his research on hypoglycaemia and diabetes, he has appeared as an expert witness in some of the world's most famous trials such as those of Claus von Bulow in America, Beverley Allitt in England and Colin Bouwer in New Zealand. His work on intestinal hormones led him to designate GIP the obesity hormone and his description of muesli-belt nutrition established him as one of the country's best-known nutritionists. A former president of the Association of Clinical Biochemists and erstwhile vice president of the Royal College of Pathologists, Vincent was a founder member of HealthWatch. He is now semi-retired and lives in Haslemere with his wife Averil. Both their children are lawyers.

NOTES ON CONTRIBUTORS

Professor **Paul Aichroth**, MS, FRCS, was a consultant orthopaedic surgeon at the Westminster, Chelsea & Westminster and the Westminster Children's Hospitals over many years. His private work was undertaken mainly at the Wellington Hospital where he was Director of the Knee Surgery Unit. He is now Visiting Professor in the Department of Surgery, Imperial College, and continues teaching there. He exercises regularly!

Dr **David A Bender** has a BSc in Biochemistry (University of Birmingham) and a PhD from the University of London; since 1970, he has taught nutrition and biochemistry to medical students and general students. He is currently Sub-Dean (teaching) of the Royal Free Hospital and University College Medical School and a senior lecturer in the Department of Biochemistry of University College London. In addition to over 100 research publications in nutritional biochemistry, he has written 16 textbooks and contributed chapters to others. He is Editor-in-Chief of *Nutrition Research Reviews* and an Executive Editor of the *Journal of the Science of Food and Agriculture*.

Dr **Michael Fitzpatrick** has been a general practitioner in East London for the past twenty years. He has written on a wide range of medical and political subjects, including AIDS, addictions and health scares for both medical publications and the mainstream media. He writes columns in *The Lancet* and the *British Journal of General Practice* and is a regular contributor to the online magazine *spiked* (www.spiked-online.com). He has also appeared frequently on radio and television, and in 1997 produced a critical programme on 'parenting' for the BBC. His book *The Tyranny of Health: Doctors and the Regulation of Lifestyle* was published by Routledge in 2001. His critique of complementary medicine is included in *Alternative Medicine – Should We Swallow It?*, published by the Institute of Ideas/Hodder and Stoughton in 2002. His latest book, *MMR and Autism: What Parents Need To Know* (Routledge) was published in 2004.

The late **Maurice Hanssen**'s interest in additives began a long time before they were identified on the pack. As a director of a leading manufacturer of wines and foods, he questioned why they were using additives which seemed unnecessary and found equally good or better products could be made without using so many. Later he became a successful consultant on food and health.

Author of 28 books including the bestseller *E for Additives*, he has sold over two and a half million copies in all. As a Chambellan of the Ordre des Coteaux de Champagne and a Lauréat of the World Master Chefs Society, he believed that our food should be delicious, healthy and fun. He died in 2005.

Professor **John Henry** followed a career in general medicine and clinical toxicology at Guy's and St Thomas' Hospitals. He was appointed to the Chair in Accident and Emergency Medicine at Imperial College School of Medicine in 1997 and made a Consultant at St Mary's Hospital London. He has researched and written widely, and his interests cover all forms of acute poisoning and the medical complications of illicit drugs.

Mick Hume is editor of the online magazine *spiked* (www.spiked-online.com) and a columnist for *The Times*.

Dr **Lakshman Karalliedde** graduated from the University of Colombo, Sri Lanka and did his post-graduate training in anaesthesia at the Westminster and Royal Northern Hospitals London. At the Faculty of Medicine, Peradeniya, Sri Lanka, he developed a special interest in organophosphorus insecticide poisoning and abuse and described the 'Intermediate Syndrome' of organophosphate poisoning. He resigned his post in Sri Lanka as Head of the Department of Anaesthesiology to return to the UK where he served as Senior Lecturer in Anaesthetics at United Medical & Dental Schools of Guy's & St Thomas' before joining the Medical Toxicology Unit of the Guy's & St Thomas' NHS Trust where he has been a consultant toxicologist for the past seven years. He was lead editor of *Organophosphates & Health* (Imperial College Press) and *Handbook of Drug Interactions* (Hodder Arnold) and has published widely on organophosphate and pesticide poisoning, contributing to many textbooks including *Davidson's Principles & Practice of Medicine*.

Dr **Malcolm Kendrick** is a medical doctor who has spent many years researching the causes of heart disease. He designed and set up the educational website for the European Society of

Cardiology (ESC) and worked closely with a number of International Medical Societies to develop a Europe-wide system of Continuing Medical Education. He also set up the first website for the National Institute of Clinical Excellence (NICE). Malcolm has written widely on heart disease and has been critical of the so-called 'cholesterol hypothesis' for many years. Some of his more provocative writing on the area can be found at the website of the International Network of Cholesterol Sceptics (www.thincs.org).

Professor, Sir **Peter Lachmann** is a medical immunologist. He is Emeritus Professor of Immunology in the University of Cambridge and a Fellow of Christ's College. He is also President of the Federation of European Academies of Medicine.

He was the founder President of the UK Academy of Medical Sciences (1998–2002); Biological Secretary of the Royal Society (1993–98) and President of the Royal College of Pathologists (1990–93). He served on UNESCO's international bioethics committee from 1993–98.

For the Royal Society, he has chaired working groups on BSE and on GMOs.

Dr **James Le Fanu** is a general practitioner in South London and medical columnist of the *Sunday* and *Daily Telegraph*. He graduated from Cambridge University and the Royal London Hospital in 1974 and held junior hospital posts at Whipps Cross Hospital, the Royal Free, St Mary's and the Bristol Royal Infirmary. He has made original contributions to medical journals on many subjects including the threat of a heterosexual AIDS epidemic, passive smoking, poverty and health and the dietary causes of heart disease. His history of post-war medicine, *The Rise and Fall of Modern Medicine*, was published by Little, Brown in June 1999.

Dr **Sandy Macnair** qualified in medicine from St Andrews University and, after a stint in general practice, joined the pharmaceutical industry organising both fundamental and clinical research for several companies in Europe, Africa, Australasia and North America. Latterly, he has been an independent consultant to a number of primary food producers including those of sugar, eggs, milk and salt, with regard to their impact on the public health.

Professor **Sam Shuster** is Emeritus Professor of Dermatology, University of Newcastle Upon Tyne and Honorary Consultant to the Department of Dermatology, Norfolk and Norwich University Hospital. He qualified in medicine at UCL, followed by a PhD in physiology, and, after junior clinical and research posts in the Royal Postgraduate School of Medicine, was appointed Lecturer in Medicine in the Welsh National School of Medicine. An interest in endocrinology and metabolism led on to dermatological research, and he started the Skin Research Unit in The Institute of Dermatology, and was subsequently appointed to the Chair of Dermatology in Newcastle, then the main centre for skin research in the UK. He was President of The European Society for Dermatological Research and a member of many academic and government committees. He has published many papers and books on clinical and fundamental dermatological research, including aging, UV radiation, and basic and clinical pharmacology; he has an interest in sports medicine.

Lord Taverne – **Dick Taverne** QC – has been an influential voice in politics for many years. As a Labour MP, he become Financial Secretary to the Treasury; in 1973, he stood and was elected as an Independent Social Democrat and today he sits in the House of Lords as a Liberal Democrat. Recently his main interest has been science and society and three years ago he founded the charity Sense About Science to promote the evidence-based approach to scientific issues. He is the author of *The March of Unreason: Science, Democracy and the New Fundamentalism* published in 2005.

CONTENTS

Preface   xxiii

Introduction: Panic Nation   1

Prologue: Whose Opinion Can We Trust?   13

PART ONE: FOOD SCARES

Chapter One: Obesity   25

Chapter Two: Junk Food   37

Chapter Three: Organic Food   47

Chapter Four: The Great Cholesterol Myth   57

Chapter Five: Sugar   73

Chapter Six: Salt   83

Chapter Seven: Water   95

Chapter Eight: Tea, Coffee and Caffeine   101

Chapter Nine: Alcohol   109

Chapter Ten: Pesticides in Food   119

Chapter Eleven: Food Additives: How Safe,
How Valuable?   127

PART TWO: DIETS

Chapter Twelve: Healthy Eating 139

Chapter Thirteen: The Epidemic of Diet Books 151

Chapter Fourteen: Diet and Disease 161

Chapter Fifteen: School Dinners 173

Chapter Sixteen: You Are Not What You Eat 181

Chapter Seventeen: Food Allergies 185

Chapter Eighteen: Detoxification 191

Chapter Nineteen: Food Labelling 199

Chapter Twenty: Vitamins, Minerals and
Other Supplements 207

Chapter Twenty-one: Genetically Modified Organisms 225

Chapter Twenty-two: Transmissible Spongiform
Encephalopathies – BSE and vCJD 237

PART THREE: HEALTHY LIVING

Chapter Twenty-three: Sun and the Skin:
A Violation of Truth 259

Chapter Twenty-four: Complementary Medicine:
Integrated Waffle? 271

Chapter Twenty-five: Alternative Medicines and
Herbal Remedies 279

Chapter Twenty-six: Exercise 287

Chapter Twenty-seven: The Smokescreen of
Passive Smoking 293

Chapter Twenty-eight: The Air We Breathe   303

Chapter Twenty-nine: The MMR Story   309

PART FOUR: MYTH INTERPRETATION

Chapter Thirty: The Harm That Pressure Groups Can Cause 323

Chapter Thirty-one: The Misuse of Numbers   335

Chapter Thirty-two: Epidemiology   351

Further Reading   363

PREFACE

BY STANLEY FELDMAN
AND VINCENT MARKS

'We ought to recourse to experimentation and not
suffer ourselves to be deluded by unfounded theory
or specious argument.'
ABBÉ FELICE FONTANA, 1775

This book is an attempt to set the record straight, to counter
'unfounded theory and specious argument'. We are being
scared witless by a mixture of half-truths, tendentious beliefs and
unsubstantiated opinions that are presented in the media as
incontrovertible, scientifically proven facts. Many of these ideas
have originated from overzealous pressure groups, from
presentations by special-interest lobbies or from self-styled
gurus. The more improbable the story, the more attention it
receives from a press hungry for sensational news. These stories
are seldom analysed or their contents challenged by the scientific
community. As a result, many of these ideas have become
accepted as self-evident truths, by the public and by responsible
official bodies who lack the knowledge or the political will to
challenge them.

This creates an aura of uncertainty that makes us susceptible
to the claims of those who tell us that they can make us healthy,

prevent disease, ensure our children are all geniuses and make us live longer. Rather than risk the possibility of coming to harm, we accept even the most improbable suggestion that they propose. As though gripped by a semireligious conversion, we condemn this or that food as being 'junk'; we pay over the odds for food termed 'organic', although we know it possess no extra power; we spend millions of pounds on magic potions, treatments and herbal medicines that have been demonstrated to be useless; we eat silly diets in the ill-founded belief that they will make us happier or live longer. We are scared off GM foods, although they have been eaten without any ill effects by a third of the world for over seven years. Even though the gurus of this modern cult turn out, time and again, to be no more than witch doctors in modern dress, they still scare us to the point where we become irrational and accept their brew of pseudoscience and magic.

The idea for the book was borne out of our frustration at the credence given to the avalanche of hyped, improbable or inaccurate scare stories that defy reason and fuel what Mick Hume has described as an irrational 'epidemic of epidemics'.

The frustration and anger at the scientific community's inability to counter this insidious drip feed of scare stories came to a head at a meeting of the Millennium Club in 2004. At this meeting a group of senior academic doctors and scientists interested in healthcare problems suggested that it was time to set the record straight. The idea for this book was to persuade a group of truly independent experts to examine the scientific evidence behind some of the current scare stories and to present it in a manner that would be easily understood by the general public. The aim was to explain what is known and what is probably true about a subject and to separate this from speculation and opinion. This resulted in the First Edition of this book. The book was so popular that we have been encouraged to update it, and to add many new chapters. In this edition we have concentrated on those myths and fantasies that concern food, diet and lifestyle.

To this end we have sought contributions from experts who are scientists, academic doctors and independent journalists who have proven expertise in the subject on which they have been invited to write. Once again, we have asked them to present the facts behind these issues so that readers can determine for themselves where the truth lies.

Each contribution represents the interpretation put on the facts by its author and does not necessarily reflect the collective opinion of the editors or all the contributors.

If we have succeeded in persuading the reader to think again about the 'unfounded theories and specious arguments' with which we are bombarded, it will have served part of its purpose of being an interesting, informative and enjoyable read.

INTODUCTION: PANIC NATION

BY MICK HUME

At the start of the twenty-first century, we in the West enjoy higher standards of living, health and diet than at any moment in history. But you would be hard pressed to know it, from the miserabilist tone of much public discussion of the human condition.

At another time, the fact that people in a society lived far longer, healthier lives than their ancestors might reasonably have been thought a cause for some celebration. Today, however, we often appear unhealthily obsessed with looking on the dark side of life and worrying about our health. Even where no major health problem appears evident in the present, there is a veritable epidemic of experts on hand to assure us that we are only storing up problems for the future, warning of the threat of supposed 'time bombs', be it the 'ageing time bomb', the 'obesity time bomb', the 'mobile-phone time bomb' or whatever. As yet, these alleged health time bombs have failed to explode as predicted –

remember the epidemic of heterosexual AIDS that was supposed to kill countless thousands in the UK, or the epidemic of vCJD ('human mad-cow disease') that was meant to leave behind up to half a million dead? Yet it seems there is always another 'time bomb' of one sort or another allegedly waiting in the wings to get us. In the same way, in recent years the government chief health officer has appeared to be suffering a bad case of 'epidemicitis', at various times describing the country as being in the grip of an epidemic of everything from flu to smoking.

Look at the list of current health panics and concerns that are addressed in this book. They cover a range of issues so wide that it might seem as if no part of the human physique or psyche has been left untouched by a huge wave of fresh diseases and disorders. Everything from our cholesterol levels to our intake of such everyday items as salt is now not only put under the laboratory microscope, but is highlighted in the daily news headlines as a potential health risk.

The list of health risks with which we have to contend grows longer almost by the day. It is well captured in the following A-to-Z (well, A-to-X, anyway) list of everything that, at least according to certain epidemiologists, is supposed be capable of causing cancer today:

> Acetaldehyde, acrylamide, acrylonitrile, abortion, agent orange, alar, alcohol, air pollution, Aldrin™, aflatoxin, arsenic, arsine, asbestos, asphalt fumes, atrazine, AZT, baby food, barbecued meat, benzene, benzidine, benzopyrene, beryllium, beta-carotene, betel nuts, birth control pills, bottled water, bracken, bread, breasts, bus stations, calcium channel blockers, cadmium, captan,

carbon black, carbon tetrachloride, careers for women, casual sex, car fumes, celery, charred foods, chewing gum, Chinese food, Chinese herbal supplements, chips, chloramphenicol, chlordane, chlorinated camphene, chlorinated water, chlorodiphenyl, chloroform, cholesterol, low cholesterol, chromium, coal tar, coffee, coke ovens, crackers, creosote, cyclamates, dairy products, deodorants, depleted uranium, depression, dichloroacetylene, DDT, dieldrin, diesel exhaust, diet soda, dimethyl sulphate, dinitrotoluene, dioxin, dioxane, epichlorohydrine, ethnic beliefs, ethylene acrylate, ethylene dibromide, ethylene dichloride, Ex-Lax™, fat, fluoridation, flying, formaldehyde, free radicals, fruit, gasoline, genes, gingerbread, global warming, gluteraldehyde, granite, grilled meat, Gulf war, hair dyes, hamburgers, *Heliobacter pylori*, hepatitis B virus, hexachlorobutadiene, hexachlorethane, high bone mass, HPMA, HRT, hydrazine, hydrogen peroxide, incense, infertility, jewellery, Kepone™, kissing, lack of exercise, laxatives, lead, left handedness, Lindane™, Listerine™, low fibre diet, magnetic fields, malonaldehyde, mammograms, manganese, marijuana, methyl bromide, methylene chloride, menopause, microwave ovens, milk hormones, mixed spices, mobile phones, MTBE, nickel, night lighting, night shifts, nitrates, not breast feeding, not having a twin, nuclear power plants, NutraSweet™, obesity, oestrogen, olestra, olive oil, orange juice, oxygenated gasoline, oyster sauce, ozone, ozone depletion, passive smoking, PCBs, peanuts, pesticides, pet birds, plastic IV bags, polio vaccine, potato crisps (chips), power lines, proteins, Prozac™, PVC, radio masts, radon, railway sleepers, red meat, Roundup™, saccharin, salt, selenium, semiconductor plants, shellfish, sick buildings, soy sauce, stress, strontium, styrene, sulphuric acid, sun beds, sunlight, sunscreen, talc, tetrachloroethylene, testosterone, tight bras, toast, toasters, tobacco, tooth fillings, toothpaste (with fluoride or bleach), train stations, trichloroethylene, under-arm shaving, unvented stoves, uranium, vegetables, vinyl bromide, vinyl chloride, vinyl fluoride, vinyl toys, vitamins, vitreous fibres, wallpaper, weedkiller (2-4 D), welding fumes, well water, weight gain, winter, wood dust, work, X-rays.

Or perhaps, to put it more succinctly, *being alive can give you cancer.*

Not so long ago, few would even have been aware of the existence of many of these issues, never mind worrying about them. Yet somehow our forebears seemed to survive perfectly well in blissful ignorance, their lifespan lengthening from generation to generation, despite often pursuing lifestyles and diets that would now be considered dangerously irresponsible.

So let us stand back from those headlines for a moment and ask ourselves, how could it be that many people now apparently feel threatened by so wide a range of new health risks? How could it be that so many different dangers suddenly appear to be menacing our society at the same time – and, moreover, at a time when as a society we are in such a state of rude public health?

It seems clear that this divergence between the facts of our longer, healthier lives and the perception of such varied and rising risks to our health cannot be explained by the specifics of any particular issue. It is not the details of our salt intake or of our cholesterol levels that make so many people open to these sorts of health concerns today. Rather, there must be some broader, overarching trends at work in our culture and society that can lend new weight to the fear of previously unimagined risks.

In order to grasp what is going on here, we must first come to terms with the broader spirit of the age.

For a start, we are faced today with a powerful cultural aversion to risk. Health risks that might have once have been brushed off as acceptable or negligible are now elevated into important issues of public concern. Thus 'passive smoking' – the inhalation of the smoke from other people's tobacco – has recently become the subject of a major health crusade across the West, despite the questionable evidence of the real effect of environmental tobacco smoke on public health, and the fact that fewer people now die of smoking-related diseases than in the past. In a climate where there no longer seems to be such a thing as an acceptable level of risk, many other minor health risks can be used to spark major overnight controversies.

Where health risks are concerned, it seems the orthodoxy now is always to assume the worst-case scenario to be the most likely one, however far-fetched. Humanity has always faced risks, and there has always been a debate about how to manage them. Today, however, unlike in the past, risk is seen not as something we can handle or perhaps even turn into opportunity, but as something that we suffer from and must be guarded against.

The assumption that we cannot cope with risk and uncertainty reached a new level when the *British Medical Journal* came out with the argument that the word *accident* should henceforth be banned, since such incidents were really avoidable if we took the proper precautions. Not only, it seems, is there no longer any such thing as a manageable risk, but it is apparently no longer acceptable to suggest that accidents will happen.

Underpinning this heightened desperation to avoid or limit risk is another powerful theme of contemporary culture: the notion of human vulnerability. Once the widespread assumption might have been (based on some sound historical evidence) that humanity could survive more or less whatever was thrown at it, that the resilience that had taken us from the caves to something approaching civilisation was pretty well indomitable. Today, the opposite tends to be assumed.

The default setting for the human condition is now widely seen as being a state of vulnerability and victimhood. The autonomous individual who stands on his or her own two feet appears to be an endangered species. Instead the assumption is that we are pretty pathetic specimens who must need professional intervention and advice to protect us from the problems of everyday life. We are a society on the couch, under the supervision of the therapeutic state.

The overwhelming fear of risk and the sense of humans as near-powerless victims of life have not only stoked irrational health panics but have helped to create an unhealthy attitude to health and illness in our society.

First, it means that there is a tendency to medicalise many of our problems, to redefine personal issues and characteristics as medical afflictions requiring professional intervention. Thus, everything from childish mischief making to shyness can now be labelled as a syndrome or a disorder, and drugs or treatment prescribed. This process of medicalisation has the effect both of relieving people of responsibility for their lives (how can those suffering medical conditions be blamed for the symptoms?), and of making them even more obsessive about health issues.

Second, as Dr Michael Fitzpatrick – GP and author of *The Tyranny of Health* – has argued, these trends have created a climate in which it is now deemed perfectly normal for us to be ill rather than well, and where health has been turned from something we took for granted into the goal of life for which we must self-consciously strive:

> In the recent past, health was regarded as the normal state of affairs and illness was considered an exceptional departure from normality, a transient state through which the patient passed... At the same time, illness has lost much of its stigma and even confers a series of socially approved identities – 'person with HIV/AIDS', 'cancer survivor', 'sufferer from stress', 'victim of bullying' – confirmed by patient organisations, celebrity sponsorship, soap opera story lines, autobiographical accounts and other forms of media coverage.[3]

Who is responsible for bringing about this unhealthy state of affairs? It is common to blame outbreaks of irrationality and health panics on stupid members of the public, now sometimes known as 'the worried well', who are whipped up into a moblike frenzy by 'the meejah'. The media certainly play a key role in setting the public mood. But it is important not to underestimate the extent to which these problems emanate from the top of society downwards – starting with the government and the political class. They have done more than anybody to worry the well.

Since the panic about a SARS epidemic gripped the world in 2003, the New Labour government's policy towards issues such as bioterrorism or SARS in the UK has been based on the principle of 'organised paranoia'. That memorable but little-known phrase was coined at the time by Geoff Mulgan, then the head of the powerful Downing Street Performance and Innovation Unit. Mulgan was speaking at a conference entitled 'Panic Attack: interrogating our obsession with risk', organised by the online magazine *spiked* at the Royal Institution in May 2003. He had a wry little smile on his face when he used those words. But he definitely was not joking.

Mulgan suggested that, through elevating this organised paranoia into a principle informing policy planning, the government hoped to become better at spotting new risks such as SARS, BSE and bioterrorism 'before they become evident'. But how exactly do the seers and oracles of Whitehall hope to identify a potential risk before it has even become visible? By gazing into a crystal ball, perhaps?

Almost, it seems. The modern political equivalent of the crystal ball is the 'what if?' scenario, and this is increasingly becoming the stuff of policy-planning discussions on both sides of the Atlantic, especially post-9/11. It means that policymakers dream up fantasy disasters (what if a terrorist infected with SARS crashed a petrol tanker into a nuclear power station?), and then try to plan to deal with these hypothetical crises.

The reaction to SARS became a powerful symbol of what is wrong. Here was a new but relatively minor epidemic that, in a sane society, would demand a serious response from the medical and epidemiological authorities.

In our apparently less-than-sane society however, officials

from the World Health Organisation (WHO) downwards treated SARS as a cross between the Black Plague and a bioterror attack, quarantining entire cities and damaging whole economies. Meanwhile people across the world could be seen walking around wearing useless paper masks, a sort of modern equivalent of the medieval amulets used to ward off evil. The SARS panic turned into an outstanding example of the cure being worse than the disease, the panic causing more damage in the real world than any fantastic 'what if?' scenario is likely to.

Mulgan's remarks should serve to remind us that the suffocating safety-first spirit of the age comes from the top down. Major political academic and scientific institutions now appear to be obsessed with risk management/avoidance, and infected with the outlook of organised paranoia. The worst fear of those in authority is now to be accused of not taking sufficiently stringent precautions to ward off some potential, or even hypothetical, threat to public health.

The watershed in this came with the BSE/vCJD crisis of the 1990s. The authorities were widely – and arguably unfairly – blamed for not doing enough to foresee and forestall that disaster for British farming. The Phillips Report into the disaster advised that the government should in future adopt a strict 'precautionary approach' at the hint of any potential public-health problem. Even though the apocalyptic predictions about a vCJD epidemic on which the Phillips approach was based proved entirely unfounded, the precautionary principle has been institutionalised in government policies ever since. It essentially dictates that a lack of hard evidence about a possible risk is no excuse for postponing official intervention and public-health warnings.

The impact can be seen in something like the government-backed Stewart Inquiry of 1999 into the safety of mobile phones, which established that there no evidence of a health risk – but then concluded that, regardless of the evidence, we should all adopt a precautionary approach to using the things anyway. In 2005, the official UK Food Standards Agency launched a high-profile PR campaign around the alleged risk posed by the Sudan 1 food dye. The presence of traces of the banned colouring in some processed foods (so minute that anybody would need to eat a supermarket full of the stuff to suffer so much as a stomach ache), became the pretext for ordering the recall of millions of pounds' worth of perfectly edible food. Every expert knew there was no real risk of harm to public health; one put the risk of eating some of the contaminated processed food on a par with smoking one cigarette in an entire lifetime. But they went ahead and banned it anyway, threatening shopkeepers with prison for selling safe food, just as a precaution.

The authorities' hope is that taking pre-emptive action will reassure the public and forestall future health panics. The result, however, is often the precise opposite. In the risk-conscious climate discussed above, overblown precautionary measures only confirm many people's suspicions that there is a real problem. And self-conscious government attempts to show that it is doing something can only lead to escalating demands for it to do more.

It is possible to see how this works itself out in relation to the avian-flu issue as it has developed in the UK over the past couple of years. For its part, the New Labour government has tried to hold the line against hysteria and appear reasonable, issuing a consistent 'don't panic' message. But it has been repeatedly outbid by opposition politicians, experts, campaigners and media voices accusing it of complacency or a cover-up, and demanding more and more precautionary measures. In this, it lies at the heart of government policy on everything from food dye to mobile phones, and by emphasising the need to reduce risk. Now, fearful of being accused of not intervening enough to prevent a potential threat to public health (almost the most serious charge a politician can face these days), the government's response is to up the ante further, to try to demonstrate that it is fully prepared.

There have been many official appeals to remain calm and attempts to put the risk of bird flu in perspective (such as the chief scientist's assessment that, even if avian flu did infect our poultry population, the odds of anybody in Britain contracting it would be about 100 million to one). But these would be far more convincing if they were not accompanied by reports of the government's plans to deal with a hypothetical devastating pandemic. These measures include plans to close schools, reportedly to keep the predicted number of deaths among children down to 50,000 instead of 100,000 (that should reassure the parents); plans to dig 'plague pit-style' mass graves to accommodate the countless thousands of expected corpses; and plans to give GPs and medical staff armed escorts to beat off the predicted mobs of vaccine-hunting people. It is worth recalling that these are government measures designed to deal with a pandemic to be caused by a strain of the H5N1 subtype of the bird-flu virus that could pass easily from human to human – a strain that does not actually exist anywhere in the world, and may never do so. That is organised paranoia in action. If headless-chicken syndrome were to catch hold of the country in relation to bird flu, the infection will have spread from the top of the body politic downwards.

The confusion over bird flu confirms how the creeping spread of the politics of fear and the rise of risk-aversion makes our society easy prey to any panic in matters of personal health. We have reached the point where we often seem to live in a sort of Chicken Little culture, in which many are predisposed to panic about the sky falling in every time an acorn falls on their head (or a trace of nut appears in their food). Although the sky is not falling on our heads yet, some who should know better do seem to be suffering from clouds on the brain.

There is a crying need for a sober and rational presentation of the facts about health today, to counter the entrepreneurial scaremongers and the professional panic merchants. This book is the place to start. Ultimately winning the arguments, however, will also require waging a culture war against the miserabilist spirit of our times, which provides such a fertile environment for the spread of sick ideas about health, risk and humanity.

PROLOGUE: WHOSE OPINION CAN WE TRUST?

BY STANLEY FELDMAN
AND VINCENT MARKS

We are bombarded with advice on healthy living. If everyone agreed upon a particular formula that would ensure good health and long life we would all sign up for it. Unfortunately, there is no utopian life plan and little unanimity of opinion. As a result we do not know whose opinion to follow and whose to ignore. As a prelude to assessing the value of all this advice, we must consider whose views are sensible and reliable. Whose opinion can we trust?

Frederick II of Germany wrote in the thirteenth century: 'one ought not to believe anything, save that which can be proven by nature and the force of reason'. His views were echoed in the sixteenth century by the French essayist Montaigne: 'I would have every man write of that which he knows.' The implication was that one must distinguish between opinion, which is that which one *thinks* may be true, and fact. Only fact is a fit basis for promulgating new ideas. The basis of essay writing is to use observed fact as a springboard from which to launch opinion. The word itself comes from the French verb *essayer*, to test or try; and it was the essay form that Montaigne used as a means of trying out his own ideas.

Today, it is all too common to find would-be Montaignes starting with an opinion and using it as though it were fact. This leaves us with the difficult problem of separating reliable, objective fact from opinion. If two people present diverging views on a subject, whom should one trust? Which one is presenting fact and which opinion?

This should be a relatively simple exercise, but, because of sophistry, spin and the deliberate misinterpretation of information, it has become increasing difficult to distinguish true facts from the plethora of dubious opinions with which we are constantly bombarded. Fact is verifiable information, numbers or observations, spontaneous or experimental, that can be reliably reproduced, and is compatible with the existing web of knowledge. Unfortunately, the misinformation explosion has swamped factual stories. The improbable sells more newspapers than the probable. The more times an improbable, unsupported story is reported, the more it enters into the folklore of what 'everybody knows'.

Ask anyone how many people died in the Chernobyl disaster and the response is likely to be that 'everyone knows' it was hundreds or thousands. We have been deliberately led to believe this story by those opposed to nuclear energy. In fact the World Health Organisation (WHO) reported in 2003 that there were fewer than 40 deaths in the 20 years following the disaster. Although there was a significant increase in the number of cases of cancer of the thyroid, there was not any increase noticed in the incidence of leukaemia or birth defects.

Who is going to give us accurate, unbiased information that we can trust? We should be able to trust various governmental bodies and independent broadcasters such as the BBC. Unfortunately, even these usually reliable bodies fall into the misinformation trap. The BBC, the government, its Chief Medical Officer and the Food Standards Agency, to take some examples, may not set out to be partisan or to push deliberate falsehoods, but the information presented, even by these authoritative bodies, is subject to the bias of the presenter and his or her particular interpretation of information. The result is that too often opinion becomes presented as fact.

There seems to be a mistaken belief within the BBC that equal weight must be given to both sides of a problem. The author Douglas Adams put it succinctly when he wrote, 'All opinions are not equal. Some are a great deal more robust, sophisticated and well supported in logic and argument than others.' The concept that fair play demands that all opinions be treated equally is nonsense. But today we frequently see warriors against reason paraded as heroes on the BBC, representing this or that irrational pressure group. The BBC gives them credibility. Radio 4's *Woman's Hour* recently gave air time to an advocate of coffee enemas who claimed it had cured his cancer. They failed to explain why taking coffee by this somewhat curious route should be better than taking it by mouth. By giving this contributor the same opportunity as an expert, to present a totally ludicrous opinion on the air, the BBC implied that his views have the same legitimacy as those of an informed spokesperson on the subject. The BBC bestows an undeserved and inappropriate authority on the advocates of silly therapies, unproven diets and irrational scare stories. Their ideas gain an undeserved credence as a result of the media obsession with providing a 'balanced debate'.

The government warning against eating too much salt sits uneasily with its own advice to replace both the water and salt lost in hot weather, and also with the statement in its own briefing document, published by the Parliamentary Office of Science and Technology (POST) in 2004, that the 'Intersalt study (1997), the largest ever carried out, found no correlation between salt intake and blood pressure'.

The report of the Parliamentary Select Committee in 2004, as reported by the BBC, stated that obesity has increased 400 per cent in 25 years – when international agreement on the interpretation of the measurement of obesity by the body-mass index (BMI), was established only about fifteen years ago. Before that time the very different, Metropolitan Life Insurance tables were used as an index of obesity.

The Food Standards Agency, usually a source of reliable information, has become a political, pioneering body that believes children will not get fat if vending machines sell fruit juice and milk rather than cola, despite the fact that fruit juice contains slightly more calories. A recent pronouncement that as a result of the epidemic of obesity the present generation will have a shorter life expectancy than their parents is silly specious propaganda: how can one know the life expectancy of a generation until most of them have died?

So how can we tell?

This, then, is the problem: how do we know that what we are being told is reliable and factual? The first step is to exclude the phoneys, the Flat Earth Society proponents and those who claim that meditation, wearing blue beads or standing on your head for half an hour each day or similar will cure cancer. Their ideas are so ludicrous that they can be readily spotted. It is a failing of our society, with all its laws to protect the consumer, that we allow such charlatans to prey upon the desperate plight of sick or ignorant people.

More plausible are the self-promoting experts who try to scare us with stories of impending doom. They talk in meaningless slogans such as 'freeing your spiritual self' (from what? one asks); 'the flooding of Leningrad and London' (there was little evidence of a rise in the sea level, in the vulnerable Seychelles, in the five years up to 2003); 'concreting over the countryside' (looking down on the British countryside from an aeroplane at a few thousand feet, you cannot even spot the motorways); Frankenstein foods (GM food has been on sale in many countries for years and no ill effect has been reported); 'epidemic of obesity' (since when has fatness been a contagious disease?); and so on. The ideas behind their slogans are scientifically improbable, but refuting them with absolute certainty is virtually impossible.

So, when an interviewer asks a scientist, 'Can you rule out the possibility that London may be flooded in the future?', to which of course the scientist cannot categorically answer no, it results in the headline: 'SCIENTIST CONFIRMS LONDON MAY FLOOD'.

Having eliminated the pedlars of the irrational, one is left with the advocates of the plausible. Unless one is particularly well informed, one has to rely on the advice of an expert as to what is likely to be fact and what is opinion. The problem then becomes, who is an expert?

We tend to look to the universities for scholarly advice. By and large the older, major universities are more demanding in the qualifications of their academic staff than the newer ones, and the older mainstream areas of study have a more predictable level of scientific attainment. Experts from universities with a well-established reputation for research are likely to be more reliable, but may also be more reluctant to accept valid but novel or iconoclastic ideas. Few of us can check the curriculum vitae or the source of information used by everyone claiming to be an expert, but in certain circumstances credibility can be inferred from the publication in which it appeared. Table 1 indicates a progression of reliability of the information in peer-reviewed journals to statements by propagandists and pressure groups.

TABLE 1

Type of information	Type of author	Type of publication	Intended audience
Primary	Scientists and epidemiologists	Research papers in peer-reviewed journals	Other researchers in the same field
Secondary	Research and academic scientists	Scientific reviews in peer-reviewed journals	Academics and teachers
Tertiary	Academic authors and scientists; expert committees	Monographs, textbooks, consensus reports	Students, practitioners and popularists
Quaternary	Popularists	Books for the layman, science-based radio and TV programmes and interviews	'Intellectual' members of the public
Quinternary	Journalists	Newspapers, TV and radio, magazines,	The public
Sexternary	Copywriters	Adverts and editorials	Intended customers
Septernary	Propagandists	Press statements, interviews	The public
Others: folklore, shop assistants, 'health writers'			

Medicine is a more rigorous course of study than that of nursing or one of the allied therapies. It is reasonable, therefore, to believe that the opinion of a medical doctor is more likely to be credible than that of a therapist. Like all broad generalisations, this is subject to notable exceptions. There is no essential course of study that qualifies one to be called a 'health expert', or to call oneself a 'noninterventionist surgeon'. It is not necessary to study human physiology to become 'an expert' on nutrition or food (indeed a former chairman of the Food Standards Agency was a zoologist), whereas there is an essential core course of scientific study in order to become a doctor. Academic doctors are not necessarily more expert than practising ones, but because of the nature of their work they are more likely to question an opinion and to be more demanding in the standard of evidence before they will accept a statement as true.

Life would be much simpler and safer if we could immediately recognise an expert and rely upon his or her views as being authoritative. This was the concept behind the Lord Chief Justice's plea for arbitration panels to appoint a single expert witness whose opinion would be accepted by all in the civil courts. This would work if all expert opinions were based on agreed fact. Unfortunately, when it comes to interpreting the meaning of the facts it becomes a matter of individual, fallible opinion, or judgement. As a result, this worthy notion has had a limited impact, and we still have gladiatorial contests in all criminal cases and some civil ones between the opposing opinions of experts, a battle for the most believable – or the most glib.

So, how can we assess the views with which we are bombarded? We have to start by separating fact from opinion, then assess the reasonableness of interpretation of the evidence against scientific probability. Fact is something that is proven, can be reproduced and is consistent with other facts; opinion relies on a belief by the person making the proposition rather than proof of the proposal. We should ignore presentational gimmicks and slogans, and look for the core message. We have to assess the credibility and bias of the messenger along with his message. This is the concept behind the current philosophy of evidence-based medicine, or EBM. This is based on evaluation of the sources of information and has much to recommend it. Unfortunately, it perpetuates the Myth that it is possible to argue from the general to the particular rather than the other way round and could, if misapplied, lead to the practice of healthcare by protocol rather than the application of knowledge and judgement. Because a particular treatment is successful in the majority of patients, it does not necessarily imply that it is the best course of action in all patients.

In the preparation of this book, we have asked the authors to present what is known or is generally accepted as factual and what they consider probable and to separate it from that which is improbable or irrational. Scientists are aware that many of the commonly accepted beliefs in healthcare are based on the misconceptions that need to be exposed to scientific scrutiny. For this purpose we have asked our panel of experts, to write 'that which they know'.

At the end of the day, we must remember that, in the world of healthcare, things are getting better. The fact that we are living longer, healthier lives suggests that there cannot be anything terribly wrong with the air we breathe, the food we eat or the way we live. We must remember this in spite of the blandishments, threats, warnings and various campaigns by governments to make us eat this diet or that, to forgo a familiar habit or to exercise ourselves until we drop. It is a sobering thought, first expressed by John Locke in 1689 in his treatise *A Letter Concerning Toleration*: 'No man can be forced to be healthful, whether he will or no.' In a free society, individuals must judge for themselves what information they choose to heed and what they ignore. Whether they should be made to feel guilty for ignoring the evidence is a matter for debate.

Part One

FOOD SCARES

Chapter One

OBESITY

BY VINCENT MARKS

'Corpulence in America is regarded, along with
narcotic addiction, as something wicked, and I shall
not be surprised if soon we have a prohibition against
it in the name of national security.'
ASTWOOD, 1962

THE MYTH: Obesity is caused by eating the 'wrong kinds of food.
THE FACT: Obesity in humans is caused by eating too much.

Obesity has always been with us but, whereas in the past it was the prerogative of the rich, it is now the scourge of the poor. We are told by numerous newspapers articles, life-insurance companies' publicity material and governmental publications that it has reached 'epidemic proportions'. It is blamed on 'junk food', but the real reason for its increasing incidence is far more complicated.

Currently, obesity is labelled among the commonest causes of death worldwide and not only in the developed and affluent West – but the evidence is not there. The illnesses to which obesity predispose, such as diabetes, coronary heart disease and hypertension, are undoubtedly a major cause of death in the developed world but uncomplicated obesity is rarely so. It is nevertheless an important risk factor that can be theoretically, and in some cases practically, reduced

Obesity develops when energy intake exceeds energy expenditure. It will be maintained until this balance is reversed. The supply of food as well as the type of food is involved from the start. Until recently, food was plentiful only for the rich – the poor often lived at subsistence level, although they frequently performed more manual work over longer periods. Although now looked upon as a hazard to health, the ability to become fat in times when food was not constantly available could have had an important survival value in the past. The ability to get fat was a status symbol in deprived communities and those subject to periodic famines. It is still so in some parts of the world. People who were fat at the start of a famine would have a better chance of surviving than those who were thin.

However, being fat has become a cosmetic problem for the fashion-conscious over the past half-century or so, and it was the social desirability of being thin that produced the huge diet and weight-reduction industry – not the impact of obesity on health. This has now changed – at least in part – as the medical problems attributable to overweight and obesity have become increasing well recognised. Should we worry about getting fat? Yes, because in the long term overweight predisposes us to a variety of illnesses and a shortened life expectancy. Even though some very fat people live their full three score years and ten and more, most do not.

A lot depends on what you call overweight, fat and obese. They are not the same thing, though often loosely used as such, and definitions change. Until about twenty years or so ago the term *overweight* was applied to those who exceeded a hypothetical ideal weight derived from survival figures obtained by the Metropolitan Life Assurance Company, whose tables adorned most commercial weighing scales found in stations and other public places, but are now long since gone. A new way of expressing fatness that, made for ease of communication in epidemiological studies, became popular in the 1980s. Called the *body-mass index*, or BMI, it relates weight to height through a formula devised in the nineteenth century by a Belgian epidemiologist, Adolph Quetelet. A person's BMI is their weight in kilograms divided by the square of their height in metres. Although it has major shortcomings – it says nothing about the proportion of bodyweight that is fat, which is the real test of obesity – the BMI has become the recognised standard of measurement for fatness, although it does not relate to morbidity as well as other indicators, such as waist-to-hip ratio or even just waist measurement.

Most healthy young adults have a BMI of 20–25. Those with a BMI less than 20 are currently classified as underweight and those with a BMI of 25–30 as overweight or plump. A BMI of over 30 is arbitrarily classified as indicating obesity. Insurance company statistics and more recently large epidemiological studies reveal that people with BMIs under 20 or over 30 are poorer life risks than those with BMIs between 20 and 30. As people get older, there is a population shift from the lower to the upper half of this range. Plumpness in late middle and old age – BMIs of 25–30, especially in women – is not the health risk that it is in young and middle-aged adults; indeed it is an advantage for longevity.

Plumpness in childhood, often called 'puppy fat' when it

occurs in adolescents, is different and has only recently become the subject of intense media attention and public concern. Evidence linking it to adult obesity is conflicting. What is certain, though, is that the real hazard is *gross* obesity in childhood, which, in spite of what one reads in the media, is unusual and often due to genetic and metabolic defects, an increasingly large number of which are becoming identified.

Childhood obesity is a medical problem from the start, but how to distinguish it from benign, non-progressive plumpness has still to be resolved. Even the criteria for defining obesity in children are unclear. Though weight and height charts still have an important role to play in monitoring children's development, the BMI is less predictive of future events in them than in adults. Fat – or *adipose tissue*, to give it its technical name – constitutes a higher proportion of a woman's bodyweight than a man's. It is only when fat deposits become abnormally large – which can be difficult to determine, machines that are said to do so notwithstanding – that it becomes appropriate to talk of obesity. There are almost as many types of obesity as there are individuals afflicted by it. However, two main physical types can usually be distinguished.

Gynaecoid obesity, so called because it is more common in women, is associated with increased deposition of fat in and under the skin – especially below the waist – and is relatively benign. *Android obesity*, on the other hand, is much more malign. It is more common in men and due to massive deposition of fat within the abdominal cavity. It gives rise to what is often, but wrongly, described as a beer belly. People, including women, with this type of truncal obesity have larger waist than hip measurements, and their limbs are often surprisingly thin. They are sometimes described as apples in contrast to the fancifully described pear shape of those with gynaecoid obesity.

When truncal obesity is associated with certain biochemical abnormalities and/or high blood pressure, people with it are said to have the *metabolic syndrome*, but the usefulness of this term has been questioned. It is the catastrophic rise in prevalence of this truncal obesity, rather than of fatness itself, that is the major cause for concern. Neither type of obesity is an illness in its own right, but each predisposes to the development of incapacity or premature death. Diseases such as sleep apnoea, osteoarthritis of the lower limbs and hypertension are common to both, whereas diabetes and coronary heart disease are much commoner in people with truncal obesity

Like all conditions from which mankind suffers, obesity is the result of the interplay between nature, in the shape of genetic and antenatal factors, and nurture, principally in the shape of the availability of food. While this may seem obvious, it has not always been accepted. As recently as the beginning of the twentieth century, the link between food intake and obesity was appreciated by very few. Anecdotal personal experience suggested that fat people ate no more than thin ones – some of whom seemed to be bottomless pits into which food could be shovelled with seemingly little effect. There is no doubt that this perception is wrong.

Statistically, fat people both expend and consume more calories than thin people, although the overlap between them is enormous. This is mainly due to differences in resting metabolism – the amount of energy required just to keep the body warm – and the levels of physical activity or exercise. It is quite easy to show that quite subtle differences in food intake or energy expenditure could, over a period of many years, produce profound changes in body shape. For example, taking in the energy contained in just one knife-full of butter more than you expend every day would, after a year, theoretically cause a 2-kilogram gain in weight.

This simplistic approach to the causes of obesity belies its complexity. What is truly remarkable is how most people manage to maintain more or less the same weight once they reach adulthood without a conscious effort to control what they eat. It is as if they possessed a 'bodystat' analogous to a thermostat in a refrigerator. The mechanics of this bodystat are still being unravelled by biochemists and physiologists throughout the world, and by psychologists, sociologists and epidemiologists in individual communities.

The role of nature – genetics – rather than nurture in the process of getting fat has been known to farmers, veterinarians and experimentalists for over a hundred years, but was only recently established in human beings. This began with studies of the differences in the incidence of obesity in identical and nonidentical twins, where the effect of environment, especially access to food, could be minimised. Even more recent is recognition of the role played by intrauterine and early postnatal nutrition in the development of obesity and the conditions linked with it.

Gross obesity occurs in several very inbred strains of rodent. In one strain the specific gene responsible was given the name *ob* for *obesity*. Only mice inheriting a copy of the gene from both parents (*ob/ob*) develop a condition that led to their depositing so much fat that they weighed 4–5 times as much as their siblings who did not have the gene or had inherited just one copy of it. The fat ones lacked the ability to make a hormone called *leptin*, which, among its many properties, has the ability to suppress appetite. ob/ob mice eat ravenously until they are so fat they cannot get to their food. Even when fed only as much as their thin siblings, they still put on more weight. Over the past decade or so a similar condition has been recognised in human beings, although it is extremely rare. Another genetic type of obesity in mice causes a condition that resembles ob/ob, but is caused by an inability to respond to, rather than produce, leptin.

The idea that hormones played a part in controlling bodyweight began with the discovery that patients with thyrotoxicosis, caused by an overactive thyroid gland, often develop ravenous appetites yet lose weight. Conversely, those with an underactive thyroid often gain weight, though they very rarely become obese. Investigations into the role of the thyroid gland showed it played no part in the genesis of obesity. Later it was observed that many patients with rare tumours of the pancreas producing too much insulin also became very fat. In these patients with pancreatic tumours, insulinomas, this was because they were incorrectly advised to eat something when they felt symptoms of hypoglycaemia (low blood sugar) coming on rather than because it came naturally to them.

Now that a surgical cure for insulinoma has become simpler and safer, we no longer see the gross obesity we used to associate with this condition. Nevertheless, experience with insulinomas established a role for insulin in the genesis of obesity that has now been confirmed countless times. Paradoxically, voluntarily overeating also leads to increased production of insulin and of reduced sensitivity to some, though not all, of its actions. Which, in real life, is the chicken (overproduction of insulin) and which is the egg (overeating) is probably different from one individual to another.

Although insulin and other glandular products, such as thyroxine, cortisone and oestrogen, have long been known to be associated with obesity, it is only since the discovery of leptin that the part that hormones play in its production has been taken seriously by the scientific fraternity.

Several new hormones, many of them produced in the intestine itself, have been discovered in the past ten years or so that affect the control of appetite and disposition of food within the body after it has been absorbed. Contrary to early expectations, most fat people have more leptin in their blood than normal, so treating them with leptin is unlikely to work except in the infinitesimally small number of people with genuine genetically determined leptin deficiency, for whom it is a 'miracle drug', just as cortisone was for patients with Addison's disease and insulin for Type 1 diabetes.

Equally exciting as the discovery of leptin is the discovery that there are at least four other hormones, all produced in the intestines or stomach in response to certain foods, that can affect appetite and metabolism of nutrients within the body. Genetically engineered animals rendered insensitive to the hormone called GIP (or gastric inhibitory peptide), for example, do not become obese with overfeeding. This observation supports earlier work, derived from studies in human beings, and suggested that GIP is one of the factors that lead people to become obese and may just be related to the composition of the diet. It also makes GIP an important target for the pharmaceutical industry to develop antagonists to its actions that can be used therapeutically.

Contrary to popular belief, it is extremely difficult to become clinically obese by voluntarily eating excessively. This was established by experiments performed on healthy young volunteer prisoners. These experiments showed that mere access to unlimited supplies of food was not enough for the average person to become obese: something more was required. It clearly has something to do with appetite and the ability to overcome the feeling of satiety that most people experience when they have eaten sufficient for their physical requirements. One of the recently discovered hormones produced in the intestine, called PYY, works on the brain to suppress appetite – so does the even more recently discovered hormone obestatin.

Under experimental conditions, PYY enables obese people to resist the temptation to eat excessively. It is currently being pursued as a potential treatment for obesity. Other gut hormones affecting appetite and the sense of satiety are also known. One of them is called is GLP-1. Like GIP and PYY, it is made and released from the intestine in response to certain foods; like GIP, it is involved with the disposition of the individual constituents of the food within the body, mainly – though not exclusively – through their ability to stimulate the release of insulin. It, or something very like it, is already available commercially for the treatment of Type 2 diabetes. Ghrelin and obestatin, both discovered within the past ten years or so, are produced in the stomach and affect appetite in opposite directions: ghrelin stimulates appetite; obestatin inhibits it.

Just how important the newly discovered hormones are in deciding whether or not you become obese is still uncertain. It's one thing to discover how a hormone works under research conditions, quite another to apply it in a clinical situation.

We are still a long way from understanding how these new

hormones work in human beings under everyday living conditions. Studies on the changes produced in grossly obese patients whose only salvation comes from by bariatric surgery – operations on the stomach that are currently the only effective method of treating this life-threatening condition – will undoubtedly advance our knowledge. So will experiments and clinical trials using pure hormones as they become available, exactly as happened with insulin and diabetes.

While the availability of a plentiful supply of food is a prerequisite for the development of obesity, the relationship is far from being a simple one. Most people with access to alcohol do not become alcoholics; a few, especially those with a genetic predisposition, do. The same is true for food, but whereas it is possible to abstain from alcohol completely – and so achieve a cure of the ill – this option is not available to the obese. Obese patients may find it comparatively simple to stick to a very low-calorie, synthetic, liquid, formula diet and lose weight at just about the maximum theoretical rate – about half a pound or a quarter of a kilo a day – but as soon as they are permitted to replace one of the meals with solid food of their own choosing they stop losing weight and may even gain it.

The idea currently being propagated by single-issue pressure groups is that obesity is due to one particular type of food constituent, whether it be fat, sugar, rapidly absorbed starches or combinations of them – in particular when they are provided in the form of foods such as hamburgers, pizzas, chips, crisps and other energy nibbles. This would be laughable if it were not so misleading. Obesity is a genuine, recognisable medical problem. It will not be resolved by simplistic dogma that is based on unproven opinion rather than on evidence.

The fact that an increase in the incidence of obesity coincided with a rise in the availability of fast or convenience foods is not evidence of their role in its causation. Exactly the same argument could be advanced for the rise in the use of telephones, or – better – central heating. Human beings burn off many more calories to stay alive in a cold environment than when they are warm. It would nevertheless be as foolish to assume that the answer to obesity is to return to the days of cold and damp housing as it is to suggest that banning the sale of energy-dense fast foods, or labelling them as bad for you, will the solve the problem. Decades of dietary advice for the prevention and treatment of obesity based on avoiding first this and then that type of food have all resulted in failure.

Any new way of losing weight is likely to produce an effect lasting a year or two, especially if aided by pharmaceutical appetite suppressants. A small percentage of dieters do manage to sustain their weight loss, but this is achieved not merely by changes in their diet but by altering their whole way of life. Indeed, the few long-term, large-scale interventional studies that have succeeded in reducing the incidence of obesity, and more especially Type 2 diabetes, have relied upon intensive re-education and alterations in lifestyle to incorporate changes in exercise as well as in eating habits. The importance of moderate and regular exercise in achieving weight loss cannot be overemphasised – not because of the calories consumed in doing it but for its general effect upon the metabolism of the body.

Other factors are important also. The way food is eaten, whether as regular meals or 'on the hoof', the time of eating, the size of individual portions and what they consist of, as well as the genetic and hormonal factors in the person eating the food, all have a part to play. The old adage that it is better to leave the dining table wanting more than to leave it fully satiated is probably still as good advice as any for those genuinely wanting to avoid obesity.

This may be difficult to achieve in an 'I want it now' society, but it might be helped by teaching elementary nutrition and the long-term health risks of obesity at an early age rather than resorting to propaganda based on half-truths and unproven ideas. But for many of the morbidly obese, the ones really at risk, it is only advances in the understanding of the pathology of obesity and its specific and appropriate treatment that offer any genuine hope of sustained benefit.

Chapter Two

JUNK FOOD

BY STANLEY FELDMAN

THE MYTH: Junk food causes ill health.
THE FACT: There is no such thing as food that is bad and food that is good for you.

The term 'junk food' is an oxymoron. Either something is a food, in which case it is not junk, or it has no nutritional value, in which case it cannot be called a food. It cannot be both. Ask most people what they understand by the term and they think of McDonalds' hamburgers. None of their explanations for why hamburgers are junk food makes any sense; rather, they believe hamburgers are the cause of serious health problems because they have been told it is so. Any food eaten to excess is, as Paracelsus said in 1538, potentially harmful. Morgan Spurlock ate a diet composed solely of McDonalds' food for a month for his film *Super Size Me*. At the end of that time, he felt unwell and had put on weight. Had he eaten a similar weight of 'healthy' sardines for the same time he would no doubt have felt just as unwell and put on just as much weight! No particular individual component of any mixed diet is harmful. The concept of 'good foods' and 'junk foods' is nonsense.

Some rather ill-informed individuals have so convinced themselves of the dangers of hamburgers that they have suggested taxing them or giving them a red warning label. Quite why hamburgers should be considered such a threat to our health that they should be singled out for taxation defies reason. Why should mincing a piece of beef turn it from being a 'good food' into one that is such dangerous 'junk' that it needs to be taxed in order to dissuade people from eating it? What would happen if, instead of mincing the meat, it was chopped into chunks and made into boeuf bourguignon – should it be taxed at only 50 per cent? To try to justify this illogical proposal, these self-appointed food experts tell us that hamburgers contain more fat than a fillet steak. They fail to point out that the ratio of protein to fat in a hamburger is usually higher than in most lamb chops, and that most hamburgers contain less fat than a Sainsbury's Waldorf salad.

But, that aside, why should the fat be bad? Would these same people like to tax the cheese offered at the end of the meal because, after all, it contains the same basic animal fat as the hamburger? Or perhaps it is the hamburger bun that they feel is unhealthy. But the same self-appointed dietary experts would not object to a helping of food in the form of pasta or a slice or two of wholemeal brown bread (which, by the way, is the bread with the highest level of pesticide). The pasta, the bread and the bun produce a similar carbohydrate load in our food and are absorbed into the bloodstream as the same constituents. As for the tomato ketchup on the hamburger, it is rich in vitamin C and the antioxidant polyphenols that are supposed to keep cell degeneration and cancer at bay.

There is no such thing as junk food. All food is composed of carbohydrate, fat and protein. An intake of a certain amount of each is essential for a healthy life. In addition, a supply of certain minerals, such as iron, calcium and tiny amounts of selenium, and a supply of vitamins, fibre, salt and fluid contribute to health. Once the necessary amounts of carbohydrate, fat and protein have been taken, any long-term surplus is stored as glycogen or fat in the body. Protein is protein whether it comes from an Aberdeen Angus steak or a McDonald's hamburger. It is broken up in the gut into its amino-acid building blocks, which are identical in both the hamburger and the steak; and although the relative amounts of each particular amino acid may vary slightly, this has no nutritional significance. These broken-down products of protein are absorbed into the bloodstream to be restructured into body proteins in the various cells of the body. Any excess ends up as fat. One source of animal protein is not necessarily of better value to the body than another, nor is it more or less fattening. A diet consisting only of Aberdeen Angus steak would be as 'junky' as one composed only of hamburgers. Similarly, animal fat is broken down and absorbed in the same way whether it originated in a hamburger, a lamb chop or the cheese on top of a pasta dish.

We need some fat in our diet, not only because it contains essential fat-soluble vitamins but also because it contributes much of the taste to foods. Very lean meat is tasteless unless enriched by a sauce containing fatty flavouring. No one would suggest that eating hamburgers and chips every day would constitute a good diet, but it would be better than one made up of Waldorf salad. The answer lies in a diet that is both varied and balanced.

The idea has grown up that some foods make you fat and others are slimming. It is true that pound for pound the fat in cheese contains about twice the calories of carbohydrate or protein but one eats much more carbohydrate and probably more protein than fat each day. It is the amount you eat that makes you fat.

One thing that the fast food industry has changed is the cost of food. Some would argue that it is now so readily available and cheap that it is not sufficiently rationed by price. As a result, people eat too much. In a world where some people are starving, this seems to be a perverse reason for objecting to the contribution made by the food industry. Many people of my generation can remember chicken being so expensive it was considered a luxury reserved for high days and holydays. It does suggest that the real cause of the problem of obesity is not the food or the ready availability of certain foods, it is a social phenomenon associated with affluence and the leisure time to enjoy eating. In other words, the 'junk' appellation should not be applied to the hamburger but to its consumer and his lifestyle.

We have been so indoctrinated about the evils of junk food, a concept so closely tied up with hamburgers that, if you were to ask the man in the street which was the better meal, lobster mayonnaise salad or a hamburger, he would almost certainly condemn the hamburger. In terms of its contribution to the food requirements of the body, the lobster mayonnaise, with its high cholesterol and fat and low-value protein, approaches the junk-food profile while a hamburger with tomato ketchup is much better value as a mixed food. A tomato, basil and chicken salad from Safeway is presented as 'healthy food' although it contains roughly the same amount of fat and calories as a Big Mac and chips (*Sunday Times*, August 2004). If, instead of eating a Big Mac, people were suddenly to start eating these salads, it is unlikely they would be any healthier or lose any weight.

There is no doubt that snobbery and cost contributes to the perception of what is called 'junk'. The term is associated with foods originating in the fast-food chains of America rather than those coming from 'foody' France, home of the croque monsieur and foie gras; from Belgium, the country of moules et frites; or from Italy with its creamy pastas covered with cheese. For a century, generations of Britons ate fried fish and chips, liberally dosed with salt and vinegar, without becoming dangerously overweight. However, when the fish protein is replaced by the meat of a hamburger or by Kentucky Fried Chicken, it suddenly becomes a national disaster.

The present obsession with obesity has resulted in any food providing a high calorie content being labelled as 'junk'. It is obvious nonsense: cheese is good food, as are fish and chips and hamburgers. It is not the particular food that makes people fat, it is the amount of it that they eat. The three heaviest mammals – the whale, the elephant and the hippopotamus – are all vegetarians; they don't eat hamburgers, chips or crisps but they get fat. The whale is hugely fat – it is covered in fatty blubber – but most whales eats only plankton (which would no doubt qualify for the five-a-day portions of vegetables and fruit we are told we must eat). It is fat because it eats lots of plankton, it grazes continuously, it's the whale's lifestyle. It is not fat because it eats food containing a lot of calories. A person who also continuously nibbled food all day long would become fat even if he grazed on fruit and vegetables. A person who sits in front of the television eating bags of peanuts (a good food) is more likely to become fat than one eating the occasional hamburger.

There is often confusion between so-called junk food and fast food. A pizza can provide an excellent meal even if it is likely to be a little heavy on fats, whereas a cherry tart that took hours to make is likely to contain more carbohydrate – even before the cream has been added to increase its fat content. Neither is junk, and both contribute food essential for the nourishment of the body.

So what is junk? I suppose the nearest one comes to a substance that is not nourishing is water. Nevertheless, a fluid intake of about two litres a day (some of it as water) is essential for survival. Without salt we would all die. We need fat, protein and carbohydrate. Even fibre, which contributes so little towards our essential nutritional requirements that it could be considered a 'junk food', has a part to play in digestion. The lettuce and cucumber salad we are told we must eat every day to prevent us dying prematurely is made up of over 98 per cent water, while most of the rest is fibre and contributes little of nutritional value. We all know of children who have refused any salad or green vegetables and have grown up to be long-lived, healthy adults. Lettuce and cucumber would qualify for junk-food status but for the small amounts of water-soluble vitamins and antioxidants that they contain. Celery is said to require more energy in the eating than one gains from its consumption – that might qualify it for the label 'junk', but there is no evidence to suggest that it is in any way harmful.

Processed Foods

Since the junk food title makes no sense the food zealots have lined up another culprit in their search for something to ban, it is 'processed food'. Why processed food should be bad is not clear as it is difficult to find out exactly what they are. Since we eat relatively few foods without cleaning them, cooking them and flavouring them, it is difficult to see what particular processes are considered to be a health hazard. Those foods that are partially prepared in some way by the food industry are no different from those prepared at home although their culinary treatment is probably better controlled. The food we eat in restaurants is certainly processed but is it therefore bad? Do the food police seriously believe in some sinister plot by the food industry to introduce dangerous or harmful substances into the meals during the preparation process? Most evidence points to the meals prepared and served at home as being more likely to cause a health problem, such as food poisoning or obesity.

Certainly, some classical methods of preparation for preservation, such as pickling and salting of meat and the preparation of some bacon, introduces nitrates and salt, which in great excess may be injurious to health. Modern food technology has allowed us to avoid an excess of nitrate and salt in preserved food. All the preservatives used today are well tested and harmless even in 100 times their concentration in any food. Almost all have stood the test of time and none has ever been linked to any health hazard.

Fast Foods

What exactly are fast foods? It seems that they are bad for you but since no one claims to know what slow foods would be like it is difficult to see what it is that causes the harm. Some of the fastest cooking I have encountered was the cooking of scallops in a wok in China. The actual cooking time was under one minute. They were delicious and seemed to be without any danger to my health. Would they have been better for me if they had been cooked for ten minutes? Fast food is such a meaningless term that one has to question the authority of those who bandy it about as a form of verbal shorthand to conceal their personal dislike of foods such as hamburgers, pizzas and hot dogs. It displays a food snobbery that is so unjustified that it needs to be disguised behind a wall of meaningless jargon.

Reclaimed Meat

Whenever I carve a leg of lamb I feel saddened that I cannot cut decent slices as I get near the bone. Often this meat goes to waste. How much better it would be if it could be 'reclaimed'. It is perfectly good meat. Fortunately, when an animal is butchered, the meat that is left on the carcass, too near the bone, or in too small an area for it to be cut off to make good butcher's meat, can be recovered by high pressure techniques. This meat is termed 'reclaimed meat'. It is perfectly good, healthy protein and has long been presented and eaten as corned beef, Spam and doner kebabs. However, when the same reclaimed meat is used by the food industry for mass catering it becomes an object of disgust. The same people who today sneer at the use of reclaimed meat tell us that in wartime Britain, when Spam and corned beef formed a major part of our protein intake, the population was at its healthiest.

It is clear that there is no such thing as junk food. It is a product of non-scientific pressure groups that, out of ignorance or prejudice, try to persuade us we are on the brink of a health catastrophe. The problem is not with the food we eat, but with the lifestyle of 'junk eaters'.

Chapter Three

ORGANIC FOOD

BY STANLEY FELDMAN

**THE MYTH: Non-organic foods are covered in harmful pesticides.
THE FACT: One of the pesticides deemed 'safe' by organic
producers carries a warning that it is harmful to fish.**

As I look back to my childhood, it seems that every summer's
day was sunny and filled with joy. I cannot remember it
raining so hard that it spoiled a day out in the country. The food
tasted better, the tomatoes were juicier, the strawberries tasted
sweet and succulent and the peas that came from the pods were
so delicious that many were eaten raw before my mother could
cook them. I realise that my memory is highly selective – there
must have been rainy days, rotten tomatoes, sour strawberries
and worm-infested peas, but somehow things today never seem
quite as good as they were in our youth.

It is the same rose-tinted nostalgia that is used to promote
organic food. The cult of natural 'organic food' is based on a belief

that, while the sun may not always have shone in days gone by, the food was better and healthier before the advent of modern farming and horticulture, when the crops were liberally fertilised with manure from animal faeces or rotting vegetable waste, in the form of compost.

This belief has been energetically reinforced by the scare stories of the eco-warriors who have blamed every ill – from heart disease and cancer to global warming, pollution, less biodiversity and the rape of the countryside – on the perceived evils of modern farming.

As soon as one spurious claim is disproved another scare is invented. So vociferous and well funded is the propaganda that they have caused many otherwise sensible people, and some government agencies, to embrace the organic bandwagon, although no one has produced any evidence in its favour. By scaring the public, the organic lobby has created a billion-pound market in the UK for food that is up to 40 per cent more expensive than that produced by conventional farming and from which it is indistinguishable.

The term *organic food* is in itself misleading. The separation into 'organic' and 'nonorganic' was based on the belief that some substances contained a life-giving property: these were originally called 'organic'. In recent times it has come to mean chemicals containing molecules based on a carbon atom. So all food is organic (with the technical exception of water). There is no such thing as inorganic food. Whenever a pressure group resorts to a nonsense name, in order to suggest that it has nature on its side, that it has the monopoly on what is good, or that it is the only path that faithful followers of purity and truth can take, one should smell a rat.

The Soil Association, the high priests of this cult, believe that chemicals, whether organic or inorganic, are bad, a danger to the consumer, and will possibly bring death to the planet. Natural substances, by contrast, are apparently good. Yet all infections are caused by natural, organic bacteria; many organic substances produced in plants and berries, such as the belladonna of the deadly nightshade and the prussic acid in almonds, are highly poisonous; the 'natural' copper sulphate that is recommended as an organic treatment for fungal infections is so toxic to marine life that copper-based antifouling of boats has been banned in many countries. If a fungicide is not used and the ergot fungus infects cereal crops, then the unsuspecting organic consumer may end up with gangrene of fingers and toes.

In all fairness to the Soil Association, it does permit the use of pesticides provided they come from an approved list. Some have reassuringly innocent names such as 'Soft Soap', which turns out to be octodecanoic acid and carries a label warning that it is dangerous to fish.

The main thrust of the argument used by adherents of this cult seems to be that organic fertiliser, by which it is implied that it is produced from animal excreta or rotting vegetable waste, is necessary in order to produce food that is both nutritious and safe. This supposition is difficult to support. Manure is teeming with bacteria, many of which are pathogenic, and a few lethal. Compost rots because of the action of these bacteria, and, while they are in the main less harmful than those in manure, most sensible consumers would be reluctant to ingest them in the produce they purchase.

The root systems of plants can absorb only those nutriments

that are in solution. They cannot take up particulate matter. Before the plant can use any fertiliser, organic faeces, rotting vegetable waste or chemical additive, it must first be broken down and rendered soluble in water. This necessitates reducing organic matter to its basic chemical form. It is true that in organic fertiliser these are usually more complex chemicals, but they must be rendered into the same simple basic chemicals in the plant before they can be used to encourage its growth.

There is absolutely no rational reason why all the breakdown products of organic fertiliser should not be supplied in a basic chemical form rather than leaving it to the bacteria in the soil to produce them from compost. At the end of the day, the plant uses both chemical and organic fertiliser in the same way in the same chemical processes that are essential for its growth. The main difference is that chemical fertiliser is produced with a standardised value of its content, and does not contain the dangerous bacterial pathogens present in organic waste.

It was reportedly Prince Albert who started the vogue for using natural, organic household waste to fertilise the kitchen garden at Osborne House on the Isle of Wight. Prince Albert died of typhoid fever, a disease caused by ingesting food contaminated with the faeces from a carrier who may not have exhibited symptoms of the disease.

The other canon of organic law is the avoidance of known effective pesticides and the preference for naturally occurring compounds such as sulphur and copper-based chemicals to control infestations. This again is illogical. It is based on the belief that the organophosphate pesticides are poisonous and naturally occurring chemicals are not. This ignores the fact that sulphur and copper-based ones are also poisonous. Both organophosphate pesticides and naturally occurring chemicals can be poisonous; it is all a matter of dose. The German-Swiss doctor and chemist Paracelsus (1493–1541) pointed out 'nothing is without poison; it is the dose alone that makes it so'. When one looks at those parts of the world where pesticides are not freely available (usually because of cost), it is found that over a third of all the food produced is eaten by pests, whereas in the Western world, where pesticides are used, the loss is reduced by 41 per cent (figures from the WHO and UN Environment Programme, 1990).

The level of pesticides in our food is carefully monitored and kept below a very conservative safety level. The chemicals have a short half-life and have not been shown to accumulate in the body. Their level in food is way below that at which it is likely to cause symptoms, even in the most sensitive individual. Although pesticides in food have been blamed for a variety of ill-defined syndromes, including cancers, extensive medical studies have failed to implicate them as the cause of any known clinical condition. There are no mysterious unknown disease states caused by the prolonged intake of small doses of these chemicals. Since they do not accumulate in the food chain or in the body, chronic toxicity is improbable. As Sir John Krebs, the former chairman of the Food Standards Agency, pointed out in *Nature* in 2002, 'a single cup of coffee contains natural carcinogens equal to at least a year's worth of synthetic carcinogenic residues in the diet'.

The various conditions that have been attributed to these chemicals by the food faddists bear no relationship to any of the known effects of the pesticides. There have been sufficient cases of self-induced organophosphate poisoning to recognise the symptoms of poisoning (pesticides are a common form of suicide in Third World countries). It starts with excessive salivation and lachrymation and is invariably followed by painful gut cramps and an uncontrollable twitching of the muscles. Pesticides are not commonly associated with any allergic conditions.

Virtually all the chemical pesticide residue that occurs in food is found on the outside of fruit and vegetables and is easily washed off. If the choice has to be made between pest-infected food, food exposed to bacterial pathogens and minute harmless amounts of pesticide, then to choose not to use them is the equivalent of a patient with pneumonia refusing antibiotics in favour of leeches and bleeding.

The inconsistent approach of the advocates of organic food becomes apparent when one considers organic eggs. These have to come from organically reared chickens. To be an organically reared chicken, the bird has to eat 80 per cent organic food for six weeks. No effort is made to control the other 20 per cent, which may contain potential carcinogens or toxic material. At the end of that time, any eggs it lays will be deemed organic and therefore much more expensive. Organic eggs and chickens should not be confused with free-range chickens, which can roam more freely and eat whatever they like. Organic chickens are not kept in battery cages. To conform with the organic requirements, they must be allowed 1 square metre of space per 25 lb of chicken.

There are many mysteries about what constitutes organic food. If a banana is squashed and its juice extracted to produce 'banana flavouring', it can be analysed and shown to be the chemical amyl acetate. However, if one produces amyl acetate by adding vinegar to amyl alcohol it cannot be called 'organic'. It is the same chemical, it tastes the same, it smells the same but it is not natural and it is therefore presumed to be bad. The same logic suggests that acetic acid is somehow different from the acid in vinegar, or citric acid from that of lemon-juice extract.

It has been suggested that prepackaged, cleaned lettuce is dangerous, as it is washed in a solution containing chlorine. The initiates of this scare fail to point out that the amount of chlorine residue in the product is less than that found in most swimming-pool water and in some drinking water.

A walk around the organic shelves of a supermarket leaves one amazed at the gullibility of its patrons. The produce is not particularly inviting in its appearance, and its taste is, for the most part, identical to that of the normal produce. A ten-year, obsessively controlled trial of foods grown in similar positions, on the Boarded Farm study in Essex, compared organically grown crops with those produced by conventional farming, using integrated farm management. The study revealed that the best results, judged by soil quality, effect on bird life, biodiversity and yield, came from the integrated farm management fields. Blind tasting of the crops from these studies failed to reveal any consistent difference between organic and nonorganic produce. This is hardly surprising, since taste is largely a result of the genetic makeup of the particular strain of the crop that was planted, the time it has spent maturing before being picked and the climatic conditions during its growth.

Although most produce, be it organic or not, tastes better

when freshly picked, the use of preservatives can prolong the freshness of some produce. Some preservatives are available for use in organic foods but they are seldom used in organic vegetables and fruits, which consequently have a short shelf life – as evidenced by wilting lettuces and bendy cucumbers.

Today, the zealots of the cult of organic food are making ever more irrational inroads into the way we live. They are promoting organic clothing and toiletries with the implied assurance that these are somehow less likely to cause allergies and skin disease. There is no evidence to support this claim, which plays on the fears of parents with children who suffer from skin allergies.

So why do people pay up to 40 per cent more for organic products? Is it a cynical confidence trick to exploit consumer ignorance? Is it the belief that, should little Johnny turn out to have allergies/asthma/autism or a brain tumour, this might have been prevented if he had been brought up on organic food and worn pyjamas made from organic cotton? Or is it simply a matter of choice? It is difficult to believe that the proponents of organic produce are all part of an evil conspiracy to defraud the public, although they often use unworthy, unscientific scare tactics, conjuring up all sorts of disasters to frighten the nonbelievers. Most just seem to be victims of their own propaganda, who yearn after bygone days when the sun shone all the time.

However, there is another side to the story. The food industry has to accept some of the blame. It has too often put cost before quality, marketed fruit picked before it has had time to ripen and mature on the tree, and encouraged the production of food that looks good on the supermarket shelf rather than produce that tastes good when eaten. I believe that our memories of apples picked straight from the tree, tasting crisp and juicy, of strawberries that were sweet and succulent and peas that one could not resist eating raw have some factual basis. It is our desire to get back to the days of real, fresh, ripe fruit and vegetables that has encouraged the spurious market for organic food.

Chapter Four

THE GREAT CHOLESTEROL MYTH

BY MALCOLM KENDRICK

'For every complicated problem there is a solution that is simple,
direct, understandable, and wrong.'

H L MENCKEN

THE MYTH: A high cholesterol intake causes heart disease.
**THE FACT: Cholesterol levels are not affected by cholesterol
intake, and in any case there is no evidence to suggest that
cholesterol and heart disease are linked.**

If you eat too much cholesterol, or saturated fat, your blood
cholesterol will rise to dangerous levels. Excess cholesterol
will then seep through your artery walls causing thickenings
(plaques), which will eventually block blood flow in vital arteries,
resulting in heart attacks and strokes.

Scientific hypotheses don't get much simpler than this, the
cholesterol, or diet-heart hypothesis, which has broken free
from the ivory towers of academia to impact with massive force
on society.

It has driven a widespread change in the type of food we are told to eat, and consequently the food that lines the supermarket shelves. Many people view bacon and eggs as a dangerous killer, butter is shunned, and a multibillion-pound industry has sprung up providing 'healthy' low-fat alternatives.

At the same time, millions of people are prescribed statins to lower cholesterol levels, and each new set of guidelines suggests ever more lowering of cholesterol is needed. When it comes to explaining what causes heart disease, the cholesterol hypothesis reigns supreme.

Landmarks in the development of the cholesterol hypothesis

1850s: Rudolf Virchow notes the presence of cholesterol in atherosclerotic plaques. Suggests excess cholesterol in the bloodstream may be the cause.

Early 1900s: Ashoff feeds rabbits fat and cholesterol, notes the development of atheroma.

1912: First heart attack described by Herrick.

1940s: Epidemic of heart disease hits USA, interest in the area explodes. Many researchers blame high fat/cholesterol diet.

1948: The Framingham, study on heart disease starts. Still running today.

1954: Ancel Key's seminal Seven Countries Study published. Demonstrates clear links between saturated-fat intake and heart disease.

1961: Framingham confirms link between raised cholesterol levels and heart disease.

1960s: First cholesterol-lowering drugs developed.

1970s: Brown and Goldstein find gene leading to extremely high cholesterol levels (familial hypercholesterolaemia) and premature heart disease.

1980s: Statins launched.

1985: Nobel Prize for Brown and Goldstein.

1990s: Statins trials demonstrate that cholesterol lowering protects against heart disease.

Presented in this way, it's not difficult to see how the cholesterol hypothesis became the dominant hypothesis, effortlessly swatting alternative ideas into touch. Indeed, to question this theory is to risk being placed on the same shelf as flat-earthers and creationists.

However, all is not what it seems. The cholesterol hypothesis can be likened to a cathedral built on a bog. Rather than admit they made a horrible mistake and let it sink, the builders decided to try to keep the cathedral afloat at all costs. Each time a crack appeared, a new buttress was built. Then further buttresses were built to support the original buttresses.

In a similar way, although direct contradictions to the cholesterol hypothesis repeatedly appear, no one dares say, 'OK, this isn't working, time to build again from scratch.' That decision has become just too painful, especially now that massive industries, Nobel prizes and glittering scientific careers have grown on the back of the cholesterol hypothesis. The statin market alone is worth more than £20 billion each year.

In reality, cracks in the hypothesis appeared right from the very start. The first of these was the stark observation that cholesterol in the diet has no effect on cholesterol levels in the bloodstream:

> There's no connection whatsoever between cholesterol in food and cholesterol in blood. And we've known that all along. Cholesterol in the diet doesn't matter at all unless you happen to be a chicken or a rabbit.
>
> ANCEL KEYS, PHD, PROFESSOR EMERITUS AT THE
> UNIVERSITY OF MINNESOTA, 1997

A bit of a blow to a cholesterol hypothesis, you might think, to find that dietary cholesterol has no effect on blood cholesterol levels. However, as everyone was, by then, fully convinced that something rich and 'fatty' in the diet was the primary cause of heart disease, no one was willing to let go.

So the hypothesis quietly altered from cholesterol in the diet to saturated fat in the diet – or a bit of both – as if, in some way, cholesterol and saturated fat were similar if not almost exactly the same thing.

In reality, this could hardly be further from the truth. Saturated fat and cholesterol have completely different functions in the body, and they have very different chemical structures.

A saturated-fat molecule (top left) and a cholesterol molecule (right).

As James Black warned over two hundred years ago:

> A nice adaptation of conditions will make almost any
> hypothesis agree with the phenomena. This will please
> the imagination, but does not advance our knowledge.
>
> JAMES BLACK, *LECTURES ON THE ELEMENTS OF CHEMISTRY*, 1803

Unfortunately, this adaptation did not work. It's true that Ancel
Keys appeared to have proved the link between saturated-fat
consumption and heart disease, but, when it came to the major
interventional trials, confirmation proved elusive.

The MR-FIT trial in the USA was the most determined effort to
prove the case. This was a massive study in which more than
350,000 men at high risk of heart disease were recruited. In one
set of participants they cut cholesterol consumption by 42 per
cent, saturated-fat consumption by 28 per cent and total calories
by 21 per cent. This should have made a noticeable dent in heart-
disease rates.

But nothing happened. The originators of the MR-FIT trials refer to the results as 'disappointing' and say in their conclusions, 'The overall results do not show a beneficial effect on coronary heart disease or total mortality from this multifactor intervention.'

In fact, no clinical trial on reducing saturated fat intake has ever shown a reduction in heart disease. Some have shown the exact opposite:

> As multiple intervention against risk factors for coronary heart disease in middle aged men at only moderate risk seem to have failed to reduce both morbidity and mortality such interventions become increasingly difficult to justify. This runs counter to the recommendations of many national and international advisory bodies which must now take the recent findings from Finland into consideration. Not to do so may be ethically unacceptable.
>
> PROFESSOR MICHAEL OLIVER, *BRITISH MEDICAL JOURNAL*, 1991

This passage followed a disturbing trial on Finnish businessmen. In a ten-year follow-up to the original five-year trial, it was found that those men who continued to follow a low-saturated-fat diet were twice as likely to die of heart disease as those who didn't.

It's not as if this were one negative to set against a whole series of positive trials. In 1998, Uffe Ravnskov looked at a broader selection of trials. 'The crucial test is the controlled, randomised trial,' he said. 'Eight such trials using diet as the only treatment have been performed but neither the number of fatal or non-fatal heart attacks was reduced.'

As Ravnskov makes clear, no trial has ever demonstrated

benefits from reducing dietary saturated fat. At this point most people might think it was time to pull the plug.

Far from it. In 1988, the Surgeon General's office in the USA decided to silence the naysayers by putting together the definitive report proving a causal link. Eleven years later the project was abandoned. In a letter circulated, it was stated that the office 'did not anticipate fully the magnitude of the additional external expertise and staff resources that would be needed'.

Bill Harlan, a member of the oversight committee and associate director of the Office of Disease Prevention at National Institute of Health, says 'the report was initiated with a preconceived opinion of the conclusions, but the science behind those opinions was not holding up. Clearly the thoughts of yesterday were not going to serve us very well.'

The sound of a sinking cathedral fills the air with a great sucking, slurripy noise. But still no one let go. Instead, more buttresses were desperately thrown at a rapidly disappearing pile of rocks.

Variations on a theme emerged. It is not saturated fat, *per se*, that causes heart disease. It's the ratio of polyunsaturated to saturated fat that is critical. Or is it the consumption of monounsaturated fats, or a lack of omega-3 fatty acids, or an excess of omega-6? Take your pick. These and a host of other add-on hypotheses have their proponents.

As of today no one can – or will – tell you which type of fat, in what proportions, added to what type of antioxidant, vegetable, monounsaturated fat or omega-3 is the true culprit. Hugely complicated explanations are formulated, but they all fall apart under scrutiny.

This may all seem incredible, such has been the level of antifat propaganda, but it is true. With the exception of Ancel Keys's flawed Seven Countries Study (he preselected the seven countries for his study in order to prove his hypothesis!), there is not one scrap of direct evidence.

But, of course, there are two parts to the cholesterol hypothesis: diet and raised cholesterol level. Leaving diet behind, surely it has been proved beyond doubt that a raised cholesterol level is the most important cause of heart disease.

Cholesterol levels and overall mortality

Before looking at the connection between blood cholesterol levels and heart disease, I think it is worth highlighting a critically important – remarkably unheralded – fact: after the age of 50, the lower your cholesterol level, the lower your life expectancy. Perhaps even more important than this is the fact that a falling cholesterol level sharply increases the risk of dying, of anything, including heart disease.

The dangers of a low cholesterol level were highlighted by a major long-term study of men living in Honolulu: 'Our data accord with previous findings of increased mortality in elderly people with low serum cholesterol, and show that long-term persistence of low cholesterol concentration actually increases the risk of death.'

The danger of a falling cholesterol level was first discovered (somewhat ironically) in the Framingham study: 'There is a direct association between falling cholesterol levels over the first 14 years [of the study] and mortality over the following 18 years.'

It seems almost unbelievable that warnings about the dangers of a high cholesterol level rain down every day, when the reality is that a low cholesterol level is much more dangerous than a high level.

Given this, why would anyone want to lower the cholesterol level? On the face of it, it would make more sense to take cholesterol-raising drugs. Especially after the age of 50.

Cholesterol Levels and Heart Disease

The reason why everyone is so keen to lower cholesterol levels is that supporters of the hypothesis have decreed the following:

A high level of cholesterol causes premature heart disease.

A low level of cholesterol is caused by an underlying disease. It is the underlying disease that kills you, not the low cholesterol.

Therefore, if you lower the blood cholesterol level you will reduce the risk of heart disease, and you will not increase the risk of dying of any other disease.

FIGURE 3

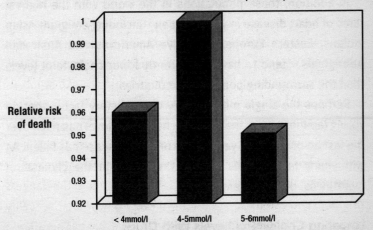

RISK OF CARDIOVASCULAR DEATH AT DIFFERENT CHOLESTEROL LEVELS (WOMEN)

This could be true, but it is worth reviewing some of the evidence that linked raised cholesterol levels to heart disease in the first place. Let's begin with women.

Perhaps the largest single analysis of cholesterol levels, and death from cardiovascular disease (and other diseases), was published in 1992. This review included more than 100,000 women, aggregated from a number of different studies and countries.

To quote from the study, 'The pooled estimated risk for total cardio-vascular death in women showed no trend across TC [total cholesterol] levels.' In short, for more than 50 per cent of the world's population – women – raised cholesterol is not a risk factor for heart disease.

Moving to men, it is true that under the age of 50 there does seem to be an association between raised cholesterol levels and heart disease. But, after that age, when more than 90 per cent of heart attacks happen, the association disappears.

In addition, those populations in the world with the highest rates of heart disease in younger men – including emigrant Asian Indians, Eastern Europeans, Native Americans and Australian Aboriginals – tend to have significantly lower cholesterol levels than the surrounding populations/countries.

Perhaps the single most directly contradictory fact is that, in young Japanese men, the average cholesterol level has risen over the last 20 or so years, yet the rate of heart disease has fallen. As with many facts in this area, if they don't fit the cholesterol hypothesis, dismiss them.

Lowering Cholesterol Levels With Drugs
Surely, despite everything written up to this point, all previous

arguments are refuted by the knowledge that lowering cholesterol levels with statins protects against heart disease. As all good scientists know, 'reversibility of effect' provides the most powerful supportive evidence for a hypothesis.

However, the flipside to this argument is as follows. How can lowering cholesterol levels prevent heart disease in people who do not have a high level? The most often-quoted clinical trial in the last few years is the UK-based Heart Protection Study (HPS). A veritable triumph for statins, demonstrating protection in almost every group studied.

What is most intriguing, however, is that protection was apparent if the starting cholesterol level was high, average or low. How can this be explained? At this point we enter *Alice in Wonderland* territory. A rational person would accept that a normal cholesterol level cannot be a risk factor for heart disease (or anything else for that matter). Therefore, people with normal cholesterol levels can gain no benefit from having their levels lowered.

So, if statins do protect those with normal, or low, cholesterol levels – which they clearly do – they must be doing this through some other mechanism of action, unrelated to cholesterol lowering. In fact, there is a growing body of evidence to support the idea that statins have a whole series of different protective actions.

However, accepting that statins work 'in another way' would demolish the final buttress keeping the cholesterol hypothesis afloat. And so the latest argument is that no one in modern society has a normal cholesterol level. An article in the *Journal of the American College of Cardiology* best sums up this line of thinking. Under the heading, 'WHY AVERAGE IS NOT NORMAL', O'Keefe, the lead author, makes the claim, 'Atherosclerosis is endemic in our population, in part because the average LDL [low-density lipoprotein, or 'bad' cholesterol, of which more later] level is approximately twice the normal physiologic level.' In short, according to O'Keefe, our cholesterol level should be about 2.5 mmol/l, not 5.2 mmol/l.

This argument, if true, does neatly demolish the question, 'How can people with normal, or low, cholesterol levels be protected against heart disease?' O'Keefe and others would argue that we all have a high cholesterol level. Everyone is ill, and all shall have statins.

One oft-quoted fact that seems superficially supportive of O'Keefe's hypothesis is that peasant farmers in China have very low cholesterol levels and a very low rate of heart disease (although their average cholesterol levels are actually about 4, not 2.5).

But, when you study the figures with more care, they reveal something else. As usual, those with low cholesterol levels have by far the highest mortality rates. Liver failure and liver cancer are common causes of death. However, there is a simple explanation for this association.

Many Chinese peasant farmers have chronic hepatitis, which creates low cholesterol levels, and also leads to liver failure and liver cancer, which is why people with low cholesterol levels die young.

Does this mean that a low cholesterol level protects against heart disease? No. What the Chinese data tell us is that those with higher cholesterol levels are *not* chronic-hepatitis carriers, so they live longer and have more chance of developing heart disease in old age. On the other hand, those with low cholesterol levels cannot die of heart disease, because they are already dead.

Without chasing too many mad arguments around, the simple fact is that everyone in the West does not have a raised cholesterol level. Repeated studies have shown that a perfectly normal or healthy cholesterol level lies between about 4 and 6, and lowering it cannot protect against heart disease, otherwise we will have introduced a new concept into medical science. Normal is unhealthy and must be treated.

People are grasping at straws in their attempt to explain why statins protect against heart disease in those with normal cholesterol levels, and in women and the elderly, where a raised cholesterol level is not even a risk factor. The only possible explanation for the results of the statin trials is that statins do not work by lowering cholesterol levels.

The cholesterol hypothesis is a complicated mess

The cholesterol hypothesis has always exuded the siren song of simplicity. However, once you start to examine it in any detail, the simplicity rapidly mutates into complexity.

Even at the very start people, should have known that cholesterol in the diet was never capable of appearing, unchanged, in the bloodstream. Cholesterol is not soluble in water (thus blood), which means that, after absorption, cells lining the gut pack cholesterol into a small protein/lipid sphere, known as a *lipoprotein*, before releasing it into the bloodstream.

Thus, you do not have any cholesterol floating about in the blood: it is all contained within lipoproteins. You do not actually have a cholesterol level. Instead, you have a level of different lipoproteins, with the low-density lipoprotein (LDL), or 'bad' cholesterol, being the so-called dangerous one.

Next question: what raises the LDL level? Eating too much fat, or cholesterol? The first problem here is that the cells lining the gut do not make, or release, LDL – they make other forms of lipoprotein. So, no matter what you eat, it can have no direct effect on LDL levels.

So where does LDL come from? LDL is, effectively, the shrunken form of a very low-density lipoprotein (VLDL). VLDLs are made in the liver and used to transport fat, and cholesterol, from the liver to other cells around the body. As VLDLs lose fat they shrink, transforming into LDL.

Therefore, in order to find out what makes LDL levels rise, we must surely find out, first, what makes VLDL levels go up; and what makes VLDL levels go up, primarily, is eating excess carbohydrates. What makes them go down is eating fat!

Recognising this, and a host of other problems, the supporters of the cholesterol hypothesis have twisted and turned. As of today (and this will certainly change), the original – dietary – cholesterol hypothesis has become the following: if you eat too much saturated fat, the body will reduce the number of LDL receptors (things that remove LDL from the bloodstream), forcing the LDL up. A more tenuous, and unproven, link could hardly be imagined, but that is what is left of the originally super-simple cholesterol hypothesis. The diet part, anyway.

But the difficulties of trying to establish a dietary link to heart disease actually pale into insignificance when you start trying to work out how the raised LDL itself level may cause heart disease.

If it were simply a case of excess LDL seeping through the artery wall when the level gets too high, then why doesn't this happen in all artery walls, everywhere? If I lie too long in the sun I expect to get sunburned on every bit of skin exposed. I do not expect to get discrete patches of sunburn. Yet we do see little 'patches' of atherosclerosis. Some people die of heart disease and are found to have perfectly clean arteries, apart from a single killer plaque. So why did the LDL seep through at only one place? What protected the rest of the arterial system?

And why do veins never develop atherosclerotic plaques. They are exposed to exactly the same LDL level as the arteries. They are thinner than arteries, but their general structure is identical. (I should add that if you use a vein as a coronary artery bypass graft (effectively turning it into an artery), it will develop atherosclerosis.)

These questions represent only the tip of a huge iceberg. In an attempt to answer some of them, the cholesterol hypothesis has turned itself into the following, complicated mess. LDL, when it is oxidised, travels through the lining of the artery wall (endothelium) into the middle part of the artery. (How oxidised LDL passes straight through an endothelial cell into the artery wall behind is unexplained.)

In this oxidised state it attracts white blood cells from the bloodstream They, in turn, migrate into the artery wall and start to 'digest' the oxidised LDL in order to remove it (This bit is plausible.) However, white blood cells, once they have started to digest oxidised LDL, cannot stop. They get bigger and bigger until they burst. This, in turn, attracts more white blood cells to the area, which then burst. (White blood cells that just burst? This makes absolutely no sense whatsoever. Why on earth would the body develop a scavenger system that automatically self-destructs?)

The burst white blood cells, in turn, release substances that trigger a whole cascade of inflammatory reactions in the arterial wall. After a period of time you have a mass of dead white blood cells, cholesterol, oxidised LDL remnants, and a whole series of other inflammatory agents all focused in one area, trapped in the artery wall. (Well, this is what is found in a plaque, among many other things.)

Anyway, that is allegedly how a plaque starts and grows. I have kept that explanation as simple as humanly possible, but it seems absurdly unlikely. Oxidised LDL – what happened to normal LDL? Well, there's no way anyone can see of getting that through an arterial wall. Exploding white blood cells – another buttress ?

In truth, the current ideas on plaque formation used to keep the cholesterol hypothesis afloat are complex nonsense,. But the entire area is now protected by a ring-fence of scientific jargon that frightens off all but the most dedicated seeker after truth.

To those who have studied the hypothesis with a critical eye, it seems unbelievable that it can possibly still be standing. Dr George Mann pronounced it dead in an editorial in the *New England Journal of Medicine* in 1977, referring to it as the 'greatest scam in the history of medicine'. Yet this hypothesis has never had more followers than today. It is time, I think, that it was consigned to the dustbin of history. It is neither simple nor direct – nor understandable. The only certain thing about it is that it is wrong.

Chapter Five

SUGAR

BY VINCENT MARKS

THE MYTH: Sugar causes coronary heart disease, diabetes, hypertension, gout, tooth decay and obesity.
THE FACT: It really contributes only to tooth decay and its adverse effects can be offset by the addition of fluoride to drinking water and toothpaste.

Sugar has had a bad press. The nutritionist Professor John Yudkin described it as 'pure, white and deadly'. A whole episode of the BBC's flagship current-affairs programme *Panorama* on 10 October 2004 was devoted to the supposed iniquities of the sugar industry. The reason for this media interest is that we know that we do not need sugar in our diet in order to survive – we can live perfectly good, healthy lives without it. Nevertheless, we like it. The question is, does it do us any harm?

Sugar means different things to different people. To a doctor, nurse or patient with diabetes, sugar in a medical context is synonymous with glucose, because it is the only simple sugar found in body fluids such as blood and urine in amounts that are easily measured. It is the form in which the sugar we eat is used by the body. To a chemist, sugar is an alternative name for one type of carbohydrate. These are carbon-containing compounds in which hydrogen and oxygen occur in the same ratio as in water. They are usually sweet to the taste. To the cook, sugar is synonymous with sucrose, a substance containing equal amounts of glucose and fructose bound to one another chemically, and comes either from sugar cane or sugar beet. Both produce sugar that is indistinguishable without the help of sophisticated isotopic analysis.

However, to those in the food industry not all sugars are sucrose. To them the term 'sugar' includes both sucrose and invert sugar. Invert sugar is made from sucrose by splitting it chemically into an equal mixture of fructose and glucose. More recently, something resembling invert sugar has been made from hydrolysed starch. It contains more fructose than glucose and is cheaper than ordinary sugar. It is widely used in the soft-drinks industry in the USA, and to some extent in Europe.

All the sugar we buy in the shops is sucrose. In its unrefined state it is inedible and brown. So-called 'natural brown sugar' is partially purified sugar, which still contains some plant colorants. It is sold at a premium to people who believe it is healthier and better for them than white sugar. It's not the same as conventional brown (table) sugar, which is ordinary refined white sugar, stained brown.

There is absolutely no reason why sucrose, taken as sugar, should figure in our diet at all. Unlike proteins, fats, vitamins, minerals and water, it is not an essential constituent of our diet, but its presence in all fruit and most commercially prepared foods makes it extremely difficult to avoid. The transformation of sugar from an expensive luxury in the seventeenth century to a substance providing some 10 per cent or more of our average daily energy intake is due principally to its sweetness. It is seldom used primarily as a source of calories, since it is always more expensive than starchy or fatty foods. Despite the current fashion for low-carbohydrate diets, some carbohydrate is probably necessary. Starch, the most abundant carbohydrate in all but the most bizarre diets, can be converted by the body into all the various forms of sugar required by the body as part of its structure as well as for energy.

Sweetness is a primary taste. Mother's milk contains lactose, a sugar with about half the sweetness of sucrose, and many synthetic milk preparations contain sucrose – it is added to make cow's milk, which has only half the lactose content of human milk, more palatable. It is this ability to make foods and medicines palatable that has led to sugar's current widespread use and production throughout the world.

No one would come to physical harm if they never ate another gram of sugar. Indeed, there is a rare disease, more common in western France and in Switzerland than in Britain, that can be treated effectively only by completely excluding sugar from the diet. This necessitates avoiding fruits and many vegetables as well as foods containing refined sugar. This disease – hereditary fructose intolerance – provides good evidence for the nonessential nature of dietary sucrose and fructose: sufferers can lead healthy lives provided they avoid fructose, and because they cannot eat sugar they usually have very healthy teeth. This demonstrates the importance of sucrose in causing dental decay – the one common ailment that can be genuinely laid at its door.

Sugar was considered a highly desirable dietary item until comparatively recently. The idea that it might not be all it was cracked up to be, and that it could be a cause of bad rather than good health, appears to have gained ground during the 1950s. It was promoted by a British naval officer, Surgeon Captain Thomas Cleave, who in 1957 coined the name *saccharine disease* to describe a number of seemingly unrelated chronic illnesses that he attributed to the large amounts of highly refined carbohydrates in the diet. These included not only sugar but also white flour and polished rice, all of which, he postulated, had had much of their health-promoting factors – most notably dietary fibre – removed, leaving behind just 'empty calories'. Professor John Yudkin, one of the most distinguished academic nutritionists in Britain at the time, working independently of Cleave, also came down heavily on the detrimental effects of sugar in his book, *Pure, White and Deadly*. He exonerated dietary starches because they produce only glucose following digestion in the gut. He believed that it was largely the fructose component of table sugar that was harmful.

Cleave and Yudkin both relied heavily on epidemiological evidence linking increased sugar use with a rising incidence of coronary heart disease, diabetes, hypertension, gout, tooth decay and of course obesity. Cleave went further and included peptic ulceration, varicose veins and diverticulitis of the colon among the various manifestations of the saccharine disease, which he blamed largely on the loss of dietary fibre during the refining process.

The rise in life expectancy in the past 50 years has been associated with an increase in the prevalence of chronic diseases. The possible link between diet and disease has led to attempts by governments on both sides of the Atlantic to find out whether changes to our diet might make us healthier. In the USA, a committee chaired by George McGovern published its 'Dietary Goals for the United States' in 1977. The main thrust of the report was that Americans should reduce their fat, cholesterol and meat intake and increase their carbohydrate consumption to a level such that it would provide 55–60 per cent of their total energy (calorie) intake. These changes were to be achieved by increasing the consumption of fruits, vegetables and whole grains, while reducing the intake of refined sugar to 15 per cent of total energy intake (this was amended in the second edition, published later in the year, to 10 per cent).

This figure was not based on any hard scientific evidence. Though the target may have been achievable, it was not reached. Indeed, there is no evidence that it would have done most of those reaching the target much good. It might possibly have reduced their incidence of tooth decay and, if combined with other dietary restrictions, lessened the risk of obesity. Similar advice was offered by NACNE (National Advisory Committee on Nutrition Education) – an ad hoc British committee whose final report was never issued officially. (It was claimed that it was never officially endorsed, due to a dirty-tricks campaign by the food industry.)

In the 1980s, behavioural disorders in children were added to the list of diseases that Cleave and Yudkin had ascribed to sugar. As a result of this crescendo of accusations about the role of sugar in disease, the Center for Food Safety and Applied Nutrition in America commissioned the most thorough evaluation of the health aspects of sugars and sweeteners ever undertaken. The US Food and Drug Administration (FDA) Sugars Task Force, as it was called, took into account that in America, but not in Europe, only half of the sugar consumed per head of the population was sucrose; the rest was largely high-fructose corn syrup (HFCS), whose production in Europe was held back to protect the sugar-beet industry. If fructose was the real culprit, these studies should have revealed it. The task force found that there was absolutely no evidence that sugar, including those sugars with a high fructose content, caused any of the long list of diseases laid at its door, including diabetes and behavioural disorders in children. The only exception was tooth decay (this problem has been partly overcome in the UK by the addition of fluoride to drinking water and toothpaste). Only in the case of hereditary fructose intolerance and a few other equally rare genetic disorders can sugar be considered a specific health risk.

This is not the impression given by most health writers, who do themselves and their readers a disservice by extrapolating from animal experiments, in which huge amounts of sugars are added to animals' diets, to human beings eating a normal diet. There probably are some people, especially but not exclusively children, who drink inordinately large amounts of sugary drinks or eat too many sweets that supply energy but none of the other essential nutrients contained in natural plant and animal foods. People often do not realise how much sugar they consume in various products, especially in fruits and fruit juices. One grossly obese patient told me that she drank four litres of pure fruit juice a day. What she did not realise was that this contained 400 grams of sugar providing 1,600 calories, even though no sugar or syrup had been added. While it is true that sugar in fruit is associated with trace elements, vitamins and dietary fibre, whereas sugar from a packet or in prepared foods is not, the sugar in both is otherwise exactly the same.

The way in which sugar is eaten does, however, have an effect upon some functions of the body. Taken in large amounts on an empty stomach, sugar, especially glucose, can cause such a sudden rise in the blood-sugar level that it produces an excessive corrective response producing a fall to a level that may temporarily interfere with brain function. This condition, referred to as *reactive hypoglycaemia*, is easy to produce in the laboratory, but rare in real life. It became a fashionable condition in the 1970s – when a diagnosis of hypoglycaemia was in vogue, and was more socially acceptable than the generally more realistic ones of neurosis, chronic alcoholism and anxiety states. Hypoglycaemia provided a bonanza for health writers, who could lay at sugar's door yet another supposed evil. They even went so far as to describe sugar, in blazing headlines, as a poison or toxin that ruined the lives of millions of unsuspecting victims. They claimed, without scientific evidence, that removing sugar from the diet cured these conditions. Today a diagnosis of hypoglycaemia is largely confined to rare cases of disease affecting one or more of the bodily organs that produce a low concentration of glucose in the blood.

There is no doubt that sugar makes food palatable and in this sense contributes to obesity, which is an important cause of diabetes and heart disease. It is sensible to try to reduce the intake of sugar in children, especially in carbonated soft drinks, because large amounts contribute to making them fat and cause dental decay. Adults should make their own choice whether to drink water, fruit juice or unsweetened drinks, provided that they make their choice knowingly and not on the basis of spurious benefits suggested by an advertisement.

Artificial sweeteners

The onslaught against sugar by health-food writers is mild compared with that against artificial sweeteners. These are in the main substances that are intensely sweet and can be added to foods to increase their palatability but not their bulk or calorie content. The first was saccharine, which remains popular with manufacturers and customers, though a minority find that it leaves a bitter aftertaste and avoid it.

At first, saccharin use was confined to sweetening drinks and foods designed for people with diabetes. But now it and the many other intense sweeteners that have been discovered and licensed by the various food regulatory authorities are used in the production of foods and drinks aimed at preventing obesity – which is a much bigger market. Of the many substances that have been found to possess intense sweetness, only a very small number have survived the intense safety testing now demanded of them, which generally takes at least ten years. It is never completed, since the licence can be withdrawn at a moment's notice – as in the case of cyclamate, for example – only to be restored when further testing shows the alarm to have been a false one.

There is, however, no internationally agreed standard and different national licensing authorities have different criteria. Saccharin, cyclamate, aspartame and sucralose are the most important intensive sweeteners that are licensed by most but not all of the world's food-safety regulators. The conditions under which they can be used depend partly on regulation partly on their own chemical properties – whether they will withstand cooking for example.

Notwithstanding the extensive testing and constant post-marketing vigilance they undergo, each of the intense sweeteners has been the subject of scare stories – none more so than aspartame. This is probably the most widely used intense sweetener worldwide, after saccharine, but also one of the most vilified. This began with rumours that it caused all manner of illnesses – rumours that were based mainly on a fraudulent scare story put out in the 1980s under the pseudonym of Nancy Markle. Although most well-informed modern detractors admit that this was a fake and claim to rely only upon peer-reviewed scientific data to support their case, their arguments are weak and fly in the face of overwhelming evidence of safety from experimental and human epidemiological studies.

The latest attack on aspartame and the subject of a debate on its safety in the UK Parliament was based on a life-long rat study from an Italian research institute. This showed that in female rats – but not male rats fed exactly the same dietary regime – a significantly large number had histological evidence of lymphoma or leukaemia when they died than those whose diet did not include aspartame. What the aspartame detractors fail to mention is that the authors themselves say, buried away in the results section but not mentioned in the discussion or conclusions, is that 'no substantial difference in survival was observed among treated and control groups, males or females'. In other words aspartame does not limit life (of rats) – it just changes the condition from which they die (but only if they are female).

Coincidentally the Italian study showed that the increase in brain tumours that had been the basis of an earlier aspartame health scare could not be confirmed, emphasising once again that reliance upon a single study or even multiple studies, no matter how well conducted, cannot be relied upon as providing the absolute truth.

Pointing out that the health scares generated about the intense sweeteners does not mean that I endorse their use. There is no convincing evidence that they actually help reduce the incidence of obesity, although theoretically they should. The greatest users of foods – and more especially drinks – sweetened with intense sweeteners are the obese, not the slim members of the community.

The motives of people opposing the use of artificial sweeteners, like those opposing the use of sugar, are not necessarily the same, nor are they based upon scientific evidence. Resentment against their manufacturers undoubtedly plays a major role, as does the Myth that natural foods are safer and better than purified or synthetic ones. It is no surprise that many of the health-food writers who castigate the licensed intensive sweeteners advocate the use of an equally intense but 'natural' sweetener known as stevioside (or stevia). The only trouble is that stevia consistently failed to pass the toxicity testing required for a certificate of safety from regulatory bodies throughout the world except those where it gets by under a 'grandfather clause'.

Because there are no specific health reasons for using or not using high-intensity sweeteners or sugar in foods and drinks, people who prefer sweetness should not be made to feel guilty by those who improperly condemn them as noxious substances. After all, as Mary Poppins reminds us, a spoonful of sugar helps the medicine go down!

Chapter Six

SALT

BY SANDY MACNAIR

THE MYTH: If everybody ate less salt, this would lower the national average blood pressure and prevent thousands of premature deaths each year from strokes and heart attacks.
THE FACT: Most of us can handle up to a tenfold increase without significant changes in blood pressure. There is some evidence that a low-salt diet increases the risk of premature death.

A study of 10,000 men and women in 32 countries in the Intersalt Study published in 1988 showed that the average daily intake in almost every country where salt is freely available is between 6 and 12 grams. The British average is 9 grams, almost exactly the worldwide average, and this suggests that we have it about right. However, an expert committee of nutritionists that was set up by the Department of Health in 1987 to review recommended daily amounts of vitamins, minerals and other nutrients concluded in 1991, that 4 grams of salt per day would be sufficient for 97 per cent of the population.

The expert committee made no allowance for the salt lost in sweat, although they did acknowledge that unaccustomed hard exercise or exposure to high temperatures could induce salt losses in sweat of as much as 20 grams a day. This of course left no margin for those unacclimatised to heat on exposure to a sudden heat wave. Recent heat waves in Europe and the UK have resulted in thousands of deaths among the elderly as a consequence, in large part, of an enhanced risk of heart attacks and strokes caused by sodium depletion.

Human evolution

Humans belong to the order Primates, which includes apes and monkeys. Within that order is the family Hominidae, comprising humans and the great apes. The hominoids evolved from a common ancestor about 14 million years ago in the Rift Valley in Africa. It is probable that, in the process, the hominoid ancestors, common to both the great apes and the hominids, became separated. The population on the eastern, more arid and open, side of the Rift evolved into the hominids and those on the western side, remaining in the hot, humid rain forest environment, continued along their evolutionary track to become the great apes.

The unique features of the Rift provided the ecological niche that facilitated the evolution of *Homo sapiens*. Principal among these was the fact that there were rainy seasons and dry seasons. The absence of the rich, year-round variety of the plant foods of the rainforest required these early humans to look to the only alternative food sources: fish from the lakes and meat from the nomadic herbivores. The lakes filled during the seasonal rains but had little or no outlet to the sea and most or all of the water they lost in the dry season was by evaporation.

The shores of the lakes of the Great Rift Valley abound with crystalline salt deposits The evolution of man's large brain, three times the size of that of the chimpanzee, was extraordinarily rapid, occurring in less than two million years and was clearly dependent on an adequate source of the essential fatty acids provided by Rift Valley lake fish.

Studies by the palaeontologists Bramble and Lieberman reported in 2004 found that the fossil evidence from an examination of their leg bones suggested that man evolved as a long-distance runner. Unlike the great cats and the hunting dogs, humans are poor sprinters. The human approach was to hunt their quarry by day and, by outrunning the target animal, to pursue it until it was exhausted, when it could be despatched with hand-held weapons. Moreover, the seasonal availability of a glut of meat followed by a dearth in the dry season required the development of long-term preservation of supplies; it would not have taken *Homo sapiens* long to discover that burial in the lake shore salt pans would keep a carcase safe and its meat palatable for many months.

Thermoregulation in extreme heat

Dependence on long-distance running in the heat of day, close to the equator, required the parallel evolution of an effective means of dissipating waste heat. Where the ambient temperature is considerably lower than core body temperature, the normal mechanisms combining radiation, conduction and convection suffice to lose the heat. When the ambient temperature approaches or surpasses the body temperature, evaporation of water provides the only effective means of losing heat. This necessitates sweating and the production of sweat requires adequate supplies of salt as well as water.

Homo sapiens is one of the very few land mammals with almost no body hair. Virtually the whole skin surface is peppered with the openings of the 4 million or so sweat glands whose sole function is to respond to a rise in core temperature by producing sweat. Heat is lost by the evaporation of the salty sweat on the surface of the skin. The evaporation of 1.7 litres of water results in a heat loss of 1,000 kilocalories.

Each sweat gland is a coiled tube that starts below the skin surface and from which emerges a duct carrying its secretions onto the skin surface. The coil is a secretory organ that actively extracts salt and water from the blood. The 'precursor sweat' produced in the coil contains much the same concentration of salt as in the plasma, some 8 grams per litre. The sweat duct is lined by cells, which recover some of the salt from the 'precursor sweat'. The sweat in an unacclimatised subject, by the time it finally emerges onto the skin surface, contains about 3 grams of salt per litre. In those who are fully acclimatised, the salt concentration can be as low as 0.3 gram per litre or one-tenth of that in the unacclimatised.

Acclimatisation, which takes a week to ten days of continuous heat, also increases the capacity of the glands to secrete precursor sweat, raising the maximum sweat output from about 1 litre per hour to twice or three times that rate. Salt lost in sweat in the unacclimatised can be as high as 30 grams per day, while in the fully acclimatised it may be as little as 3 to 5 grams, despite an increase in the volume of sweat produced.

The role of sodium in the body

In solution, sodium chloride ionises to form a positively charged sodium ion and a negatively charged chloride ion. The sodium ion is the most important of the several ionic constituents in the 15 litres or so of body water outside the tissues of the body (i.e. the extracellular fluid or ECF). Sodium ions are essential for virtually all bodily processes including nerve conduction, hormone secretion, digestion, detoxification and consciousness.

Not only does sodium play a critical role in the function of every cell but its presence in the ECF at an exact concentration equivalent to 8 grams of salt per litre provides the mainstay of the osmotic pressure that holds the volume of the ECF and the blood plasma stable within narrow limits. Not surprisingly, the body has evolved a series of interlocking feedback systems to ensure that the volume and ionic composition of body water in its various compartments are rigorously monitored and constantly corrected. Within the kidney there is a system of enzymes and hormones that continuously sample the salt content of blood flowing through it. If sodium is on the low side then a hormone in the blood, angiotensin II, is activated, causing the smaller peripheral blood vessels to constrict with a rise in blood pressure, which, among other things, raises the rate at which water is filtered from the blood by the kidney.

At the same time a hormone released from the adrenal glands (aldosterone) enhances the reabsorption of sodium from the urine being filtered out by the kidney and from any sweat passing down the sweat ducts towards the skin surface. The net effect is to conserve what sodium there is within the body and avoid sodium depletion while excreting excess water so that the concentration of sodium in the ECF and blood plasma returns to normal. The process is reversed if the level of sodium is too high. Another hormone, the antidiuretic hormone, is released from the pituitary gland beneath the brain. Its effect is as its name suggests: simply to inhibit the excretion of water by the kidney while the sensation of thirst is experienced by the individual, who promptly begins to seek water and, by drinking, increases the body water with a reduction in the sodium concentration in the ECF.

The effect of salt intake on blood pressure

The average salt content of the human body is about 250 grams, of which approximately half is in the ECF. Salt is absorbed fairly quickly from the diet causing an increase in the salt content of the ECF. This produces the sensation of thirst as the body attempts to restore the status quo.

Those who advocate dietary salt restriction suggest that the rise in ECF volume following the consumption of a salty meal causes a rise in blood pressure. However, there is no evidence that hypertensive people (those given to high blood pressure) have an increased blood volume. There are several studies that show that athletes, who, in spite of having a 20 per cent greater blood volume than similar but untrained individuals, usually have lower blood pressures. The blood pressure is controlled by sensors in the large vessels carrying blood to the brain, which monitor the stretch in the vessel wall with each pulse of blood leaving the heart. The critical set point is the pressure required to maintain an adequate blood supply to meet the needs of the brain. This system monitors the output from the heart on a beat-by-beat basis and reacts within seconds if a change is needed. It is almost entirely independent of the blood volume.

To understand the role of the kidneys in controlling the amount of sodium in the body it is helpful to consider the principles that govern their work. Of the 5 litres of blood pumped out by the heart every minute, about one litre flows through the kidneys and of this about one-tenth is filtered off by the glomeruli – the part of the kidney that filters the fluid part of the blood from the cells. This filtrate is almost completely, but very selectively, reabsorbed and returned to the bloodstream. Those constituents that the body needs, such as amino acids, sugar and most of the water, are returned to the blood while waste products, such as urea and the end products of protein metabolism, remain in the filtrate. The water and dissolved constituents that remain then enter a final collecting system and are delivered to the bladder as urine.

In the course of a day, the amount of water filtered from the blood amounts to 170 to 180 litres. The amount of salt in this filtrate is nearly 1.5 kilograms (1,500 grams), of which all but about 9 grams is reabsorbed. The real work of the kidney is in reabsorbing about 170 litres of fluid and over a kilo of salt. If the kidney is slow to excrete salt then it is simply responding to hormonal signals to conserve salt in the face of an apparent shortage.

Having regard to the importance of sodium chloride in the human body and the extraordinary complexity and precision of the feedback systems that have evolved to ensure stability of the sodium concentrations within and around the cells, it is not surprising that the effect on blood pressure of reducing salt in the diet is for most people zero or very close to zero. The amount of salt excreted in the urine precisely matches the intake after losses in sweat have been accounted for.

Studies on the effect of dietary salt restriction upon blood pressure reveal that normal healthy subjects show, at most, a tiny reduction of the average pressure of one or two millimetres of mercury. Of course, none of these feedback systems operates perfectly for everybody. In a trial of the effects on blood pressure of salt restriction in normal healthy individuals at the Indiana

University Center for Research in Hypertension, the dietary salt intake of 36 men and 46 women was reduced progressively over a two-week period. They aimed to get from the average American salt intake of 9 grams per day to about half of that and to keep it there for the three months of the study. The average daily salt intake was actually reduced from 9 to 3.9 grams during the trial and the average blood pressure, which had been 107.3/71.7 millimetres of mercury at the beginning, was, after the twelve weeks on the salt-restricted diet, down by a negligible 1.7/1.9 mm.

Very similar results have been obtained in recent composite analyses of numerous randomised trials of salt restriction. The researchers (E R Miller and her colleagues) went on to publish the changes in pressure for each individual in their study. These demonstrated that, although 43 of the 82 subjects in the group showed little or no change, there were 25 whose pressure fell and 14 who showed a rise. These pressure changes, when presented as graph, showed a classical bell-shaped curve, indicating that there is considerable random variation among individual responses.

In a subsequent study involving 64 boys and 85 girls, very similar results were observed: in the 12-week period of salt restriction (down to less than 3.5 grams of salt per day), the blood-pressure changes followed a similar bell-shaped curve varying between plus and minus 15 mm, as in the adults. In the children the average blood pressure of the group did not change at all.

The Indiana University Center for Research in Hypertension also carried out studies on a group of eight volunteers who were given diets in which the daily salt content was adjusted upwards every three days, from 0.6 grams to of 87 grams (about ten times their normal intake). They were given plenty of water to drink and they gained some weight due to temporary water retention. Although the mean blood pressure of the group rose from 110/66 mm to 130/85 mm on the highest intake, it was still within normal limits. Interestingly, one volunteer showed no change in his blood pressure over the whole range. Even with this enormous salt intake, he was troubled only by waking several times in the night with a full bladder!

Mario Timio and his colleagues reported on a twenty-year follow-up study in 144 nuns in an Italian Benedictine convent who were compared with 138 laywomen from the same region. Both groups consumed the amount of salt typical for European women in general, about 7 grams per day. The nuns followed St Benedict's dictum, *ora et labora* (pray and work), while the laywomen followed their usual way of life. Blood pressure and diet, in addition to other things, were examined at four-year intervals and, although the blood pressures of the lay women rose as they got older, those of the nuns remained steadfastly the same throughout. This single small study suggests that the rise in blood pressure that occurs with age in the majority of men and women in industrial societies is unlikely to be caused by the salt in the diet.

Can sodium restriction be harmful?

There are three concerns with regard to the safety of mass sodium restriction. First, as we have seen, in any group of normal healthy individuals, there are as many people whose blood pressure will rise when their salt intake is restricted as there are in whom the blood pressure will fall. In them, the risk of a heart attack or a stroke is increased. The UK government has been pressurising manufacturers to take much of the salt out of staple foods such as bread, cheese and breakfast cereals, covertly and without giving consumers the choice. It is assumed, without any evidence, that this enforced salt restriction will do no harm.

There are few studies of the long-term consequences of a low-salt diet in terms of mortality from cardiovascular disease. This is particularly troubling when what evidence there is suggests possible harmful consequences. In a study in 1995, of the relationship between dietary salt intake and heart attacks among men with high blood pressure, Michael Alderman and colleagues followed up 2,937 subjects for an average of nearly four years. The frequency of heart attacks was lowest in the group with the highest salt intake. In a 1998 study Alderman and his colleagues followed up the 11,348 Americans whose diet had been checked in the National Health and Nutrition Survey in 1971–5. They found that those with the lowest salt intakes showed the highest death rates from cardiovascular disease. These studies do not prove that there is a hazard associated with a low-salt diet but they give cause for concern.

This concern is supported in a study by Dr Keatinge and his colleagues in 1986 into the marked rise in recorded deaths from heart attacks and strokes in a British heat wave in 1976, published in the *American Journal of Medicine*. Maximum temperatures of 34.6°C were followed by peak mortalities from coronary and cerebral thrombosis one or two days later. In a laboratory experiment, they studied the effect of heat on young unacclimatised volunteers by exposing them to moving air at 41°C for six hours, during which they lost nearly 2 litres of sweat containing 12 grams of salt. In spite of the fact that water is freely available, the blood volume declined and clotting factors in the blood became more concentrated, a condition likely to promote thrombosis in elderly people. The important point is that in Britain, with our temperate maritime climate, very few of us, except those training as long-distance runners, are acclimatised to heat.

Conclusion

The charge that is levelled is that we urbanised humans eat far more salt than is good for us and that it causes some, perhaps most, of us to develop high blood pressure as we grow older. This is intuitively improbable. Man, in his evolution from tree dwelling vegetarian to omnivorous hunter, required an intake of salt above that of other primates. Left to his or her own devices, the average adult will take between 6 and 12 grams per day. There is no evidence that salt intake is correlated with the prevalence of high blood pressure or that salt restriction will reduce blood pressure in young normal individuals; indeed it is clear that in a significant proportion (up to 20 per cent) the blood pressure may rise, sometimes alarmingly, if salt intake is reduced. It cannot be assumed that the reduction in salt intake by a population as a whole is either reasonable or safe.

The champions of salt restriction across the population as a whole are, with few exceptions, either nutritionists or epidemiologists who do not appear to understand the complex physiology involved in sodium and water homeostasis. The tribal peoples of the rainforests in such parts of the world as South America and Papua New Guinea are held up as an example of people who eat little salt and whose blood pressure does not rise with age. They have indeed had to adapt to an environment in which there is virtually no salt. The blood pressures of these peoples do not rise as they get older but very few live to a ripe old age and their growth is stunted. On the other hand, the Japanese, whose average salt intake is among the highest in the world, are also the longest-lived race in the world.

Without adequate randomised trials to show that it is effective and establish its long-term safety, in particular to show reduced cardiovascular mortality, the imposition of a low-salt diet by government diktat appears particularly foolhardy and without any scientific basis.

Chapter Seven

WATER

BY STANLEY FELDMAN

THE MYTH: Binge drinking water is good for you.
THE FACT: It merely causes more trips to the toilet.

It seems that a bottle of water has become a fashion accessory, with young people binge drinking its contents at every occasion. Are we in the midst of yet another 'epidemic', one that dehydrates us to such an extent that we need constantly to top up our body's water level?

It is difficult to discover how this unlikely fashion started. The fluid needs of the body have been known for over 50 years, and we have managed to survive without swigging water at every opportunity. Perhaps the fashion can be traced back to the WHO's quite reasonable suggestion that about two litres a day of clean water is required, in addition to other nutritional needs, for all adults. There is evidence that the bottled-water industry has taken this as the basis of a sales pitch. In a BBC broadcast (*You and Yours*, December 2004) their representative insisted that water *meant* water, and out of preference it should be bottled water. Other fluids would not do, because they were not the pure 'clean water' referred to by the WHO.

Water Balance

Let's look at the reason behind our need for water. Life began in the oceans where water was plentiful. Only millions of years later, when the salt content of the seas increased to toxic levels, did a desalination mechanism become necessary in order to prevent a build-up of salt in the body. The kidneys carried out this function. When life emerged from the seas on to land, access to water became difficult and conservation of fluid became the priority for the kidney. As land-based life developed its ability to forage for food, a need to rid the body of excessive quantities of other salts and chemicals contained in this new diet, became necessary. Although the kidney became the principal organ for removing these unwanted substances from the body, it still retained the ability to conserve water by concentrating the urine. As the kidney can only excrete water-soluble chemicals, it needs a supply of water to fulfil this function. The amount of water required will depend on the amount of waste substances produced as a result of metabolism and the efficiency of the kidney at concentrating the urine.

Man is particularly vulnerable to a shortage of water: it is not only essential so that the chemicals that are the end product of metabolism can be excreted in the urine, it is also a crucial part of our metabolic heat-loss mechanism. Out of every 100 calories we burn in our bodies at rest, about 80 calories end up as heat. In order to cope with this inevitable heat production, man has evolved into a very sweaty organism – it is principally by the evaporation of sweat that we lose heat. The dangers associated with an inability to sweat have been known since ancient times, when god figures often died after they were covered from head to toe in gold paint for ceremonial purposes. More recently it was found that patients encased in whole body plasters often developed dangerously high temperatures. Sweating is so efficient that a man can exist in a room hot enough to cook a steak providing the atmosphere is dry; however, if the humidity is high and sweat cannot evaporate, he will die. Even at a room temperature of 20°C we lose heat by sweating – one does not have to be pouring with sweat to lose significant amounts of water. It is estimated that in temperate climates the average adult loses about 500 millilitres of water as sweat without even being aware of the loss. The loss of water will be higher if he or she does hard physical work, or if the ambient temperature is raised.

We also lose water during breathing. We breathe relatively dry air into our lungs, and exhale fully saturated moist air. One only has to breathe out on to a cold mirror to demonstrate the amount of water contained in our breath. The more rapidly and deeply we breathe, the more water is lost in this way. In normal circumstances we lose about 500 millilitres of water every 24 hours by this means.

Most of our water loss, however, is from the kidneys. The amount is variable as it depends upon the food we eat and the efficiency of the kidneys at concentrating urine. An average person on a mixed diet loses between 800 millilitres and one litre of fluid by this means.

A litre from the kidneys, half a litre through the breath and half a litre through sweating: we can now see where the fluid requirement of two litres a day comes from. It is neither a

minimum nor a maximum figure as the amount needed varies
with lifestyle, ambient temperature and the amount of physical
work done.

Fluid Intake

With a normal mixed diet we take in about one litre of fluid as
an inevitable consequence of the food we eat. A cucumber is 98
per cent water; fruit, seafood and fish are about 80–90 per cent
water, and even meat contains about 20–30 per cent water –
one only has to leave a piece of fresh meat out of the
refrigerator for a few hours to see how much fluid oozes out.
Some meats have added water injected into them: ham, bacon,
turkey and chicken often have up to 30 per cent of their weight
added as water. Only those on a very low-roughage, high-
protein diet, or those on a starvation slimming diet, fail to take
in at least one litre of fluid with their food. If in addition one
drinks a bowl of soup and two cups of tea or coffee, or a glass
of beer a day, one will have fulfilled the body's fluid
requirement. Extra water is unnecessary unless it is a hot day or
you have been doing hard physical work. It seems that the same
people who complain most vociferously about the practice of
adding water to meat to make it 'more succulent' (without
reducing the price per kilo) are the very ones who insist upon
adding water to themselves, by drinking from a bottle.

Is there any harm in drinking extra water? Not really, except
that it means extra trips to the toilet, and there are a few – usually
elderly – people in whom the brain's control system that normally
adjusts our thirst to our fluid needs is not robust and who may
suffer a water overload. It has been suggested rather fancifully
that one can 'detoxify' oneself by binge drinking water. This is

nonsense. Alcohol and other non water-soluble chemicals are detoxified by enzyme activity in the liver at a rate that is independent of the amount of water that is drunk.

Is there any time we need more than two litres of fluid a day? If the ambient temperature is high, the loss through sweating is increased even though one may not be aware of it; if the body temperature is raised, for example during a fever, extra water and salt is essential; if the rate of metabolism is increased during exercise, heat is produced and extra water may be necessary to replace that lost in sweating; and if breathing is increased, for example to meet the needs of physical work or as part of the adaptation to a high altitude, then there will be additional water loss and the need for an increased intake.

But, provided one is living a normal lifestyle and eating a sensible mixed diet, there is no need to carry around a bottle of water. One can be reassured that it is very unusual for fit people in temperate climates to suffer from dehydration. We have an exquisitely sensitive mechanism that tells us when we need to drink more fluid: it is called thirst.

Chapter Eight

TEA, COFFEE AND CAFFEINE

BY VINCENT MARKS

THE MYTH: Tea and coffee contain caffeine which causes untold misery and ill health.

THE FACT: Tea and coffee are among the healthiest drinks known and have health-giving properties that are equal but different.

Tea and coffee are the two most widely drunk beverages in the world. They provide the body with water in a palatable and safe form without increasing the intake of calories, unless spoiled by spiking them with sugar. This makes it all the more surprising that both are constantly denigrated in the health columns of our newspapers and women's magazines. It has been so since they were first introduced into Europe in the seventeenth century. Originally the objections to tea and coffee were on 'moral' grounds, much as with alcohol, and their association with a decadent lifestyle. For the past 50 years or so it has been exclusively on health grounds. Barely a month goes by without a new scare in the media linking coffee, or less commonly tea, with some disease.

Why, then, does virtually every fad diet and health writer claim that they are harmful? Are these two universally drunk beverages really so bad? And, if so, how and why? The reason usually given is that both tea and coffee contain caffeine, which is a drug and therefore an unnatural stimulus that must be harmful to the body. The same reasoning is applied to other caffeine-containing drinks such as Pepsi-Cola and Coca-Cola and other cola-containing drinks, such as Red Bull. Mysteriously, it does not appear to apply to drinks that contain guarana, which is lauded as 'natural' by many health writers but is caffeine under another name.

Tea and coffee are much more than mere solutions of caffeine in boiling water. They were often said to have medicinal properties, which, if modern evidence is to be believed, may well be true. Caffeinated beverages have been implicated in mental ill health, anxiety, high blood pressure, heart disease, insomnia, peptic ulcerations, constipation, foetal abnormalities and spontaneous abortion, headaches, malabsorption and nutritional abnormalities, including diabetes, discoloration of the teeth, hyperactivity in children and, most extraordinary of all, dehydration. Unlike those concerning alcohol, most of the allegations made against caffeine as a cause of ill health or disruption of society are untrue or so exaggerated as to be pernicious.

The best-known charge is that caffeine produces anxiety. This is undoubtedly true – but only when taken in immoderate amounts. This property of caffeine was recognised by the medical profession within a few years of the introduction of coffee into Britain during the seventeenth century. It was originally called the *syndrome of coffee* but is now more commonly referred to as *hypercaffeinism*.

How much caffeine is too much? The answer depends on the individual and the circumstances. A dose of 400 mg of caffeine, the equivalent of roughly eight cups of tea or six cups of instant coffee, taken over a 24-hour period, day after day, by a regular user, produces no adverse effects in the vast majority of people. Taken all at once, it has an effect on almost everyone. In caffeine-sensitive people it produces a sense of anxiety, amounting to panic. It may cause tension, rapid heartbeat and a temporary mild rise in blood pressure, while in the habitué the effect is scarcely noticeable. There are large interpersonal differences in its effect due to the rate at which caffeine is metabolised in the body and the dose contained in the particular drink.

Caffeine virgins are much more sensitive than habitués to all of its pharmacological effects but just how common anxiety is, as a symptom of caffeine intoxication, is difficult to determine. My colleagues and I attempted to assess the prevalence of caffeine-induced anxiety in patients some years ago by measuring the concentration of caffeine in the blood of patients in whom nervousness was a feature. It could be incriminated in very few patients.

Symptoms of caffeine overdose are frequently caused by the body's inability to detoxify it rather than with the amount taken. This is especially true in pregnant women, because their ability to render caffeine inert is reduced early in their pregnancy. It leads many of them to reduce the amount of coffee and tea they drink, or to abandon it altogether, sometimes even before they knew they were pregnant.

Caffeine has been accused of causing ADHD (attention-deficit hyperactivity disorder). Perversely, it has also been used to treat it. It has many pharmacological properties that are similar to Ritalin. Young children tend to metabolise caffeine more slowly than adults. As a result, it can reach toxic levels in their blood after smaller doses.

The main source of caffeine in children's diets is in drinks of the cola variety. Unfortunately, they are also a rich source of calories so that overindulgence carries the twin risk of contributing to obesity and caffeine intoxication. However, there is absolutely no reason, on health grounds, to forbid their occasional use.

The idea that tea and coffee are inferior to water in quenching thirst and maintaining the body's water balance is promoted by many health writers looking for something new to say. They base their argument on unproven statements, which are probably wrong, reiterated in most pharmacology textbooks that caffeine is a diuretic. The truth is exactly the opposite: tea and coffee are excellent for restoring water lost from the body. Nevertheless, because caffeine gives many people a sense of urgency to pass urine, the impression has grown that it is a significant diuretic. It isn't.

Tea and coffee are excellent sources of water and can safely be drunk in large quantities. They are acceptable to most elderly people and provide virtually no calories. They do, however, contain other ingredients or substances with seemingly beneficial effects. Both contain lots of antioxidants and coffee has a preventative effect on the development of Type 2 diabetes.

One of the most serious allegations against coffee is that it causes foetal abnormalities. But for every epidemiological study suggesting that it does there is at least one, generally better documented, refuting it. Many of the studies on which this suggestion has been based come from toxicological studies of caffeine in rodents.

Caffeine does raise the blood pressure under experimental conditions – especially in caffeine virgins. This effect is hardly ever seen with ordinary everyday usage. Although this has been well established, the rumour persists, perpetuated by those more intent on promoting themselves than the truth. Caffeine is not a cause of high blood pressure.

Caffeine has a reputation for causing irregularities of the heartbeat. Like its effect on blood pressure, this is likely to occur only if a lot of coffee is drunk in a relatively short time or it is metabolised slowly, as in the case of the coffee virgins. The acute pharmacological effects of caffeine wear off more quickly the longer it is used. This phenomenon, known as *tachyphyllaxis*, is well known to pharmacologists.

Caffeine can affect the onset and depth of sleep and is widely used for this purpose. The effect is quite small and the amount of caffeine in a single cup of tea or small cup of instant coffee is unlikely to have much effect. A few people, especially those whose average daily caffeine intake is small, may prefer to drink their coffee or tea decaffeinated, but for most of us this is quite unnecessary.

Is caffeine addictive? It is only in so far as most people who take caffeinated drinks continue to do so – but to compare it to tobacco and alcohol, as some writers do, is nonsense. Unlike genuinely addictive drugs, caffeine does not produce either physical or psychological damage when used properly. The only evidence of its 'addictiveness' is that habitual users may experience mild to moderate headache when they have not had any caffeine for 24 hours or so. The headache is never incapacitating and rapidly relieved by a single cup of tea or coffee Untreated, the headache passes off over a couple of days.

Caffeine increases calcium excretion by the kidneys – not by much but sufficient to support the notion that tea and coffee cause osteoporosis. Although some early epidemiological studies did suggest this, more thorough studies have failed to confirm it. Indeed the milk usually added to tea and coffee is one of the more important sources of dietary calcium – especially in the elderly.

All in all, caffeine is a pretty safe constituent of the diet, but, like any substance in our diet, it can cause trouble when taken in too large an amount. For most of us its ability to increase alertness and ward off tiredness are benefits not to be readily forgone.

Caffeine is not an essential constituent of tea and coffee, as the rapidly expanding sales of their decaffeinated versions testify. Indeed, through genetic engineering it is possible to produce the native product devoid of caffeine. Caffeine adds flavour to drinks and foods containing it and may account for the popularity of the carbonated cola drinks (which have little else to recommend them except their ability to provide water in a form that many children like).

Tea and coffee both contain caffeine and various antioxidants, although they do differ in many respects. There are, however, marginal preferences based on taste, custom, availability and price. Both coffee and tea – even the black variety drunk in this country – are extremely good sources of antioxidants. Although these are popular among health promoters and foodies, proven evidence of the benefits of antioxidants is hard to come by. Both drinks supply other beneficial constituents of the diet although these are poorly characterised. Coffee, for example, has been shown, when consumed frequently over many years, to be associated with a reduced risk of developing Type 2 diabetes, and a research group at Surrey University is close to identifying the active agent – which believes it is not caffeine. Both tea and coffee consumption have been associated with a reduced risk of developing some forms of cancers but the evidence is inconclusive.

Coffee drinking is associated with raised blood levels of homocysteine, a 'risk factor' for coronary heart disease. There is, however, no convincing evidence that coffee drinking actually causes heart disease.

Tea interferes with the absorption of *medicinal* inorganic iron, but not with natural *dietary* iron. Any association between tea drinking and anaemia, especially in the elderly, is coincidental and not causal. This does not stop ill-informed health writers describing tea as a cause of iron-deficiency anaemia and suggesting that it should be omitted from the diet.

Because tea contains small amounts of oxalic acid, which is a component of many renal stones, the rumour was started that tea is a cause of kidney stones. The reverse is the truth. The water in tea helps reduce the risk of kidney stones. The amount of oxalic acid contained in tea is infinitesimal compared with other foods that health-food freaks recommend such as rhubarb, spinach and beetroot. The concentration of oxalic acid in tea was wrongly quoted by these rumourmongers. They attributed the amount of oxalate in a litre of tea to just one cupful, or about five times too much. Remember Mark Twain's advice: 'Be careful about reading health books. You may die of a misprint.'

For a short period after it was first introduced to Western Europe, cocoa drinkers were considered a dissolute lot, but in recent times they are just considered dull. Cocoa itself is the third most popular caffeinated drink drunk by adults and is pretty innocuous. Recent evidence, however, suggests that, like tea and coffee, it may actually be a healthy addition to the diet. This will not come as any surprise to those who have always believed in the health-encouraging value of chocolate – especially the dark unsweetened variety.

It is a puzzle as to why the same people who are most antagonistic to drinking coffee are among the most vocal advocates of the perverse practice of coffee enemas – a potentially and sometimes actually dangerous procedure. There is neither scientific nor aesthetic justification for this bizarre practice. Caffeine can be absorbed from the colon when it is administered as an enema – but any benefit obtained from it when taken this way is much more easily obtained by drinking it.

A word about decaffeinated coffee. Modern methods of decaffeinating coffee use 'liquefied' carbon dioxide and are by their very nature noncontaminating. Nevertheless, the allegation that toxic chemicals are used in the decaffeination process and remain in the final product are trotted out regularly by health-food writers and self-promoting, so-called 'experts'. Whether you decide to use decaffeinated coffee or the genuine article should be determined entirely by individual taste and not by any purported health benefit or disadvantage.

Chapter Nine

ALCOHOL

BY VINCENT MARKS

THE MYTH: Alcohol is a dangerous health risk.
THE FACT: Moderate alcohol intake increases longevity.

Alcohol is both a food and a drug of addiction. This chapter addresses both of these properties.

Man's use of alcohol is shrouded in prehistory. Wine, mead and cider were drunk before records began. Beer was brewed from cereals in Egypt as long ago as 5000 BC. Three thousand years ago in China, distillation was used to make what we now call spirits, although it did not reach Europe until around the fifteenth century. Today, alcohol is used in every country in the world, even where it is forbidden by law on religious grounds.

Customs and Excise records relating to alcohol go back to 1680, and show just how much it contributed to the diet at that time. Average consumption in 1700, the peak year, was sufficient to provide about 50 grams (6 units) per head for the total population (including men, women and children). It was taken almost entirely in the form of beer and was probably the only bacteriologically pure drink available to town dwellers.

Alcohol must have contributed 20 per cent or more of the daily calorie intake, compared with about 6 per cent today. Even this relatively small amount is significant and should be taken into account in any calculation of energy intake. Beer brewed in former times contained a substantial proportion of the daily vitamin and mineral requirements, but nowadays few beers contain more than trace amounts of these substances. Spirits contain no extra nutrients, and were the origin of the 'empty calorie' concept.

Britain still consumes far less alcohol than many other countries. The French are the world leaders in alcohol consumption. They take it mainly in the form of wine, but their consumption is going down, while ours, made up mainly of beer, is going up. Alcohol intake reached its nadir in Britain in the late 1940s, when it was around one-third of the present levels. Since then it has risen slowly, but inexorably. This is largely due to an increased consumption of wine, which until recent times was considered a luxury, enjoyed by the rich.

Alcohol intake varies from one part of the country to another, and among different communities. Scotland has a higher per capita alcohol intake than southeast England, but it also has a higher proportion of teetotallers. This may be due to the particular type of alcohol abuse prevalent among the Scots and other north Europeans, which can be described as 'drinking to get drunk'. By contrast, the people of the Mediterranean take their alcohol mainly in the form of wine, with their meals. This gives rise to a very different type of alcohol abuse.

The pros and cons of alcohol

Unlike in times gone by, when beer and spirits were the only germ-free drinks available, alcohol owes its present popularity to its pharmacological effect. It causes euphoria and reduces inhibitions.

It is possible to draw up a balance sheet pitting the good effects of alcohol against the unfavourable ones. The unfavourable effects dominate the attention given to alcohol in the media. It is this, together with people's personal experience and upbringing, that formulates attitudes to alcohol. It is strange that, whereas two of the three great monotheistic religions use alcohol in their rituals, the third forbids any contact with it.

Alcohol abuse is one, if the not the main, cause of antisocial behaviour. This can take the form of public drunkenness and irresponsible behaviour, especially by members of a crowd, and violence towards oneself as well as towards others. Alcohol impairs work performance, even when taken in modest amounts. Anyone who has counted the number of errors they make while using a computer after drinking even modest amounts of alcohol with their lunch will have personal experience of this. The banning of alcohol on university campuses and other workplaces at lunchtime has much to be said for it – alcohol and work just do not go together.

Currently over 90 per cent of men and 85 per cent of women in Britain drink alcohol at least occasionally, and 6 per cent and 2 per cent respectively drink the equivalent of more than a bottle of wine a day. In a survey conducted in 1997, 12 per cent of young men and 5 per cent of young women between the ages of 16 and 24 admitted being drunk once a week during the previous three months. The percentage is probably higher today. Three-quarters of all stabbings and two-thirds of all murders in Britain are committed under the influence of alcohol, as are half of all street crimes and a third of sexual offences. Chronic alcohol abuse is the most common cause of domestic violence, and is responsible for the break-up of many families.

Fifteen per cent of road-traffic deaths are associated with excessive alcohol use, either by drivers of cars and motorcycles, or by pedestrians. This is less than it was before the campaign against drink-driving got under way some 30 years ago, but it is still too high. Many of the offenders are chronic alcoholics whose compulsion to drink is so great that that they either do not recognise their impairment or are indifferent to it. Many are otherwise decent, ordinarily law-abiding people who do not appreciate that one does not have to be drunk for one's judgement to be impaired. The legal limit in the UK for alcohol in the blood is a pragmatic compromise. It is 40 per cent higher than recommended for safety by most EU countries.

Few people realise how much alcohol they can drink over a given time and remain within our liberal drink-driving restrictions. The unit concept of alcohol intake has gone some way towards helping us understand the effect of alcohol intake on the blood level. One unit in the UK is about 10 millilitres or 8 grams of pure alcohol, and is the amount contained in a single 25-millilitre measure of spirits. It is substantially less than the amount of alcohol contained in half a pint of decent beer, or a quarter of a pint of strong cider. An average dinner-table 120-millilitre glass of wine contains nearly 1.5 units of alcohol, and the 250-millilitre giant-size glasses now served in some pubs provide 3 units. Four units of alcohol taken on an empty stomach can bring the average sized man, weighing 70kg, dangerously near the UK limit for driving and well above it in countries with lower limits. A typical person disposes of alcohol by destroying it in his or her liver, at a rate of around 8 grams or 1 unit an hour. The exact rate varies: it is determined largely by one's genes. Nothing one can do will increase the rate of alcohol disposal, although some drugs decrease it. Alcohol drunk hours earlier may still be present in the body long after it might be supposed to have disappeared, especially in those who metabolise it slowly. This is why some drivers, after a heavy drinking session the night before, may have above the legal limit of alcohol in their bodies the morning after.

The higher the alcohol levels in the blood, the greater is the depression of mental function. While the adage 'don't drink and drive' cannot be faulted, it may be unduly restrictive. The effect of alcohol depends upon the amount drunk and whether it is taken with food. Assuming that no alcohol had been taken in the previous twelve hours, it is possible for a man to drink half a bottle of wine (3–4 units) at the rate of half a unit per hour with a meal and to remain within the legal limits. These amounts are unsafe when the alcohol is taken on an empty stomach, and need to be reduced by a third for women weighing less than 70 kg. Just because a driver is legally safe, he is not necessarily a safe driver, as his reaction time will be slowed at alcohol levels well below the legal limit.

It is not only the damage that alcohol does to society through its effect upon behaviour that makes alcohol a concern, but also its effects upon health. The causal links between chronic excessive alcohol consumption and cirrhotic liver disease is so well established that the prevalence of cirrhosis in a society has been used as a marker for alcoholism. Other organs that can be affected by alcohol are the pancreas, bones, blood, the various endocrine glands and of course the nervous system, where, in its most malignant form, it produces permanent and irreversible damage. There is some weak epidemiological evidence linking alcohol use to various types of cancer. This is difficult to reconcile with the much-promoted anticancer effect of the antioxidants in many alcoholic drinks.

With such a weight of evidence against alcohol, is there anything to be said in its favour? Should it not be banned as a dangerous drug of addiction that causes far more ill health and deaths than cannabis, cocaine and heroin combined?

Not only was the impracticability of this demonstrated by the failure of Prohibition in America, but also the desirability of banning alcohol is far from established. To ban alcohol would deny us access to what is possibly a health-promoting agent. Leaving aside the fact that the alcohol industry is one of the largest employers of labour in the country and makes an enormous contribution to the economy, as well as to our export and internal revenues, there is good evidence that, used properly, alcohol increases longevity and prevents some of our most common diseases, as well as providing the lubrication of social intercourse.

Life-assurance companies have known for generations that moderate alcohol use is associated with longevity. It is only in the past 30 years or so that it has been established that this is due to alcohol's effect on reducing deaths from coronary heart disease. It probably also reduces the incidence of Type 2 diabetes, an increasingly important cause of chronic illness, invalidity and death.

The evidence for alcohol's beneficial effects upon coronary heart disease comes from an ever-growing list of epidemiological studies from all over the developed world, which is consistent with age-old evidence from autopsies carried out on chronic alcoholics. These autopsies found that, whatever else may have ailed them, the coronary arteries of alcoholics were unusually free from disease. The effect is more or less specific to the coronary and other major arteries. How alcohol exerts its beneficial effects, and whether the effects are due to the alcohol itself or to some substances associated with it in alcoholic beverages, is not known. One of the strongest cases that can be made for the beneficial effects of alcohol is its action in raising the concentration of the high-density lipoproteins (HDL) in the blood, the carrier of what is often referred to as 'good cholesterol'. There is good evidence that this is linked to a reduced risk of coronary-artery disease. Although far from proven, there is good evidence that alcohol from wine is more beneficial than that from beer or spirits. The most ardent advocates of the benefits of wine drinking attribute it mainly to the antioxidants, more of which are to be found in red than in white wine. Nevertheless, wine is an important constituent of the so-called Mediterranean diet, which dietary experts have declared to be healthy. Against these very positive effects of alcohol must be weighed the fact that alcohol can be a cause of high blood pressure.

The evidence as to what constitutes an optimum alcohol intake is reasonably clear. For men it is about 2–4 units a day on average, and for women it is 1–3 units. The level at which the health benefits are outweighed by the penalties are less clear. Few studies have tackled this problem, but one, which involved an average 15-year follow-up of 36,000 healthy men carried out in Nancy, France, suggested that up to 60 grams of alcohol a day produced the same life expectancy as life-long teetotalism. An optimum alcohol intake of up to 30 grams was associated with a significantly longer life expectancy. It would seem that drinking up to three glasses of wine a day increases life expectancy, but drinking more than six glasses reduces it.

What defines alcoholism? There is no universally acceptable definition, since alcohol can produce problems in so many different ways. It is probably better just to speak of alcohol abuse. I believe that anyone who incurs a personal health penalty, or produces social disruption, by drinking alcohol is abusing it. The level of alcohol at which this occurs varies from one individual to another, and upon the circumstances in which it is taken. Regular consumers of more than one bottle of wine a day – or 6 alcohol units taken in any form – must be putting themselves at unacceptable risk, whereas those drinking just half that amount can be considered prudent and health-conscious.

Accepting the evidence that alcohol in moderate amounts – from as little as 7 units a week to as much as 28 and possibly 40 units a week – can bring health benefits, are there any people who ought not to drink at all? The answer is yes. Those with a strong family history of alcoholism are better off never starting to drink rather than running the risk of being unable to stop. Those who have already had difficulties with alcohol are better off becoming completely abstinent rather than trying to moderate their drinking. Others who should not drink are patients receiving prescription drugs that interact with alcohol. These are too many to mention by name, but the common blanket prohibition of alcohol to patients prescribed antibiotics is unjustified except in special circumstances.

Pregnant women – or, to be more precise, their foetuses – are especially at risk from a devastating condition known as *foetal alcohol syndrome*, and the more common but infrequently diagnosed condition of *foetal alcohol effects*, a common cause of preventable mental handicap. Quantities of alcohol that present no danger to the non-pregnant woman can do so to a foetus. The occasional binge drinker is as much at risk as the chronic alcoholic. No one knows at what stage of a pregnancy the foetus is most at risk or at what level of alcohol intake it becomes a problem. To cover their own backs, some doctors advise total abstinence from alcohol during pregnancy. This advice, which is almost certainly unjustified on the basis of the evidence, imposes an unnecessary burden of guilt upon women who may have drunk the occasional glass of wine before they had been warned of the risks.

Telling the truth about the advantages as well as the disadvantages of alcohol as a constituent of the diet and letting people make their own judgements is, I believe, a better option than that advocated by the World Health Organisation, which takes the view that the health advantages of alcohol relative to its disadvantages have not been unequivocally established. This may be true from the point of view of society as a whole, but to the vast majority of people who use alcohol moderately and intelligently it produces an undeserved sense of guilt. The fact is that alcohol is with us to stay, and we must learn how to use it wisely.

Chapter Ten

PESTICIDES IN FOOD

BY LAKSHMAN KARALLIEDDE

'A person injured by a burning firewood panics on
seeing the harmless white light of a firefly.'
OLD SRI LANKAN SAYING

THE MYTH: Our food is doused in harmful pesticides.
**THE FACT: Pesticide residues are not allowed to exceed
onehundredth of the amount that causes even a slight reaction
in the most sensitive species.**

The public is justifiably concerned by reports of horrendous consequences of food contaminated with pesticides. What are the facts and how far are these horror stories justified?

Pesticides have been manufactured with the intent of destroying life – those of the pests – insects, weeds and fungi – that destroy crops and reduce their yield. These infestations are a major factor contributing to global malnutrition. They were initially introduced to destroy those insects that are the vectors of diseases such as malaria, bilharzia, trachoma and fly-borne gastroenteritis. Malaria alone causes huge global misery. It is estimated that each year there are about 3,000,000 deaths due to malaria and about 5,000,000,000 episodes of clinical illness necessitating anti-malarial therapy. Fly-borne gastroenteritis is the biggest single killer of children in Africa.

Pesticides are dangerous. Ill health and deaths have been caused by the oral intake of large quantities of insecticides by people trying to commit suicide. Although common in Asia and South America, such incidents are rare in developed countries, where pharmaceutical agents and toxic household products are likely to be used by those attempting suicide.

Just as the careless use of a car may lead to death and injury (globally, 25 per cent of all 'injuries' are road-traffic-related), the misuse of pesticides will cause ill health. In contrast to cars, pesticides are used mainly by those with a poor educational and scientific background. Ignorance and misunderstanding leads to misuse. In many parts of the world no licensing is required and no training offered to those responsible for spraying crops with pesticides. It is usually impoverished, illiterate farmers, some on the verge of starvation and living in developing countries, who carry out the spraying of pesticides. They often live in single-roomed dwellings, where they cook, eat and store the pesticide alongside their food. Their primary aim is to generate sufficient income from their produce for the survival of their families.

The vast majority of them know nothing about the toxicity of the pesticides they use and apply these dangerous chemicals, often in uncontrolled mixtures, in amounts that often exceed those recommended. They cannot afford to buy any of the necessary protective equipment or to obtain modern spraying equipment. There is a sense of desperation that forces them to take risks and work much longer hours than are acceptable in developed countries. They frequently spray pesticides all day, with a total disregard to weather conditions and wind direction. The equipment they use is often old and faulty, which causes widespread contamination.

Under these circumstances it is not surprising that there are cases of ill health among those using pesticides. There have also been reports of poisoning following the accidental contamination of food, especially cereals, rice, sugar and salt used in relatively large amounts in the preparation of meals. Virtually all these cases of contamination have taken place in poverty-ridden communities where facilities for safe, separate storage of pesticides are beyond the reach of the populace.

Accidental contamination of this kind in Asia and South America is very different from the problem of pesticide residues in the food eaten in developed countries. The former implies some form of pollution, involving much larger amounts of pesticides than those found as residues. The presence of a residue implies a much less harmful situation, either because of the circumstance in which it occurs or the amount involved. Although there have been reports of food contaminated with naturally occurring toxins from plants and bacteria and chemical contamination causing ill health and even death in developed countries, there are no reports in the literature of any such effects ever being caused by residues of pesticides.

The scenarios of ill health and danger due to pesticides are entirely a result of unusual, unacceptable and unfortunate practices that are rife in developing countries. They are not encountered in developed countries such as the UK, where regulatory and monitoring process are active, aggressive and advanced.

The food chain

Safety is important to all involved in the food chain. How important are pesticide residues in this process when compared with the other problems associated with our diet? Something is badly wrong when pressure groups and scaremongers cause us to be concerned about the inconsequential amounts of pesticide residues in our food. The real problem is the way we feed ourselves and the food itself. None of these diet-related problems can be even remotely attributed to pesticide residues in food. The problem in the developing world occurs when the farmers of these poorer countries struggle to compete with the flood of subsidized food from the rich world's abundant farms. They find it necessary to use more and more pesticides to produce bigger and better crop yields. It is this vicious circle that causes the real problem with pesticides.

Not all pesticides leave residues in food, and most of the residues that can be found are on the surface and can be removed by peeling or washing. If pesticides were not used, the cost of fruit and vegetables would soar, less would be eaten and the nation's health might deteriorate. The risk from reducing the fruit and vegetable content of our diet outweighs any minute potential risk due to a tiny amount of pesticide residue.

How much pesticide?

The use of pesticides on edible crops and in horticulture is controlled in the European Union by Directive 91/414.

In technologically advanced countries such as the UK, pesticide residues are constantly monitored, using the most advanced equipment available, to ensure that the public are provided with a consistent supply of high-quality clean food free of unwanted chemicals Various factors are taken in to consideration, such as the *acceptable daily intake* (ADI). This is the amount of a pesticide that can be consumed safely every single day of one's life. To arrive at this amount, there are studies of the chemical's absorption rate, distribution, metabolism and excretion. This is then set against all the known data for its toxicity. The actual dose accepted is calculated from information gathered from the most sensitive endpoint – long before the signs of any true ill effects become apparent – in the most sensitive species. The level of safety found in these tests is then usually reduced a hundredfold to give the acceptable maximum level, the ADI, in food. This hundredfold reduction in the acceptable toxicity comprises a factor of 10 for potential interspecies extrapolation and a further 10 for interspecies variability. Where the pesticide has appreciable acute toxicity (the sort of chemical used only in exceptional cases as a single dose) a second reference dose is given. This is the *acute reference dose* (ARfD) and is the amount of a pesticide that, on the basis of current knowledge, can be consumed with complete safety at a single meal or in a single dose. The calculations are done separately for toddlers and adults. The *maximum residue level* (MRL) of pesticide is arrived at in a similar way to the acceptable dose levels. These MRLs take into consideration any special risks to babies, children and the elderly. Occasional instances where the MRL has been exceeded have been seized upon in the media as evidence of a dangerous failure of the system. They interpret the MRL as a safety limit. It is not: it is 100 times the level that causes any effect in the most sensitive animals. Exceeding the MRL indicates a failure to use pesticides correctly, but, as an isolated incident, it should not give rise to any concern by the consumer.

The toxic effects of the organophosphorus insecticides are well documented in the medical literature. Scaremongers have speculated that long exposure to the toxic effects of low doses may be responsible for virtually all of the medical problems suffered by humanity (as well as the early demise of thousands of animal, bird and plant species). They have fostered fears of carcinogenicity and birth defects in spite of an absence of any toxicology data to substantiate their claims. The fact that the only scientific report that relates low-dose exposures (as opposed to doses taken orally with suicidal intent) to any medical problem has followed the occupational use of pesticides by those involved in preparing the solutions used for sheep dips seems to have passed them by. There is no evidence to suggest that the long-term exposure to the minuscule amounts of pesticides on some produce is likely to cause any ill effects. There have never been any reports of any effects on health due to pesticide residues on food, even when it exceeded the MRL.

Currently, EU MRLs are replacing UK MRLs. About 280 active substances are now approved for use as agricultural pesticides in the UK and a list of around 680 have been approved in one or other of the EU states. In 2003, in the UK, more than 3,500 samples of food were collected from retail outlets and tested. In addition inspectors from the agriculture department, DEFRA, collected 500 samples from ports, wholesalers, import points and retail depots. Where there is wide seasonal variation in the source of supply, as for most fruit and vegetables, samples were collected each month for the whole year.

Of the total of 4,071 food samples analysed in 2003, no residues at all were found in 75 per cent of them. Residues below the MRL were found in 24 per cent of the samples. In fewer than

1 per cent of the samples, the residues exceeded the MRL. In all, the Pesticide Residue Committee reported the results for more than 170,000 pesticide/commodity combinations. As part of the violation-investigation programme, fruit and vegetables coming from a source where the produce has exceeded the MRLs in the past are targeted for special attention. When a crop is found that has exceeded the MRL, it is seized and destroyed.

Illness due to pesticide residues is exceedingly rare and mostly confined to countries without well-developed regulatory systems or is the result of accidents. In spite of this, it has been suggested that sporadic cases of poisoning might easily be missed or misdiagnosed. It is reassuring that, among the thousands of publications relating to the toxicity of organophosphorus insecticides, a search of all the relevant literature has not revealed a single incident that has been associated with residues marginally exceeding MRLs.

The main problem with the pesticides remains one of the contamination of foodstuffs used in large amounts in the preparation of meals, be that during the preparation itself, the storage or the transportation. This is almost exclusively a problem of their uncontrolled use in the developing world. These two scenarios – one relating to residues, the other to contamination – are separate and should not be confused. The regulatory mechanisms to monitor pesticide residue in fruit and vegetables in developed countries are as robust and thorough as possible. They operate with a large margin of safety and are constantly being reviewed to ensure that consumers of any age can eat as much fruit and vegetables as they like without any fear of ill health due to pesticides.

Chapter Eleven

FOOD ADDITIVES: HOW SAFE, HOW VALUABLE?

BY MAURICE HANSSEN

THE MYTH: E numbers are harmful and undesirable.
THE FACT: E numbers are perfectly safe, and their use is well controlled.

A survey by the Consumers' Association in 2004 found that a third of people try to avoid food additives for fear of adverse effects on their health. It is true that some additives can cause problems for a few of us and equally true that the modern food supply chain could not exist without them. We are blessed with foods that can be very safe and stay fresh for a longer time than ever before. It is also possible to disguise a product so that, although it is very high in fats and water and contains little of nutritional worth, it tastes delicious and fools our senses into believing that it is good for us.

Additives have been used for thousands of years. Today almost all wines have added sulphites to prevent them from going off or fermenting. Some asthmatics find that this can trigger an attack but, like the ancient Greeks who burned sulphur over their amphorae of wine to produce sulphites, we just enjoy the fruits of the vine. Since November 2005, it has been necessary to declare the presence of sulphites (E221–8), as California has done for many years. Medieval chefs decorated their elaborate confections of marzipan with bright colours to entrance the senses. Gold and silver (E175 and E174) have been used to decorate confectionary and festive dishes throughout recorded history.

Our ancestors well understood the preservative properties of salting and smoking and also curing meats with saltpetre (E252) and brine to provide meat and fish throughout the year.

The industrial revolution brought in the roller-milling of wheat to produce white flour, but, in an effort to make flour whiter, some unscrupulous millers added white lead, thought to have caused more deaths than influenza in the nineteenth century

Such abuses were brought to light by a Jewish/Huguenot chemist, Frederick Carl Accum. In 1820 he published *A Treatise on Adulterations of Food and Culinary Poisons*. This was a devastating exposé of many dangerous practices of the time. The preface reminded readers, 'However invidious the office may appear, and however painful the duty may be, of exposing the names of individuals who have been convicted of adulterating food, yet it was necessary for the verification of my statement.' The UK Food Standards Agency wisely adopts the same policy today.

In spite of Accum, it was not until public pressure forced the government to enact the Food Labelling Regulations of 1984 that manufacturers were obliged to disclose ingredients including additives. This became mandatory on 1 January 1986; *E*, standing for *European*, numbers were designated for a wide range of additives, which steadily grows, giving us a list that now identifies some 320 substances.

The identification of illegal additives in foods is as important today as in Victorian times. The difficulty is finding a substance that you do not expect to be there. We expect and look out for preservatives in sausages and can check to see if they are at legal levels, but antifreeze in wine? In July 1984 an enquiring Austrian VAT inspector wondered why a winery was claiming back VAT in significant quantities of diethylene glycol antifreeze in the summer. He had uncovered the Austrian wine scandal. Adding this antifreeze makes cheap wines taste like top-class vintages, but unfortunately a daily intake of just 3.0 ml or half a teaspoon is enough to cause kidney damage and 100 ml is fatal. A bottle bought in Barnsley, Yorkshire, of one of the 82 implicated brands contained 1.5 ml, so a heavy drinker would be at substantial risk.

More recently, in 2004, the Food Standards Agency reported on products, mostly from India, that contained the potentially carcinogenic red colour Sudan 1. By the end of the year the agency had identified lists of products occupying eight closely crowded pages. These included curry and tandoori mixes, jerk seasoning, chilli and tomato sauces and relishes, chutneys, pesto, couscous, and balsamic-vinegar-based sauces, to mention but a few. Luckily, the tip of an iceberg was discovered, and the investigations that followed yielded results that shamed many distinguished brands.

E does not stand for *Evil* or *Evade*. E numbers provide the information upon which we can make informed choices, be they on environmental, ethical, gastronomic or health grounds. With hindsight, the labelling requirement that allows additives to be described either by the E number or the chemical name has made life less easy for the consumer. Often the two are mixed, making the named additives look more like normal ingredients, so confusion persists.

When I wrote my book *E for Additives* in 1984, I found that I had a problem with fewer than one in five additives, and more than two decades later there is a significant reduction in the use of some additives that can cause intolerances or adverse effects in small, but significant, groups of people. My concerns are now about the many foods aimed at children and the less well-off, which are close to nutritional rubbish.

Aspartame (NutraSweet) has been attacked, mostly by activists in the USA, as being harmful. I am sure this is a false judgement based on unscientific evidence. The campaigning against aspartame resulted in its being reassessed by the EU Scientific Committee for Foods in 2002, which decided it was safe. Sweeteners are given a very rigorous examination by regulators because, unlike the majority of additives, they may well be used every day for many years.

The point has been well made earlier in this book that toxicity is dose-related. Drink 9 litres of water in half an hour and you will probably die. Any additive or ingredient in excess can harm – that is why the Joint Expert Committee on Food Additives (JECFA) assesses many additives for ADIs (acceptable daily intakes), which are translated into EU levels by the European Food Safety Authority (EFSA).

E numbers

Additives are grouped into six general categories according to their purposes. Labels have to define the use before stating the numbers. You might read, 'colours E102, E110, preservatives E211, E220'. All ingredients are listed in descending order as mixed with additives in their appropriate positions by weight or volume. All this is valuable information, so that when you read the label you can decide if the food is for you. The Food Standards Agency list of EU-approved additives can be found online at: www.food.gov.uk/safereating/additivesbranch/enumberlist.

Colours

There are 44 colours, numbered from E100, curcumin, an extract of yellow turmeric, to E180, litholrubin, a reddish azo dye that is safe.

Azo colours have a particular molecular configuration which means that some of them produce adverse reactions in sensitive, allergic people, especially asthmatics, those with eczema and the aspirin-sensitive. These can cause nettle rash, wheezing and watering of the eyes or nose. They are E102, E110, E122, E123, E124, E128, E151, E154, E155 and E180.

Coal tar colours used to be derived from coal and were discovered by Sir William Perkins in 1856. They revolutionised the dyeing of cloth. Some coal tar dyes are also azo colours. They include the above plus E104, E127, E131, E132 and E133. Some of these colours have been implicated in hyperactivity in children. It has been suggested that avoiding them can control this serious problem without the potential side effects of putting young people onto strong drugs such as Ritalin. Many other colours have a long history of safe use, and indeed coal tar and azo dyes are harmless for the vast majority.

Preservatives

The 39 preservatives are used to prevent some foods from deteriorating and to prevent food poisoning. They number from sorbic acid E200, which occurs naturally in the berries of the mountain ash and inhibits yeast and mould growths in unpasteurised cheeses and milk products, to E285, borax, with an extra, E1105, lysozyme, moved over from the large miscellaneous group. Sulphites may cause asthmatic attacks and have been mentioned. Benzoic acid, E210, which occurs naturally in many berries, fruits and vegetables along with the colour tartrazine, E102, provoked an adverse response in 27 out of 34 hyperactive children.

On any risk–benefit assessment of the preservatives, the risk to most of us is very low and the benefits considerable.

Antioxidants

The fifteen antioxidants number from E300, ascorbic acid (which is vitamin C), to E320, butylated hydroxyanisole (BHA), and E321, butylated hydroxytoluene (BHT). When we cut open an apple the flesh goes brown because it has oxidised. If as soon as we cut it we add lemon juice, which contains both natural E300 and citric acid, E330, which enhances its effect, then freshness is preserved for some time.

Some antioxidants such as E300 are best at preserving non-fatty foods, whereas Es 306, 307, 308 and 309 are all forms of vitamin E that can stop fats going rancid. They are very safe and it is an advantage when cooking oils contain natural or added vitamin E, especially if they are in clear glass bottles. Light encourages oxidation; in an ideal world oils and milk would be sold in opaque containers.

The last two in the list, Es 320 and 321, BHA and BHT, have pros and cons ranging from a possible reduction in some cancers to a negative effect upon others. On the whole, they are safe, but it is probably wise to limit consumption by young children. They are used in some high-calorie fatty foods.

Sweeteners

It is with sweeteners that the logic in the numbering system breaks down. The sixteen sweeteners start with E420, sorbitol, which used to be popular in diabetic foods, but as it is half as sweet as sugar and has a similar calorie content, it has fallen out of favour. It is used in many filled chocolates and confectionary as it helps keep the contents moist in the mouth and prevents the formation of crystals. This short list of 5 numbers ends with E421, mannitol, which occurs in nature with similar properties to sorbitol but fewer calories. The list then moves to E996, lactitol, and E997, xylitol, a sweetener originally derived from the silver birch and now often used in chewing gum because it helps prevent dental caries while being sweet. E950, aspartame, is safe and tastes good without the bitter aftertaste of saccharin, E994. Two sweeteners were added in 2003, sucralose, which is 600 times sweeter than sugar and is marketed as Splenda, and E962, salt of aspartame-acesulfame. It is likely that another sweetener, E968, erythritol, will soon be approved.

One of the reasons we have so many sweeteners is that different processes and acidities need appropriate sweeteners to make the food product palatable. It is a competitive market subject to many individual preferences.

Emulsifiers, stabilisers, thickeners and gelling agents

These 60 additives, from E322 to E495, and invertase, E1103, have technical functions. These range from mixing oil and water – such as the first, E322 (lecithins), which are in all our bodily cells and are found in high concentrations in soya beans and egg yolk – to thickeners, such as E412, guar gum, which allows emulsions and thickened foods to stay in suspension to give body to the product. It is a safe group of useful additives with the exception of the misuse of the gums, especially guar and konjac, E425, in sucked sweets or in capsules. If these stick in the throat, they expand greatly and have caused death by asphyxiation. Such products are now banned.

There is a major commercial issue with the group of E450 additives, the perfectly safe polyphosphates. These additives enable the producer to combine large quantities of water with, for example, meat and ham. That is why much bacon turns into a salty slurry in the pan, and canned hams are routinely found with 30 per cent added water. Oddly, these additions are rarely reflected in a lower price.

Others

Acids, acidity regulators, anti-caking agents, anti-foaming agents, bulking agents, carriers and carrier-solvents emulsifying salts, firming agents, flavour enhancers, flour-treatment agents, foaming agents, glazing agents, humectants, modified starches, packaging gases, propellants, raising agents and sequestrants – these are included in a catch-everything-else group of 135 additives with a selection of numbers between E170, calcium carbonate, or chalk (used for firming some canned fruits and vegetables and in food supplements), and E1520, propylene glycol. This is used as a carrier and carrier solvent in colours, emulsifiers, antioxidants and enzymes.

These additives are technical aids with functions such as improving the texture or appearance, improving the flavour, pressurising aerosols, making bread and cake mixes rise and providing protective atmospheres so that oxygen cannot spoil fresh foods such as fish, meat and fruit. This group of gases such as E938, argon, E939, helium, and E941, nitrogen, are a boon to once-a-week shoppers, enabling perishable products to survive in the refrigerator far better than their ungassed equivalents.

There has been a lot of debate about the flavour enhancer E621, monosodium glutamate. With the proviso that we can all be allergic or sensitive to *something*, MSG is a valuable, safe ingredient. It has been linked to a supposed condition known as 'Chinese restaurant syndrome'. This was said to cause a selection of symptoms ranging from numbness of the neck to headaches and palpitations. Sufferers were given different drinks with and without MSG, and showed the same symptoms each time!

I have checked in Chinese takeaways and some were using a heaped teaspoon in every portion. This is bad practice and will in any case give you far too much sodium. Use the tail of the spoon.

The glutamate story is that since time immemorial Japanese cooks have used the seaweed *Laminaria japonica* to improve and bring out the flavour of foods cooked in savoury stocks. In 1908, Professor Kikunae Ikeda of Tokyo isolated the active substance glutamic acid. It was found that we have taste buds separate to the usual sweet, sour, salt and bitter, which detect and appreciate glutamates. The taste was called *umami*, which means deliciousness.

It is one of the mechanisms that bond babies to mothers,

because their milk contains 22 mg glutamate per 100 ml, ten times as much as cow's milk. Tomatoes and Parmesan cheese are also naturally rich in glutamates, hence our love of pizzas and the valuable additive E621!

Flavours

The European Union is engaged on a long-term project to validate the safety and quality of the 3,000 flavours in current use, often added in combinations of ten or twenty varieties to achieve the desired result. It seems unlikely that there is space on most labels to list a separate set of numbers, and, as adverse effects are almost unknown, it is probably not needed. They can be natural, as in vanilla, or nature-identical, as in vanillin, its key flavour component, as well as synthetic. They can be described on the label as 'flavouring' but many producers describe tastes that are artificial as, for example, 'banana flavour' when there is no banana present and as 'banana-flavoured' when there is.

Additives are desirable and useful when used in the right way. They are essential to modern food processing and some have a very long history. Abuses are possible and there is no doubt that certain groups of people can be allergic or intolerant to some additives, including colours and preservatives. The E-number system allows us to make informed choices. There is no substitute for always reading the label.

Part Two

DIETS

Chapter Twelve

HEALTHY EATING

BY VINCENT MARKS

THE MYTH: You can live forever if you only eat healthy food.
THE FACT: Life is sexually transmitted and always ends in death.

Good health is at the top of everyone's wish list – but what is it? Although we know if we are unwell, there is no completely satisfactory way of knowing if we are in good health.

A dictionary definition of health – 'soundness of body: that condition in which its functions are duly and efficiently discharged' – says nothing about future expectations. Longevity is almost as important as good health, but the two are not synonymous, as evidenced by the life histories of Florence Nightingale and Charles Darwin: both suffered ill health for much of their very long lives. Nor has good health much to do with 'fitness' (see Chapter Twenty-six, 'Exercise'). There are too many reported incidents of athletes dropping down dead at the height of their powers, and of longevity in the sedentary, to support such a connection.

Another definition of good health, and the one advanced by the World Health Organisation, encompasses the concept of social and mental wellbeing, but it is unrealistic and probably unattainable for many people for much of the time. A more useful definition is the absence of discomfort, illness or disease or the imminent expectation of it. This is the logic behind 'screening' healthy people with the aim of finding those with curable diseases such as TB or glaucoma before they cause irrevocable damage. Unfortunately, the number of diseases for which this has been established as achievable is much smaller than the optimists of testing would have us believe.

While proper nutrition does not ensure perfect health, it is a prerequisite for it. Until comparatively recently, proper nutrition was available only to the affluent and powerful. The situation changed with the advances in the science and technology of food production, preservation and transportation made during the late nineteenth and early twentieth centuries, and with our increased understanding of the science of nutrition. This has made it possible to provide most people, especially those living in what is quaintly described as the developed world, with a plentiful supply – some would say too plentiful a supply – of wholesome food and drink.

Why, then, are newspapers, television and radio so obsessed with what we eat? They claim that our nutrition is so poor that we are in danger of reversing the enormous improvements we saw during the twentieth century. If this is so, it is certainly not due to a lack of advice. However, once one starts to question the soundness of that advice and where it comes from, one begins to understand the nature of the problem.

Improvements in public health during the first half of the

twentieth century made great strides in reducing premature deaths from infections, industrial hazards and the major nutritional diseases. This led to the unrealistic belief that all illnesses, except congenital ones, are preventable if only their cause was known. Although the germ theory of disease proposed by Louis Pasteur, Robert Koch and other distinguished microbiologists of the nineteenth century explained and helped to eliminate many of the commonest illnesses in the past, it did little to help us understand the chronic illnesses that afflict the middle-aged and elderly today. More recently, it has been realised that most chronic illnesses are the result of the interplay between a person's genetic makeup and the way he or she lives. What and how much people eat is possibly the most important environmental factor in the causation of chronic illness, but there are many others.

Myocardial infarction – an acute heart attack caused by coronary thrombosis – was rare at the start of the twentieth century, but by the 1960s it was the commonest cause of death in many of the countries of the developed world, including the UK. It was labelled a disease of affluence in spite of the fact that it was more common among the poor. Epidemiological studies suggested that both genetic and environmental factors were implicated in its causation. In some families, the genetic link was direct and very obvious from one generation to the next, but in most cases the link was tenuous or nonexistent.

Lung cancer, on the other hand, whose rise in incidence was almost as rapid and catastrophic, seemed to have no genetic basis and it was Richard Doll, using epidemiological methods, who laid it squarely at the door of cigarette smoking. Doll went on to establish that people who voluntarily gave up smoking reduced, although they did not abolish, their risk of developing lung cancer. Put differently, a model epidemiological study pointed the finger of blame at cigarette smoking, but it was interventional studies that established that the link was causal rather than coincidental or due to a common factor. This level of evidence of causality has rarely been repeated – particularly in relation to diet, where, with few exceptions, the results of interventional studies have been disappointing. This may be because, while eating is obligatory, smoking is not and it is possible to give up smoking entirely.

The quality of evidence linking diet to specific diseases is poor, apart from common 'simple deficiency diseases' such as scurvy (vitamin C deficiency), rickets (vitamin D deficiency), anaemia (iron deficiency) and protein-calorie malnutrition, where corrective action is both possible and effective. Usually the evidence is unconvincing, contradictory and almost impossible to confirm experimentally.

Food habits, including portion size, are acquired at a very early age, mostly from parents but also, to a lesser extent, from one's peers. They can be extremely difficult to change, even when the motivation for doing so is great. This may be why, despite a plethora of reports suggesting the benefits of this or that diet, they have so little effect. The evidence that they do any good, except in the grossly malnourished, is very shaky. This is in contrast to the obvious benefits of sound nutritional advice and the provision of nutritious food during the first half of the twentieth century. It was during this time that the science of human nutrition can be considered to have become established. It is therefore a comparatively new science that goes far beyond diet and involves an understanding of the complex interactions between a person and his or her food and drink. This distinguishes it from dietetics, which is about the use of foods to attempt to treat or prevent disease, and catering and cooking, both of which are professions in their own right.

Human nutrition is much less well developed as a science than animal nutrition, which is driven by commercial agricultural interests and has the great advantage that it is amenable to experimental study and evaluation. Animal nutritionists can specify the chemical composition of diets, and the amounts to be fed, how often and at what times of the day in order to produce the desired effect in any particular breed of animal or bird. By the addition of lysine, an essential amino acid in short supply in many vegetables, it is possible, for example, to accelerate the growth of piglets in order to bring them to market earlier, producing a significant cost saving. Despite all their best endeavours, however, animal nutritionists do not always get it right. They knew that when cows gave higher yields of milk they needed more protein. To overcome this problem they fedthem animal proteins, but it was not until it was too late that it was found that this could disseminate the 'mad-cow disease' BSE (see Chapter Twenty-two, 'Transmissible Spongiform Encephalopathies – BSE and vCJD').

While many of the lessons learned from animal nutrition, including those conducted on experimental laboratory animals in the course of clinical research, are applicable to man, they can, at best, only point us in the right direction. Laboratory rodents survive longer when fed constantly on a diet providing fewer calories than their littermates eat voluntarily. This has led to the suggestion that you will live longer if you undernourish yourself rather than maintain a 'normal' diet. There is no reason to believe that this is true for human beings, and the evidence is that underweight is just as great a threat to longevity as modest overweight or plumpness.

Animal-feeding experiments do not permit definitive conclusions as regards human nutrition, because the differences in metabolic requirements are greater between species than within them. This obvious fact does not prevent the headline writers from proclaiming the result of some research project to be a great advance in nutrition, without pointing out that it was found in only one breed of a particular species and not likely to be reproducible in humans.

The pioneers of both animal and human nutrition were concerned with the chemical composition of both the body and food, and how one was transformed into the other. They started with our understanding of the nature and structure of proteins, the role of carbohydrates and fats as sources of energy and the need for various mineral elements such as sodium, calcium and iodine. Knowledge of the vital role played by vitamins came much later, and did not reach its zenith until the early to mid-twentieth century, when vitamin B12, the last vitamin to be named, was isolated.

Sir Robert McCarrison, in a landmark series of lectures entitled *Nutrition and National Health* published in 1936, said, 'Man is made up of what he eats.' This statement is of course true, whereas the phrase 'you are what you eat' – often found in articles written for the lay public by people calling themselves 'nutritionists', and even used as the title of a television programme – is patently rubbish.

McCarrison, an observational and experimental nutritionist of the highest calibre, differentiated good from bad diets. Poor diets, he believed, were commonplace in Britain and responsible for much of the chronic illness suffered by the working class. Iron-deficiency anaemia, for example, was rife among women. In 1936, no fewer than 52 per cent of men presenting themselves to army recruiting offices in the UK, and 68 per cent of those from the large conurbations, were rejected by the military on health grounds due to their poor nutritional status.

McCarrison advocated a diet providing whole-cereal grains, milk and milk products such as butter and cheese, pulses, vegetables and occasional meat. He was also in favour of supplementing foods with minerals, such as iron, iodine, calcium, and vitamins, which, during World War Two, when traditional foods were in short supply, were seldom present in sufficient quantities in the diets of either the well-to-do or the poor. Rationing, because it made food of suitable quality and affordable prices available to everyone, undoubtedly improved the nutritional status of the population as a whole. Since that time we have never looked back – although you would not think so from the flood of dietary advice that emanates from individuals and official and quasi-official committees, and which fills our newspapers, magazines, radios and television channels (see Chapter Thirteen, 'The Epidemic of Diet Books).

Disease attributable to poor-quality food is fortunately largely a thing of the past in the developed world. It has to some extent been replaced by anxiety about the effects of overindulgence in energy-rich foods. Less well recognised is the fact that undernutrition and malnutrition are common in the elderly, especially the sick, as well as in the socially deprived. They are not helped by being fed a supposedly healthy 'low-energy-dense diet' when they are admitted to a hospital or nursing home because it is politically correct to do so. What they need is lots of high-energy food that is palatable and they can enjoy. This often means a diet that is rich in sugar and fat. Dairy ice cream, for example, can be made to incorporate all of the essential minerals and vitamins, and is usually appreciated even by the most fastidious of eaters. Soups, on the other hand, may be tasty and acceptable but do not provide calories.

There has probably never been a shortage of individuals or committees prepared to offer advice on how to improve one's own health, but the idea of improving the health of the nation by dietary means is comparatively new. The McGovern Senate Committee in America, which set dietary goals for the USA in February 1977, was probably the first to have governmental backing. By 1988, the European office of the World Health Organisation could refer to eighteen sets of recommendations for dietary changes that might reduce the incidence of diseases common in middle life. Advice to reduce fat intake, increase complex-carbohydrate intake and reduce salt and sugar intake was a frequent theme then, as it is now. It came about largely by the selection of committee members who believed in this particular mantra, and the selective citing of research papers to reflect their collective preconceptions while they ignored those that did not.

Catchphrases and jingles, especially those with an emotive message, are easy to remember. Consequently, it is simpler to talk of 'safety' and 'toxicity' as though they were absolutes and opposites, rather than merely a reflection of the dose of the same substance. Many nutrients, especially minerals and vitamins, are toxic when used in excess, but clearly essential and, therefore, safe when used properly. But individuals differ in their requirements. Failure to recognise this simple, obvious fact accounts for a number of hospital admissions each year by people who believe that if a little is 'good' then more must be better. While this attitude has taught us much about the effects of gross dietary indiscretions, we are still abysmally ignorant of the adverse effects of modest but prolonged underprovision or overusage of essential nutrients, as well as other inappropriate eating patterns.

The truth is that we know remarkably little about the long-term effects of dietary changes – not only in the chemical composition of food but also in the way we prepare and eat it. To suggest, as is fashionable, that traditional methods of preparing food are safer and better than the current industrial methods used for prepared or oven-ready food is not based on fact but on surmise and prejudice. Recently it was suggested in a BBC Radio programme that food is less nutritious than in the past. This was based on a comparison of food tables made now and 60 years ago but it made no allowance for the fact that the greater specificity of analytical techniques used today makes such a comparison nonsensical. This sort of comparison is meaningless. Although the contributor was told this by another expert participant in the programme, he would not accept her explanation. He would not accept scientific fact.

Through food science we have a wealth of knowledge about what different methods of food preparation and storage do to its composition and texture. This is the reason why we now have not only 'use by' but also 'best by' dates on all prepared foods. The growth of consumerism – albeit frequently misguided and often based upon false logic rather than genuine knowledge – has, within the past couple of decades, brought home the cost of our lack of knowledge of human nutrition. In the land of the blind, the one-eyed man is king. Consequently, many people with a smattering of knowledge and a familiarity with the terminology claim to be experts. This, when combined with an ability to wield a pen, write persuasively and project oneself well on radio and television, produces a limitless opportunity to propagate unproven and irrational beliefs.

The increase in the number of instant experts needed to fill the acres of vacant newspaper pages has coincided with the rise of paternalism and authoritarianism among a vociferous group of individuals, some of them extremely knowledgeable and sincere, who argue that the public should be told what is and is not 'good for them' on the basis of their interpretation of the published data. Such individuals may call themselves 'health educators', but they are really propagandists. They may have enjoyed some justifiable successes, such as the requirement for more informative food labelling – but that in itself is contentious (see Chapter Nineteen, 'Food Labelling'). Exactly what information and how much of it a label could and should add is open to debate. Differentiating sugars into 'natural' or 'added', for example, is nonsensical, as is the differentiation of food into 'organic' and, I suppose by inference, 'nonorganic', rather than differentiation according to its freshness and nutritive value.

To be effective, food labelling must not only be within the law but also intellectually honest. It is common, for example, to see products from reputable manufacturers that claim to contain 'no added sugars' when they are already so full of sugar that any addition would make the product unpalatable. Fruit juices and baked beans sweetened with concentrated apple juice are examples that spring to mind. One might as well sell gin labelled 'no added alcohol' as fruit juice labelled 'no added sugar'. The suggestion, already taken up by some supermarkets and manufacturers, that foods should be labelled green, amber and red is cynical attempt at commercialism. The headline 'PEPSICO PLANS TO INCREASE "HEALTHY" PRODUCT MARKET SHARE' suggests that the company also produce 'unhealthy' products which, if it were true, would be disgraceful. They clearly do not produce 'unhealthy' foods, nor would they be allowed to do so by law, so the use of these terms is exploitative and should be avoided.

The average health and longevity of the population in Britain has never been better – despite the increase in the prevalence of obesity and the illnesses that it causes. Much of this is undoubtedly due to the availability of wholesome food whose quality is assured by rigorous monitoring and which is sold at a price that most people can afford. While the food industry can be justifiably proud of its contribution to this improvement in nutritional status, it can also be castigated for promoting its products with advertisements that, although not untrue, do mislead by implication. But the same charge can be levied at the food propagandists who make their living and reputations by vilifying the food industry for using improper but legitimate means, within the current commercial climate, to persuade people to buy their products.

In order to improve the health of the nation through dietary means, it is necessary to ensure that health education is firmly based on the science of nutrition. This requires a basic knowledge of food preparation and presentation, of cooking and catering, as well as an understanding of physiology and metabolism – all of which should be taught as core subjects at school. Only then will children, when they grow up, be able to choose the most appropriate foods to eat and not be misled by ambiguous or deliberately slanted messages from commercial or governmental sources that are fashionable but not necessarily correct. The famous food pyramid,* introduced to simplify the healthy-eating message and based upon 1980s dogma, is already outmoded and incorrect and replaced by another.

What is the best advice on healthy eating today? I believe that, as in the past, we should eat a variety of different foods from the dairy, grocer, bakery, fruiterer, greengrocer and vintner, and somewhat less frequently from the fishmonger and butcher, in portion sizes and total quantity that ensures proper growth in children and the maintenance of a body-mass index of around 20–25 in young adults and 24–28 in older adults. This, coupled with moderate daily exercise and the avoidance of 'snacking' – especially in public and places of entertainment – involves a lifestyle that becomes easier to practise once one understands the reason why it is good for one's health.

There is no food or diet that will guarantee good health and long life – if there were we would all be eating it.

* The food pyramid was a graphic device that showed so-called healthier foods at the bottom and those deemed to be less healthy at the apex.

Chapter Thirteen

THE EPIDEMIC OF DIET BOOKS

BY VINCENT MARKS

THE MYTH: Diet books help you lose weight.
THE FACT: The only weight they help you lose is confined to the wallet.

We are being fed a diet of diets in books, newspapers and magazines and on television. In spite of this plethora of diets, all the indications suggest that, as a nation, we are getting fatter. Something is not working. If only a proportion of these diets were moderately successful, then we would expect some noticeable effect on the fatter members of the population. The only people who appear to benefit from this epidemic of diets are the promoters, who obtain temporary fame and fortune, and the media that exploit these phoney diets.

Those presenting this meal of diets overlook one important, pertinent fact: if there were a diet that successfully caused a significant, sustainable weight loss it would instantly become universally accepted and replace all the others. The fact that there are so many fads and fashions in diets is evidence that none of them do what they claim: to cause a significant and permanent loss of weight.

There are perfectly good reasons for special diets to meet the needs of particular diseases and special circumstances, but most of the people who use these diets do so to lose weight. Although the majority of these dieters are women, the statistical evidence suggests that it is men who stand to benefit most by losing weight.

Diet books are big business. Many of them sell over a million copies and are translated into many different languages. They often run to several editions and create a spin-off industry of dieting products. While the fad lasts, the promoter becomes a celebrity and the diet is readily taken up by the media – always anxious to exploit a new fashion – and presented as a life-changing event.

These books claim to help you lose weight and to maintain the new slimmer figure indefinitely. There is no doubt that, irrespective of the diet recommended, in most cases they will enable the devotee to lose weight initially. If followed faithfully and conscientiously they may fulfil their claim that they will make the reader slim for a short period. Other claims, such as an improvement in the dieter's health, are invariably wrong. Many of these diets may actually damage one's health if pursued faithfully for any length of time. The failure to sustain the weight loss for a reasonable period or the occurrence of unpleasant side effects after a while explains why these diets come and go with such frequency. Long-term follow-up studies, that should be done to substantiate the claims before they are made are never done before the diet is launched.

Dr Atkins' Diet Revolution is an excellent example of the life cycle of a fad diet. Dr Robert Atkins's book was first launched in 1972 but it really took off after its relaunch in 1993. In that year the new edition (reprinted by Vermillion Press, 1999), proclaimed *Dr Atkins' New Diet Revolution*. It was described as an American blockbuster that had sold 3 million copies. It also carried the endorsement of Nigella Lawson, a TV celebrity cook who described it as 'the perfect diet for those who love food...' Not being a scientist or having any medical knowledge, she failed to point out that the diet was nutritionally unsound and, like other fad diets, potentially dangerous. The problems with this fad diet eventually led to the bankruptcy of the organisation that sponsored it after lawsuits were filed against its promoters.

By 2003, scientific studies started to appear describing the failure of the Atkins diet to sustain weight loss and highlighting its potential to damage the health of its followers. In 2004 Jody Goran, a previously healthy and normal 50-year-old, developed a near-fatal heart attack after two years on the Atkins diet. The judge felt that Mr Goran had just cause to sue Atkins Nutritionals, a company producing low-carbohydrate convenience foods, supplements and condiments. This potentially opened the floodgates to other claims. In view of the adverse publicity, Atkins Nutritionals filed for bankruptcy.

What distinguishes a fad diet from a genuine diet designed to meet a particular circumstance or to remedy a disease? What is the proper use of nutritional therapy?

To answer the second question first, *nutritional therapy* is based upon an understanding of the scientific principles governing nutrition, namely what food does to us and what we do to it. *Dietetics* is the application of nutritional science to the preservation of good health by eating a proper mixture of foods in the correct amounts and the alleviation of specific illnesses. It is practised and taught by trained dieticians.

Fad diets are designed to produce a quick fix to a chronic problem without consideration of the root cause of the condition. In most cases they are aimed at making people lose weight. Many of those who use the diet are not dangerously obese in the first place, but merely wish to be slimmer. Almost all the diets claim to be health-inducing and consistent with a normal lifestyle without any supporting evidence. They are often based on spurious or misinterpreted science and make claims such as achieving detoxification of the dieter, a claim that demonstrates a lamentable lack of understanding of how the body works. Most of their claims lack scientific credibility. Some contain a scintilla of truth but, as with all Myths, any truth is so distorted and exaggerated that it is misleading if not frankly dishonest. Most fad diets ignore all the principles of healthy eating that have been established by painstaking research since the science of nutrition was established in the latter part of the nineteenth century.

The qualifications, if any, of the authors of fad diets are often spurious. Some of the grand-sounding titles they make claim to have been awarded to them by other unqualified, self-styled nutritionists, while some have been bought over the Internet from a diploma factory. A few, as in the case of Dr Atkins, are medically qualified or have diplomas from recognised universities. Often, these self-styled nutritionists and their diets receive endorsement from a celebrity, who, although he – or more commonly she – may claim to have benefited from the particular diet, is unlikely to be in a position to judge its nutritional rationality or its safety.

Broadly speaking, fad diets can be divided into (a) those that advocate a (relatively) high-protein and/or high-fat intake and (b) those that are based on a (relatively) high-carbohydrate/low-fat intake. An alternative approach to dieting called *combining*, which is often referred to as the Hay Diet after one of its arch proponents, is based on the spurious and totally erroneous belief that the human gut is unable to cope with foods containing both carbohydrates and proteins at the same time.

The Hay Diet ignores the fact that the commonest carbohydrate-rich foods, such as bread, rice and pasta, provide about 15 per cent of their energy as proteins, which is more or less what a healthy diet should do. It also fails to acknowledge that the body's physiological response to a mixed meal is very different, and probably more beneficial, from that produced by its individual constituents.

Only a minority of fad diets – usually those, such as the Cambridge diet, relying exclusively on synthetic ingredients – emphasise that it is the amount of food that is eaten, rather than its constituents, that is important in regulating weight. Of course, if the constituents are so low in energy content that it is physically impossible to eat enough of them to meet the daily need for energy, such as the cabbage-soup diet, weight loss is inevitable until a new equilibrium is reached.

The authors of fad diets are often people with charisma and a flair for publicity. They encourage their readers, or victims – for that is what they really are – to believe that they are suffering from nonexistent or imaginary problems, such as cellulite, which makes them susceptible to illogical, silly or downright dangerous dietary practices masquerading as remedies. The idea that merely by changing the composition of your diet you can alter the site in your body where fat is deposited or removed is a sick joke, but one that has been exploited by some authors with great success

The most popular fad diets are the brainchild of a single individual whose name, geographical location or particular 'concept' is attached to it. The names of Hay and Atkins; of Scarsdale, Beverley Hills and Cambridge; and the Macrobiotic, F-plan, Cabbage Soup, G-I and Zone Diet Plans respectively, spring to mind. Channel 4 TV organised a stunt over the winter holiday season 2005–6 in which ten obese women were recruited to follow a named diet, which would be allocated at random. They were weighed and interviewed by an obesity expert before, and after several weeks on, their allocated diets. The results are shown in Figure 4. The small size of the sample and short duration of the trial do nothing to establish any new scientific facts, though none of the dieters achieved anything like the massive losses of weight sometimes claimed as occurring but are scientifically impossible.

FIGURE 4

Weight loss in ten obese women after six weeks on a named diet.

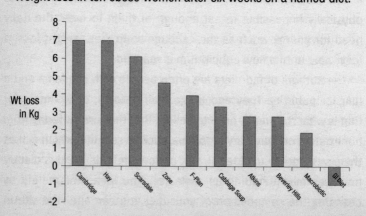

As expected, all but one of the women on the diets lost weight. The one who didn't was on a G-I diet. This so closely resembled the diet eaten by most normal, health-conscious individuals that the result came as no surprise to anyone with an interest in the subject. The televised programme was made to look more scientific than it was by appearing to measure the relative fat and water loss achieved by each of the volunteers. The method used, which is based on electrical impedance, is too insensitive to produce meaningful results in a study such as this, but helped to introduce novelty into an otherwise unadventurous programme.

Properly conducted scientific studies dating back to the 1950s established that low-carbohydrate diets always produce a more rapid initial reduction in weight than low-fat diets, due to accelerated water loss. They are, however, no more effective in producing permanent weight loss than high fat diets providing the same energy content.

Clones of me-too books soon follow the successful launch of a fad diet – each with its own style. They rarely achieve the commercial success of the original. They and the original book generally enjoy a brief period of enormous popularity while their authors make numerous radio and television appearances but gradually fade away to be replaced by other equally fatuous and fashionable ones They rarely disappear altogether, being constantly resurrected by the next tier downwards of writers: the magazine and newspaper gurus, who present them as new and original, even though they may be ten or fifteen years old.

The Atkins Diet, for example, underwent a resurrection that was even more successful than its launch. The latest fad diet, not yet arrived here from America, is the 'Jesus Diet'. It is brainchild of a Florida physician, Dr Don Colbert. It's based on asking oneself, 'What would Jesus eat?' Dr Colbert is, according to his website, known as 'The Physician To God's Generals' and the author of numerous books on biblical cures for all manner of illnesses.

The extraordinary claims for the effectiveness of fad diets are based largely if not exclusively on anecdote or on small, uncontrolled, short-duration trials.

There are some undoubted successes, such as this one, described in Atkins's *The Typical Success Story in Diet Revolution*:

Tim started Atkins because he wanted to see his kids grow up. At 35 years old Tim weighed 335 pounds [24 stone or 152 kg], far too much even for a strongly built six footer [72 inches or 183 cm; body-mass index = 46]. The day after his wife's birthday – they went for a final carbohydrate blowout – Tim started Atkins. Within two weeks he lost 21 pounds. After four weeks, 34 pounds. 'By July 27, 1999, after nine months on the program I had shed 122 pounds [55 kg] and weighed 213 [97 kg].' Without difficulty, enjoying the food and adhering faithfully to the Atkins Lifetime Maintenance phase, Tim had stayed right around the weight for two and a half years.

Long-term follow-up studies – five years or more – of people undergoing fad diets are rare and only ever conducted by scientists, never by the originators. They reveal that only 15 per cent of slimmers who responded well initially – including those doing so under medical supervision – continued to maintain their new status. This is undoubtedly the reason behind the high incidence of the unhealthy practice of cyclic weight gain and loss that results from trying one fad diet after another. None of them are sustainable and, if they were, they would undoubtedly cause one type of malnutrition or another. That is why they are fads.

Most of the early weight loss produced by a fad diet is water and is always greater with low-carbohydrate than with high-carbohydrate, diets provided they contain the same amount of energy (calories). There is a perfectly good scientific reason for this. It has to do with the fact that carbohydrates are stored in the body along with about four times their own weight of water, whereas fats are not. Moreover, fats contain twice as many calories as the same weight of carbohydrates. Even so, many of the claims made for the speed of weight loss must be fictitious; the old adage, 'If it sounds too good to be true, it's untrue', springs to mind. It is impossible to lose more than about 200 grams (8 oz) of weight a day even on a literally starvation diet once the early loss of water has been taken into account. Most of the weight change is due to loss of fat, but some is tissue protein whose function is structural – not to provide energy. It is for this reason, if no other, that rapid weight loss and adherence to a very low-calorie diet – less than about 800 –1,000 calories a day – is unhealthy.

The fact that it will not work in the long term unless you are also undergoing a change in lifestyle is of secondary importance. A diet that advertises that you can 'lose 9 lb every eleven days' has got to be a spoof; it may be true for the first eleven days but not for subsequent ones, unless it is combined with unnatural physical activity.

The other fad diets
Another species of fad-diet book is aimed not at the overweight

and obese but at vulnerable members of the community who believe, on the most slender of evidence, that they are suffering from some illness caused by food. Hypoglycaemia, food allergy and gluten sensitivity, for example, are real conditions that are grossly overdiagnosed, often on the flimsiest of evidence, and inappropriate or ineffective dietary treatment advised. What these diets have in common with mainstream fad diets is that they almost all castigate the caffeinated beverages, tea and coffee (see Chapter Eight, 'Tea, Coffee and Caffeine'), alcohol and sugar (sucrose) – even when consumed as part of a high-carbohydrate diet – as particularly unhealthy.

In conclusion, the review by Joy May Buslaff on the Amazon.com site in October 2004 of William Bennett and Joel Gurin's excellent book, *The Dieter's Dilemma*, published in 1982, sums up the situation with regard to fad-diet books – although this is not one – much better than I could myself.

Although this book is beginning to become dated, it remains in line with what scientific research keeps stating: We cannot sustain a reduction in food intake any more than we can impose a sustained change in our breathing patterns. We need science to invent an appetite-suppressing treatment that affects ghrelin, leptin, adiponectin and other hormones – the dictators of our appetite and metabolism. Until then, all we can do is choose quality foods, eat until we are satiated, and enjoy whatever physical activity suits us best. This book will not help you lose weight, but it may keep you from losing mind when all the popular diets fail you.

Chapter Fourteen

DIET AND DISEASE

BY STANLEY FELDMAN AND VINCENT MARKS

THE MYTH: Many dieases are caused by the food we eat.

THE FACT: Diseases are rarely caused by the food we eat.

There is a dramatic difference in the incidence of diseases, such as cancer, cardiovascular disease and strokes, in various parts of the world. This has led to the suggestion that it must be the result of something in the local diet, or to toxins in the food. This belief has been at the root of many of the dietary fads that have affected our eating habits. Over time almost all the suggested associations between a particular diet and a disease have proved to be illusionary. Nevertheless, the zealots who dictate our eating habits have invariably been slow to admit they were wrong. In many instances they have merely shifted from advocating one discredited food fad to another.

Dr Tim Byers, of Colorado Health Sciences, has spent the past 25 years or so trying to discover whether there is a link between any aspect of our diet and cancer, without a single success. One by one the shibboleths that he has investigated have turned out to be without foundation. This is a far cry from those prophets of doom who tell us that 20 per cent or more of all cancers are caused by the food we eat. There is very little evidence for their claims but, as with all of these proposals, it is far easier to make such a claim than it is to disprove it.

Eating red meat has been linked with cancer of the colon, but, then, since eating meat is so common, it is difficult to disprove convincingly. Certainly, cancer of the colon also occurs in vegetarians. There is just a little evidence for the carcinogenicity of substances such as acrylates formed when meat is overcooked or burned, but one would have to eat several burnt cows to get a dangerous amount in one's food.

We are told by the House of Commons Select Committee (2004) that obesity costs the health service £3.7 billion every year. There is evidence that it causes some cases of Type 2 diabetes and it is associated with a diminution in life expectancy. It undoubtedly contributes to the rate of deterioration of arthritic joints and to the development of cardiac failure, but it is not a cause of either. There is no convincing evidence that obesity causes cancer. How the Select Committee came to decide it cost £3.7 billion every year is a mystery that undermines the credibility of this contentious report.

Organophosphate pesticides have been cited as a cause of cancer of the brain. However, it does not occur in those using these substances every day in high concentrations for pest control. The proposed association has never been substantiated. Poisoning by organophosphate pesticides causes lachrymation and salivation followed, if the dose is high, by gut cramps and in extreme cases muscle weakness. None of these symptoms have been described in those claiming to have suffered from the effects of pesticides in food.

It has been suggested that the mercury in some oily fish and in the amalgam used as a dental filling has been the cause of mental deterioration (see Chapter Eighteen, 'Detoxification'). On the basis of this belief patients have had perfectly good fillings replaced. Mercury is a dangerous, toxic substance but before any effect is likely to be encountered from this cause in any patient it would be necessary to have all the teeth filled with amalgam for many years.

A health scare that crops up repeatedly is that tiny amounts of aluminium in food cooked in aluminium saucepans can cause mental degeneration. Aludrox, a drug containing a high concentration of aluminium hydroxide, has been used in the treatment of indigestion for 50 years without any evidence of an effect on the brain or any other toxicity.

Hardly a week goes by without another health scare and the prediction that if only we were to eat this or avoid that thousands of deaths would be prevented. The list of scare stories is endless. Although certain dangers are recognised, especially in the uncontrolled market of herbal remedies, the vast majority of these panic stories have no scientific support.

Equally, unscientific speculation has surrounded some of the diets and regimes that we have been told are good for us, often with support from government-sponsored bodies. We were told authoritatively that eating more fibre would prevent cancer of the bowel; it does not. We were told that cutting out fat in the diet would prevent heart disease; it makes little difference. A recent report from America found that a low-fat diet made no difference to the incidence of heart disease in more than 40,000 patients studied over eight years. We were told that eating plenty brassica vegetables, such as broccoli and Brussels sprouts would prevent cancer of the prostate; to date there is no evidence that it has any effect.

The invocation to eat plenty of fruit and vegetables is based on the belief that those living around the Mediterranean do not have as much heart disease as those in northern Europe or the USA, because they eat a diet rich in fruit and vegetables and low in fats. Those who have lived in these regions know that the actual diet of the indigenous population contains very few vegetables and is often high in fats. The claims for the beneficial effects of the antioxidants and polyphenols in the fruit and vegetables are speculative, according to the US Preventive Services Task Force. There are many other reasons why life on the shores of the Mediterranean should be good for your health!

If there is any truth in these recommendations, the effect is barely detectable, according to Dr Barnett Kramer, of the disease prevention section of the American National Institute of Health.

If a diet were proven to be particularly effective in reducing disease, it would have been instantly and universally accepted. Similarly, if there were good scientific evidence that a particular component of the diet was toxic, it would be banned. Indeed the likelihood is that too many, rather than too few, possibly harmful compounds are prohibited. The precautionary principle is applied very strictly to the food we eat.

The High-Fibre Story

Dr Denis Burkitt worked for many years in West Africa with great distinction. His experience there led him to the theory that eating a high-fibre diet prevented colonic cancer. He based this claim on his finding that the incidence of cancer of the colon was almost nonexistent among the natives in the region and he attributed this to the high-fibre content of their diet. Since he promulgated this theory a generation has been indoctrinated on the value of eating a high-fibre diet. Over the years more and more evidence has accrued to show that incidence of cancer of the colon in Africa is not very different from elsewhere in the world and that a high-fibre diet does not prevent it. This cancer has a strong genetic link. Fibre may help prevent constipation. However, in spite of the Victorian concept that constipation was a source of body toxins, we now know it does little harm. Even the very low-roughage diet of the astronauts appears to be free of any deleterious effects. There is some epidemiological evidence that fibre in the diet may help reduce the incidence of heart disease.

Salt and the blood pressure

Both the Food Standards Agency (FSA) and the World Health Organisation (WHO) recommend a reduction in the daily intake of salt in the belief it will reduce the number of people who suffer from high blood pressure. The WHO suggests a target of 4 grams of salt a day but the British FSA goes even further and suggests we should aim to reduce the intake to 1–2 grams. As a result, the food industry has been cajoled into reducing the salt content of many of its products to the point where they are tasteless. We are being warned that we will die of strokes or heart failure unless we reduce the amount of salt we take with our food.

Serious doubts about these recommendations have been raised by the mixed messages coming from the scientific studies on the subject and the unequivocal evidence that people have died from eating too little salt.

If there is a strong association between the amount of salt eaten and the blood pressure, then reducing the amount eaten should lower the blood pressure in the most patients. It does not do so. In the Report of the Cochrane Committee, an independent scientific body, in 2002, on 3,500 patients, collected together from eleven peer-reviewed trials, where the participants were subjected to a strictly controlled low-salt diet for over one year, it was found that there was no discernible effect on the blood pressure as a result of a controlled reduction in salt intake.

The largest study, the Intersalt study quoted in the Parliamentary Office of Science and Technology (POST) report, 'Improving Children's Diet', concludes that 'in the study on over 100,000 adults in 32 different countries no statistical overall association was found between salt intake and blood pressure'. This study is particularly significant, because it measured salt excretion. This is a much better way of telling how much salt is taken in over any length of time than calculations based on the intake in the diet, since the amount of salt in most foods, even in bread, varies greatly.

Really sick patients, such as those recovering from major abdominal surgery or operations on their heart, are often maintained for days or weeks on fluids fed directly into their veins. The content of these fluids is worked out on the basis of the minimum amount required to keep these sick patients alive. Depending upon the nature of the condition being treated, the basic requirement for a 70 kilogram adult is for 3 litres of water, 2,000 to 3,000 calories as dextrose and a minimum of 9 grams of salt. This regime has been used for the past 50 years without any report of an ill effect due to too much salt, or of its causing a high blood pressure, even though the amount of salt given is above the present average daily intake and much higher than recommended by the FSA. It was shown by Alderman and coworkers, writing in the journal *Hypertension* in 1995, that reducing the intake of sodium may cause the plasma renin level to rise, an effect that causes reduced organ-blood flow, a rise in blood pressure and an increase in the work of the heart.

Those zealots advocating a reduction in the salt content of processed food point to a paper in which the results of 28 very different studies were cited, the largest of which demonstrated that a progressive increase in salt intake caused a rise in blood pressure. These studies were lumped together and treated as a single investigation. The soundness of this analytical technique, known as *meta analysis*, is open to serious doubt. The dangers of mixing together the results of different studies using different-sized groups and differing criteria of analysis, and carried out by different researchers using different methodologies, are obvious (see Chapter Thirty-one, 'The Misuse of Numbers'). Unless the trials are strictly controlled and of a uniform pattern they have little true scientific credibility.

In some of these studies the results of only four weeks' study were included. The nature of the diets varied greatly and in some studies it led to a significant loss of weight that might have been expected to cause a fall in blood pressure. The best conclusion the investigators who presented these results could reach was that 'it is not clear whether sodium intake in isolation is a factor in the development of hypertension'. Hardly a ringing endorsement of the view held by those advocating a very low-salt policy with so much certainty.

Deirdre Hutton, chair of the Food Standards Agency, has stated that cutting down on salt in the diet would prevent 35,000 people dying each year in the UK! This figure suggests that there is something very wrong with our primary-care medicine. All GPs are told to measure their patients' blood pressure each year (for which they receive extra pay) and to treat with drugs any in whom the blood pressure is raised. If in spite of this there were 35,000 people left out, who subsequently died as a result of high blood pressure, it would suggest that something was badly wrong. Of course the figures quoted are nonsense.

We must be certain that the benefits of salt restriction outweigh the risks. As Sandy Macnair points out in Chapter Six, the evidence that salt is bad for us is open to doubt. Against the equivocal evidence that salt can be dangerous there is no doubt that a lack of salt can cause death.

Four healthy young athletes died on the Great North Run in 2005. On this occasion the half-marathon took place in hot and humid conditions, Although the athletes had access to fluids, including so-called isotonic fluids, during the run, they were not prepared for the huge salt loss that accompanies strenuous exercise in hot weather. They almost certainly died of heatstroke – an inability to sweat enough to lower their body temperature. There are many other reports of fit adults dying of heatstroke after an unusual exertion. Heatstroke is caused by lack of salt. One cannot sweat without salt and it is impossible to lose heat in temperate and hot climates without sweating. These tragedies are almost certainly the result of too little salt in the body. If all the runners obeyed the Food Standards Agency and restricted their salt intake the death rate would be much higher.

Without salt, many foods, especially watery ones, such as

soups and vegetables, are tasteless. Salt has been used for centuries in the pickling and conservation of food. Many people in the developing world, who do not have access to refrigerators, would suffer from malnutrition during the winter months, when fresh food is scarce, if they were to reduce the use of salt in their food. Animals seek 'salt licks' because their instinct, developed over many millennia of evolution, drives them to eat as much salt as possible as an essential part of their diet.

Against the evidence for the essential role of salt in our lives, there needs to be strong, unequivocal evidence that it is bad for us before we restrict its intake. There is little evidence that it is likely have much effect on high blood pressure, most of which is due to a hardening of the arteries that inevitably occurs as one gets older (there is another rare but more lethal form of high blood pressure, called *malignant hypertension*, which may be helped by a low-salt diet). No one should die as a consequence of a high blood pressure. A raised blood pressure can be controlled by drug therapy. This is a safe and proven way of reducing the incidence of strokes and heart failure. It is much more effective than any possible benefit that may result from reducing the salt intake in food. It does not need the imposition of a low-salt diet or of the food police and it carries less risk for the patient

Does Diet Cause Disease?

In the view of Dr Arthur Schatzkin, chief of nutritional epidemiology at the National Cancer Institute in the USA, those who develop a disease, especially cancer, want to know *why* it happened to them. They want to be able to pin their disease on some causative agent. Doctors are well aware of this phenomenon. It is common for their patients to blame their disease on some casual outside occurrence. Cancer of the breast is often said to have started after a blow on the chest, while heart disease is frequently attributed to some emotional disaster. Although most people accept that colds are caused by a virus, it is still common for it to attributed to a draught. The present suggestion that high blood pressure is due to our being fed too much salt is in the same pattern as that proposed by Schatzkin. We like to feel that our disease is due to some outside agent or cause. The most rigorous and the largest ever report on the effect of diet on the health comes from the Rockefeller University in New York (2006). This study was conducted prospectively on just under 50,000 American women who were followed over eight years. It found no evidence that the diet consumed influenced the pattern of any illnesses in the group. There was no correlation between fat intake and heart disease, colon cancer or cancer of the breast.

The media have contributed to the belief that many diseases are caused by malign outside influences and that by avoiding a particular food or environment, or by eating this or that compound, we can prevent thousands of deaths every year. They have failed to differentiate between a proven cause for a disease, such as that between smoking and cancer of the lung, and a *possible tenuous unsubstantiated* link between a food or toxin and some disease. There has been a too ready assumption that a chemical that produces cancer in rats in high doses is also likely to be carcinogenic in trace amounts in humans, that an atmospheric pollutant that smells bad is harmful and one that is coloured must be toxic.

Too often, ill-founded media speculation has been responsible for whipping up senseless public anxiety to a point where it has led to the intervention by the authorities. Government agencies fall over themselves to ban this or that food ingredient on the very slimmest of evidence without a full risk–benefit evaluation. The lack of objectivity in many of these claims is evidence of a failure to understand science and the relationship between toxicity and dose.

After expensive campaigns to promote failed beliefs such as a low-fat diet as the answer to heart disease, a high-fibre diet to prevent colon cancer, smothering oneself with sunblock to prevent malignant melanoma, and eating five pieces of fruit or vegetable to stop cancer, one would have expected government agencies to be more circumspect in their enthusiasm for banning the contents of various foods, especially those enjoyed for hundreds of years without any obvious side effects. It is noticeable how few countries share the enthusiasm of the British food police to stop people eating what they enjoy.

Chapter Fifteen

SCHOOL DINNERS

BY STANLEY FELDMAN

THE MYTH: School dinners are harming our children.
**THE FACT: For many it's the one healthy, sustaining meal
each day.**

Up and down the country tens of thousands of children have
been eating lunch at school, five days a week, unaware
that they were being poisoned, fattened up like turkeys before
Christmas, having their arteries stuffed full of cholesterol and
their brains addled by the food they were eating. Then along
came Jamie Oliver.

There is little doubt this TV chef caused a seismic change in the
public attitude to school meals. His highly entertaining television
programmes caused such a strong reaction that serious, sensible
columnists of world-renowned newspapers suggested he should
be canonised as the saviour of our children. The government,
ever willing to ride a wave of popular sentiment, agreed. Saint

Jamie was honoured and his words became the epistle of a new litany. Since they could no longer enjoy cheap hamburgers and sausages, the cry was, 'Let them eat organic pulses, pasta and salads drenched with olive oil!' It was good entertainment but bad science.

In this frenzy of self-doubt no one paused to ask the pertinent question, 'What evidence is there that five school lunches, out of the potential for 21 meals each week, actually cause any harm?' We know that smoking causes cancer of the lung and heart disease, that alcohol, in excess, causes liver disease, asbestos causes a particularly nasty cancer of the lung, that too much fatty food causes obesity and obesity causes our joints to wear out, but what disease follows from eating five school meals a week? For some children it is the only good food they get.

During the course of the programmes we were led to believe that school meals were the reason for the 'epidemic of childhood obesity' described in the Parliamentary Select Committee report on obesity in May 2004. The report itself was highly contentious. It presented a picture of a baby said to be 'choking on its own fat' on its cover. Indeed the baby was dying of obesity but this was because it was suffering from a very rare inherited genetic disorder, the ob/ob (leptin deficiency) syndrome, and had nothing to do with diet. It went on to suggest that almost 15.5 per cent of the school population is obese and it expected this to rise to 25 per cent in a few years. It suggested that all these children were likely to suffer from diabetes, cancer and an early death.

In the flurry of the responses to this alarmist document and without any proper assessment of the problem, many millions of pounds were promised to fight childhood obesity and several new quangos with silly targets were established. The more one delves into the origins of these figures, the more doubtful they become. The National Audit Office survey in 2002 gave a figure for childhood obesity of 6.75 per cent, measured by the more or less arbitrary International Standard (up from 5.9 per cent in 1998). The definition of obesity varies from study to study, and this is different in different age groups. This was acknowledged in the Parliamentary Office of Science and Technology (POST) report 'Improving Children's Diet' (2003) which concluded that 'different cut-off points have been used to define obesity in children ... it is only recently [2000] that the definitions have been formulated'.

In the 1980s, a person was defined as overweight if he or she was 5 per cent over the average and obese at 20 per cent overweight. In the mid-1990s the body-mass index, or BMI, gained acceptance as an index of obesity and with it came an increase in the number of children described as obese. It rose to around 6 per cent of the children measured at school. However, the criteria of what constituted obesity varied according to the age group studied. Age has a profound influence on the percentage of obese children reported: at six years the incidence is half that at fifteen years. The higher incidence at fifteen is not surprising, since many children, especially girls, put on weight at puberty – it used to be called puppy fat! There is little doubt that there is a tendency for more children to be fat today than about ten years ago, but the most reliable evidence suggests that the increase in the pre-puberty age groups is about 1 per cent in the past three years – hardly an epidemic.

Although four cases of Type 2 diabetes were diagnosed in older children in 2002, it remains an uncommon condition. According to the Department of Health's statistics, there has been no significant increase in the incidence of Type 2 diabetes in children in the five years up to 2002. High blood pressure in children is rare unless there is a specific disease process at work. It is noticeable that the incidence of fat children is not evenly spread: there is a distinct divide between the fatter children in the north and those in the more affluent south of England.

If Jamie Oliver is to be believed and school meals are making our children dangerously fat, it prompts the question of the effect of the meals that the children do not eat at school. If it is the five meals taken at school that makes them fat and not the others, then they would have to contain a huge content of calorie-containing fatty and carbohydrate food. Most schoolchildren indulge in a considerable amount of physical exertion and they need a sensible intake of calories to meet this demand, unlike the inactive time at home in front of the television.

Perhaps the problem is that school meals are inculcating bad habits and it is these that are responsible for obesity in children. If this were so, and bad eating habits infected every school meal, like a virus, then a high proportion of children eating school meals would get fat or at least the fatties would be evenly distributed throughout the land. This is not so. Childhood obesity shows a socioeconomic difference – it is commoner in lower-income families than in others. Fat children are much less likely to be found in fee-paying schools. This politically embarrassing fact points towards the children's lifestyle, rather than the school dinner, as the cause of obesity.

It fits with the observation that in the past ten years the sale of fattening 'snack foods' has increased fivefold and the sale is generally higher to children in poorer households. They are consumed in vast quantities by those who sit in front of the television in the evenings. If schools have any role at all in helping to establish good dietary habits they should teach that obesity is caused by eating too much food rather than the nature of the diet and that eating between meals is bad for you. The first step in any campaign to persuade children to eat less is to discourage them from eating snack foods and to look upon confectionary as a treat.

Jamie Oliver points the finger at the fat in school meals, which he claims is 'stuffing the arteries with cholesterol' and causing heart disease. Many large trials have demonstrated that a low-fat diet, while it may reduce blood cholesterol levels for a brief period, does not produce a long-term effect. The fat in your diet is not the same as the cholesterol in your blood and in the arteries. Most of the cholesterol in the atheromatous plaques in blood vessels is manufactured by enzyme activity, an activity blocked by statin drugs. The claim that school meals are a particular cause of heart disease is nonsense. It demonstrates just how far Jamie Oliver has wandered from his sphere of expertise, which is in the kitchen, cooking food.

In one programme Jamie Oliver produced an X-ray, which he claimed proved school meals cause constipation. They do not. The X-ray appeared to show a condition known as *megacolon*, in which the nerve supply to the bowel is defective.

Do school meals impair concentration and lead to poor behaviour? All the scientific studies contradict Oliver's claim that they do. It is usual to find that children are more alert and concentrate better after a meal high in carbohydrate. Two recent studies published in the *British Journal of Public Economics* found that children perform best in examinations after they have eaten a meal of so-called junk food or one rich in carbohydrate.

Do school meals lack essential dietary ingredients? Probably not, if cooked properly, although a case can be made for including more dishes with a significant fish oil content, such as salmon, mackerel and sardines. However, they are not as popular with children as spicy foods and hamburgers. Do school meals contain too much salt? The government advisory body, Committee on Medical Aspects of Food and Nutritional Policy (COMA), has decreed that they do but the evidence for any ill effect is lacking. Various reports, including that from the WHO, suggest that a daily intake of 4 grams is adequate. In physically active, lively children this may be insufficient, particularly after a period of strenuous exercise in hot weather. Children need salt; foods without salt, such as boiled fish and unsalted vegetables, are likely to be left uneaten.

We are told fizzy drinks are bad without being told why. It cannot be the bubbles: they are made up of carbon dioxide, and we produce litres of the stuff in our bodies every day. Is it the sugar? If it is, why replace them with fruit juice that has as much or more sugar per 100 millilitres? Nevertheless, whatever is drunk, cold tap water should be available.

What has been missed in the enthusiasm with which the media have cashed in on the controversy surrounding school meals is that children like them and eat them. The principal reason for their existence is to ensure no child goes hungry. To be able to achieve almost universal acceptance of a meal containing sufficient carbohydrate, fat and protein and micronutrients to sustain the needs of a growing child, at a price that can be afforded, is a major achievement. To abandon the present system for one made with local products and expensive organic foods cannot be justified on scientific grounds. The outbreak of fatal food poisoning (*E coli* 0157) in schoolchildren in Wales in 2005 came from their eating locally produced meat products. It suggests that such a change is not without risk.

Let us look at some of the alternative meals that have been suggested.

- Brochette drizzled with olive oil – this is an expensive version of bread and dripping but, being foreign, it is presumed to be good.
- Tagliatelle with leeks and cheese – high in carbohydrate and fat with a high salt content.
- Pasta with a basil and garlic dressing – I cannot imagine this would have a great following among the 8–10-year-olds.

Most schools that have introduced these foods have found a 10–15 per cent increase in the number of children who bring sandwiches in for lunch. For my money, I would prefer my child to have a diet made up of a hamburger or a sausage, which he would be likely to eat and enjoy, rather than any of these salad- or pasta-based regimes, which he would leave on his plate. Since the purpose of school dinners is to stop children being hungry, it defeats its purpose if children refuse to eat them.

School meals are not perfect. They have to be affordable and that restricts the choice of what goes into them. The most important thing is that they are safe, that they are prepared and served in a controlled manner that minimises the risk of bacterial or toxic contamination and does not destroy their vitamin content. Any meal served to children should be balanced and contain a mixture of protein, fat and carbohydrate. The servings should be supervised to ensure a mixture of all three principal ingredients are on every plate and that too much of any one is avoided. They should be palatable and attractive to the children who must be tempted to eat them. They should be varied from day to day and as many new choices introduced as the children will accept.

Provided that these criteria can be achieved there is no need to try to use school meals as a lesson in intercultural culinary customs or to follow the latest adult food fad promoted by a celebrity cook. After all, the primary purpose of a school is to teach its pupils and render them literate and numerate, not to try to give them a range of expensive meals that they do not like and will not eat.

Chapter Sixteen

YOU ARE NOT WHAT YOU EAT

BY STANLEY FELDMAN

THE MYTH: You are what you eat.
THE FACT: You are the product of your DNA.

Television can be a medium for entertainment and for enlightenment; occasionally it can successfully combine both. Unfortunately, when enlightenment plays second fiddle to the need for entertainment, the balance is lost and truth and science are too easily traduced. This is seen frequently, and with particularly devastating effect, in programmes concerning the food we eat and the way we live.

The attention-grabbing title of the TV series *You Are What You Eat* ignores the obvious fact that we are *not* what we eat. Eating chicken does not make us cluck, nor does consuming a bunch of carrots make us a carrot. Even the wider, looser interpretation given in the programme, that we are composed of the all the substances found in the food we eat, is factually wrong. If we eat a beetroot we do not turn red, because we excrete the colour-forming sugars in our urine; they do not become part of our body. We do not incorporate the fat we eat in cheese into our tissues. Our body fat has a very different composition from that of cheese. If we take in too much salt it does not stay long in our body before the kidney excretes it in the urine.

No matter what the original nature of the food we eat, it is digested in the gut into its various simple building blocks. Carbohydrate ends up as simple sugars, fats mainly as fatty acids and protein, whether they come from a turkey twizzler or an Angus steak, end up as a series of amino acids. As far as the body is concerned, it does not matter whether these amino acids came from a hamburger or a veal chop, a prime cut of meat or the wall of the gut, from protein in the skin or from a slice of liver, it will still end up in the body as the same series of amino acids. These will then be used to make the specific proteins required by the body or broken down, metabolised and excreted in the urine.

The composition of our body remains the same irrespective of the nature of the food we eat. Only part of the fat in our body comes from constituents in the fat in our food. Both the carbohydrate and protein that we eat can be metabolised so as to contribute to our fat stores. The body is a chemical factory. Food is constantly being broken down into its constituent units in the gut before it enters the bloodstream. It is then reassembled in the body into the different complex fats, proteins and sugars that the body needs. These chemical processes are carried out by enzymes whose activity is controlled by the DNA in our cells. It is not influenced by the food you eat. Examining one's stools, as advocated by the presenter of the TV programme, tells you nothing about this process.

The failure to come to terms with this scientific fact has led to the development of a mythology of good and bad food. It as if the food we eat passed unchanged, directly into our body where 'bad food' causes heart disease, obesity and cancer while 'good food' prevents us from being ill. The belief has gained ground that if only we eat the right food we would be slim and happy and would live for ever. This is obvious nonsense.

The head of the Food Standards Agency, Dame Deirdre Hutton (a civil servant without any medical background), is on record as saying she believed that by getting rid of processed food and so called 'junk food' we will all be healthier, slimmer and long-lived. She intends to campaign against those foods that she considers harmful by labelling them with a traffic-light system to warn the unwary of their danger. This ignores the fact that there is no such thing as a bad food. It is not what you eat that determines whether it will contribute to a healthy life but whether it is eaten as part of a sensible mixed diet. Oxygen is toxic in high concentrations, and so is water. Any person who only drank water or breathed 100 per cent oxygen would die. No one should be deceived into believing that eating a lot of a food with a low energy value is less fattening than eating half the amount of one with twice its calorie content.

There are substances, such as selenium and vitamin D, that are toxic in large amounts but are essential for life in small amounts. Are these bad or good foods? It is this basic misconception that has led to the prevalent idea that it is what you eat that is important and that an expensive cut of meat must somehow be better for you than cheaper alternatives; that some fizzy drinks cause you to get fat while a glass of fruit juice, which contains just as many calories, does not; that water injected into chicken meat, ham and bacon is bad, but vegetables and salads, which contain over 90 per cent water, and a glass of water with your meal are good. As a result of this misconception, silly diets have been described for losing weight, preventing heart attacks, increasing mental powers and for detoxification after overindulgence (this ignores the fact that it is the liver enzymes that are responsible for detoxification, not the diet or the amount of water drunk; see Chapter Eighteen, 'Detoxification').

The price paid for the media's preoccupation with the ratings is a disastrous loss of scientific objectivity. In their obsession with entertainment the media have turned celebrity cooks into the arbiters of good and bad nutrition and self-styled 'nutritionists' into experts on diet and health, and have promoted catchy aphorisms that stick in the mind and mislead viewers. The end result has been proliferation of absurd diets, scare stories and food programmes that claim that one particular food is good while another is junk. Pseudoscientific terminology is used as a cloak for ignorance and absurd claims are made that fly in the face of known physiological fact, while science is ignored. If we fail to respond properly to science and allow ourselves to be deceived by the zealots of the various pressure groups, with their mystic belief systems, we will return to the Dark Ages, when truth was perverted and science denied.

At the end of the day we are the product of our genetic DNA and not any of the food we eat.

Chapter Seventeen
FOOD ALLERGIES
BY STANLEY FELDMAN

**THE MYTH: Eighty per cent of people suffer from some
food allergy.**
**THE FACT: True food allergies are rare; intolerance and
idiosyncratic aversions are common.**

I came across a patient wandering the corridor of the hospital
clutching an iron bar. On asking him why he held the bar, I
received the reply, 'I am allergic to static electricity.'

More and more people are being diagnosed as having an
allergy to a particular food. Frequently it is made in an attempt to
give patients the feeling that they are being listened to and their
symptoms taken seriously. The diagnosis is often made when the
patient's symptoms fail to suggest a particular organic disease or
a disease affecting a particular organ. The more bizarre the
patient's symptoms, the more likely it becomes for an unusual
allergy to be suggested by the puzzled medical adviser.

In many cases, such as the one cited above, the mere fact that the patient believed that at last someone had recognised the cause of his problems gave him comfort. Had he given even a few moments' consideration to the impossibility of being allergic to static electricity, the treatment would have failed and his symptoms would probably have recurred. In many cases, the diagnosis of 'an allergy' produces a placebo response that may relieve symptoms.

True allergy exists and its frequency is increasing. It is the result of an idiosyncratic abnormal immunological response to a substance that the body encounters from time to time. It is often associated with foods, and can produce life-threatening responses, as anyone with peanut allergy can testify. Often, especially in allergic responses such as hay fever and asthma, it is difficult to pinpoint the exact cause of the allergy.

There is no doubt that in addition to true allergies there are a growing number of people who become *intolerant* of certain foods. Food intolerance is uncomfortable but it does not produce the reaction in the body that is seen with true allergies. Its effects are limited to the gut and are not life-threatening. Most people who have been labelled as 'allergic', having suffered from some vague symptom at some time, accept the diagnosis and adjust their lifestyle to accommodate it, even though it may not be correct. The conviction that they are allergic becomes so fixed that they find it impossible to expose themselves to the supposed cause without suffering from discomfort. Many of these people are the victims of nonmedical nutritionists who frequently make the diagnosis of allergy without any supporting evidence or on the basis of totally spurious test such as the vega test (monitoring the body's electromagnetic field and its response to certain foods), which is entirely without merit.

An allergic response has a specific scientific connotation. It occurs when a sensitised individual is exposed to a specific allergen. The antibody, which is formed as part of the sensitisation process, normally soaks up the offending antigen, preventing it from causing any damage. In the allergic individual this effect is enormously exaggerated. There is a massive antibody–antigen reaction, which triggers off the release of excessive amounts of natural substances that behave as toxins. These cause the blood vessels to become porous, allowing fluid to escape from the bloodstream into the tissues. This results in a massive swelling of the face, mouth and larynx. It is also associated with a precipitous fall in blood pressure and with skin rashes and difficulty in breathing due to an asthma-like constriction of the air passages.

This type of reaction occurs only when a sensitised individual is exposed to the specific sensitising antigen to which he has developed an antibody. The body's immune system develops a memory for that particular antigen, usually a protein or a part of a protein. Sometimes the memory is imperfect, in which case the recognition is less specific and the antibody may react with a range of similar substances. This type of nonspecific response may occur with various types of nut in patients with peanut allergy. The antibodies associated with allergic reactions usually belong to just one of the five main types of antibody produced in the body. It is often possible to determine that an allergic reaction has taken place – or is likely to take place – by measuring the level of antibody in the blood.

Many sensitised individuals show a positive skin test. This is performed by injecting a drop of the presumed antigen, diluted in saline, into the skin to form a small blister. Sensitised individuals usually, but not always, develop a reddening and swelling of the surrounding skin.

The reactions involved are complex and varied but without a detectable level of immunoglobulins, in the form of either immunoglobulin E (IgE) or IgG, in the blood or a positive skin test it is not possible to be sure the reaction was allergic. Truly allergic responses can and do cause death. Because of the seriousness of this diagnosis it should not be made lightly, especially if supporting biochemical evidence is not found following an attack. The nature of the antigen should be established and the risks explained to the patient.

Although it is becoming increasingly common, true food allergy is still rare. The antigen is almost always a protein or a part of a protein called a *peptide*. Fish, especially shellfish, are a common cause of allergic responses but the commonest cause in the UK is the protein in peanuts and peanut oil. This may cross-react with proteins and peptides in other nut oils. Peanut oil is commonly used as a solvent for other less soluble fats. If it is in a food product it should always be clearly stated on the label.

It is possible to become sensitised to substances other than protein but this is far less common. It occurs where a substance, such as a drug like penicillin, combines with the person's own proteins to become an antigen. When this occurs, the next time the patient is given that drug he or she may develop an allergic reaction. A reaction to penicillin-based drugs is one of the most frequently encountered examples of this type of allergy.

Intolerance

Food intolerance is far more common than allergy; it is also less well understood. The commonest of these is intolerance to gluten. Since gluten is present in most wheat-flour products, it makes life uncomfortable unless a wide range of foods are avoided. In its most severe form, known as *coeliac disease*, gluten sensitivity can be fatal.

Lactose intolerance produces discomfort when milk products are consumed. Since lactose is present in breast milk, the intolerance usually develops later in life. When it occurs in newborn infants it presents a serious problem. They have be fed with a milk substitute in which lactose is replaced with sucrose as the source of carbohydrate. Lactose intolerance is more common among Asiatic and African adults living in the West, because milk is not ordinarily a major part of their diet. Similarly, it is unlikely that one is born with intolerance to glutamate, the supposed cause of the well-documented Chinese food syndrome, since glutamate is present in mother's milk.

A good example of food intolerance is *scombrotoxin poisoning*, which occurs in a few people when they eat mackerel and certain other types of fatty fish. It used to be thought of as an allergy, but was shown to be due to contamination of the fish flesh with a toxin (scombrotoxin) obtained from an alga that the fish had eaten. At one time it was thought to be due to histamine produced in the flesh of nonfresh mackerel. This has subsequently been shown to be wrong.

It is easy to dismiss these conditions as a failure of the metabolic pathway, such as the deficiency in lactase found in many patients with lactose intolerance. However it is difficult to demonstrate such a mechanism in many of these patients although intolerance to a particular foodstuff is present. However, whatever the cause, if the food to which they are intolerant is removed from the diet, their symptoms improve.

This type of intolerance becomes commoner as one gets older. It is self-reinforcing: once the label of a food intolerance has been given, it is difficult for the patient to sample even a trace of the substance without developing marked symptoms. The typical symptoms associated with intolerance of a particular food are abdominal distension, bowel cramps and diarrhoea. In severe cases it may cause sickness.

A diagnosis of food allergy or intolerance should not be arrived at casually. Whenever possible, it should be confirmed by scientifically valid tests. A diagnosis cannot be made by inspecting the stools of a patient or by looking at the tongue. It is too easy to dismiss a patient's symptoms as being due to an allergy, as in the case of the patient diagnosed as having an allergy to static electricity. To do so will result in many people going around carrying their own food version of that patient's iron bar.

Chapter Eighteen

DETOXIFICATION

BY VINCENT MARKS

THE MYTH: One can detox one's body by diet.
THE FACT: The liver does the detoxification and this process is not affected by diet.

F ood – especially that of plant origin – contains lots of toxic substances. These are invariably natural in origin and have developed over aeons to make those parts of the plant that contain them unacceptable to marauders, whether bugs, insects or mammals. Vegetables are frequently inedible, indigestible or frankly toxic unless they are cooked. Many varieties of bean are toxic unless the lectins they contain are cooked at a sufficiently high temperature and for long enough to render them safe. Uncooked and unripe potatoes are not only unpalatable but will actually kill any rats that are fed on them.

Cooking is one of mankind's most important inventions. It renders many of our most staple foods digestible and nutritious and detoxifies others. Even so, the food that we eat will always contain substances that can harm us. Some of these toxins are produced from food by the bacteria that live in our gut. Fortunately, like other animals, we have a highly developed system for rendering most toxins harmless. This process is called *detoxification*. Only when the quantity of toxin absorbed exceeds the body's capacity to deal with it does poisoning occur.

A lot has been known about poisoning from ancient times but the scientific study of rendering poisons harmless, or detoxification, is comparatively new. The principal means by which the body ultimately rids itself of toxic or unwanted substances is by renal excretion. However, only water-soluble chemicals can be excreted in the urine. It falls to the liver to turn insoluble toxic substances into soluble ones ready for renal excretion. This is the process called detoxification. Substances such as the metals lead, iron and mercury cannot be readily detoxified and as a result they accumulate in the body. The study of the mechanisms of detoxification can be dated from the appearance in 1957 of a book by Professor R T Williams at St Mary's Medical School London called *Detoxication Mechanisms*. He described, for the first time and in depth, the metabolism of both natural and synthetic noxious substances, which he called *xenobiotics*. Until then, the way they were handled by the body had been ignored. Recently, interest in the subject has burgeoned, but it remains poorly understood by the public.

Through common usage, 'detox', short for detoxification, has come to mean the process wherein patients are admitted to hospital to overcome the effects of addiction to drugs or alcohol. However, this intervention does nothing, apart from withholding the noxious substance, to accelerate the actual process of detoxification. This is determined by the physiological state of the patient's liver and its genetic make-up, and proceeds at its own predetermined rate. This type of detoxification can be helpful by correcting the dietary deficiencies that are common in drug abusers and alcoholics.

Metabolic detoxification takes place mainly, though not exclusively, in the liver. It employs whole batteries of enzymes, which differ from one group of toxins to another. These are the enzymes that rid the body of medicinal drugs as well as of toxic materials generated by the breakdown of substances present in our diet, such as the amino acids derived from proteins.

The liver is well placed to act as the detoxification factory of the body, being the first organ encountered by blood as it comes from the gut carrying dietary toxins, as well as the nutrients. Special receptors on the surface of the liver cells recognise and remove most of the potentially toxic materials before they enter the general circulation and reach cells of the body.

The conversion of substances into ones that are highly water-soluble ready for excretion in the urine does not always result in the formation of less toxic compounds. For example, in this process the liver converts methyl alcohol, or meths, from a relatively innocuous substance into formaldehyde, which is very toxic. Sometimes the process can be a disadvantage. Removal and detoxification by the liver may prevent a medicine, taken by mouth, from reaching the rest of the body in a form that is potent through a process referred to as the *first-pass phenomenon*.

The diets that are claimed by some to help the body to do its job of detoxifying natural and synthetic toxicants (poisons) in our food are completely useless. They are no more than an updated version of purging, used long ago by the medical profession, but now assigned to the rubbish heap of history. Treatments, such as the coffee enemas, advocated by many fringe practitioners do not detoxify anything

There are a few rare forms of toxic damage than can be rectified by modern scientific methods. The most important of these are caused by certain metals such as lead, mercury, cadmium and aluminium, which cannot be handled by the liver. Cases of poisoning from these agents are fortunately uncommon. They must be correctly diagnosed, as the treatment is not without danger. The amounts of these metals ordinarily consumed are infinitesimal, but we can now measure them by the exquisitely sensitive analytical techniques available today. Genuinely toxic effects are produced only in cases of long-term industrial exposure or pollution, by contamination of food and drink, and in certain rare hereditary diseases. Chelation has a place in the treatment of these rare conditions.

Chelating agents are chemicals that bind very tightly to certain metals and make them available for excretion in the urine. They are not without danger and it is irresponsible nonsense to advocate their use in the absence of a clear indication for doing so. They should never be used for ridding the body of the harmless, minuscule amounts of nonessential metals ordinarily present in our food.

Mercury poisoning has been well studied. It was common when it was used in the hat-making industry. Inhalation of the metallic fumes produced a form of brain damage that provided the medical basis for the Mad Hatter in *Alice in Wonderland*. Mercury poisoning almost disappeared from the scene when the toxicity of metallic mercury, or quicksilver, was recognised. It was given a new lease of life by the occurrence, in Japan, of a brain disease caused by eating fish caught in Minamata bay. The bay had become contaminated with *methylmercury*, a form of organic mercury (to distinguish it from inorganic or metallic mercury), released by local industry in its effluent. Fish swimming in the bay absorbed and retained the organic mercury in their bodies to such an extent that when eaten in large amounts – as they were by some of the poor fishermen and their families – they developed a form of brain damage. This was different in nature from that produced by metallic mercury, but still attributable to mercury. No fewer than 2,000 people were afflicted by Minamata disease, as it became known, of whom 50 per cent have died. Organic mercury poisoning is real and deadly, but fortunately very rare, except as a result of industrial poisoning.

The ability to measure and record the composition of our food soon established that other varieties of fatty fish – including those swimming in the open seas – had the capacity to remove the infinitesimal amounts of organic mercury present in their environment and store it in the bodies. Although apparently not harmful to the fish themselves, the amounts of mercury in their flesh, and more especially their fat, is easily measurable by modern analytical techniques. This led to the inevitable scare that tuna and certain other large oceanic fish predators whose flesh contains organic mercury are not the good 'brain food' we have been led to believe. It is now labelled as a potential brain poison – especially for pregnant women, since it can affect their unborn baby. The quantities of mercury involved are of a different order of magnitude from those found in fish from Minamata bay and to compare the risk of eating oceanic tuna with that of eating fish caught in the bay is ludicrous. Nevertheless, it was done by many regulatory authorities just to be on the safe side.

But, while the mercury scare from eating oceanic fish has

gradually faded, another involving mercury has taken its place. It is that the inorganic mercury in our dental fillings is poisoning us. The amounts that actually get into our bodies from dental fillings are so small as to be meaningless. In spite of this, some dentists have capitalised on the fear, created by the presence in one's mouth of such a potential poison, to persuade their patients to have their amalgam fillings removed and replaced by new synthetic materials. It has been calculated that the exposure to mercury experienced during the removal of the amalgam fillings represents the equivalent of a lifetime of exposure to them left *in situ*.

The situation as regards dentists and their assistants is totally different. They are exposed to mercury vapour while preparing amalgam fillings and from any spillage that may occur. It can, in exceptional circumstances, reach toxic levels and produce symptoms. It is understandable therefore that dentists are chary about using mercury amalgam now that better materials are available. The European Commission has suggested banning the use of metallic mercury in barometers, thermometers and blood-pressure machines – to mention just a few of the household items that use it – because of a perceived threat to the health of the workers making them. One is bound to ask, Has the fear of mercury poisoning gone too far?

Although cooking is probably one of man's greatest detoxicating inventions, it does have its downside. Certain types of cooking can reduce the amounts of nutrients, more especially some vitamins, present in foods, while others can produce substances that cause cancer in animals. Only boiling or steaming is exempt from this. In the past, barbecuing and grilling were singled out as especially capable of producing potential

carcinogens from harmless ingredients. In 2002, Swedish scientists working in the National Food Administration laboratories threw a bombshell into the arena with the discovery that some cooked foods contain the neurotoxin acrylamide. They were able to do so because modern analytical methods are so sensitive that infinitesimal amounts of a substance can now be detected and measured in almost anything as long as they are looked for. No one doubts that we have been eating food contaminated with acrylamide since cooking began – the cause of the present panic is that until recently we just didn't know it was there.

Acrylamide is formed by any type of cooking that subjects food to high temperatures. Frying, grilling, barbecuing and baking are the most likely methods of producing acrylamide. Acrylamide was not considered a toxin until about 20 years ago, when it was shown to damage the nervous system of laboratory animals if it was added to their diet. Subsequently, it was found to be a low-grade carcinogen under similar conditions.

There the matter would have rested had it not been for the discovery of acrylamide in a variety of food products. This raised concern about their safety. It was directed especially at industrially prepared foods rather than home-cooked ones. Particular opprobrium was attached to those labelled as junk foods and its presence was used as a weapon with which to denigrate them. During the early part of the 2000s, a huge amount of energy was expended by researchers in the food industry to determine the cooking conditions that favour acrylamide formation and how to reduce it. Meanwhile, clinical researchers and epidemiologists have undertaken studies to determine how toxic the tiny amounts of acrylamide in food really are.

None of the numerous and very large epidemiological surveys that have looked into the potential carcinogenicity of acrylamide in foods, such as crispy bread, potato crisps and coffee, have found any association between computed lifelong acrylamide ingestion and any type of cancer – or any other illness for that matter.

Undeterred by the lack of evidence of toxicity of acrylamide in prepared foods, several people, mainly if not exclusively from California, have started lawsuits against certain food manufacturers claiming, under Proposition 65, that they had been poisoned by improperly labelled food.* The US Congress is discussing the legality of Proposition 65 as applied to the labelling of foods containing acrylamide.

Acrylamide and mercury represent two very different types of substance that are present in everyday foods. Any attempt to reduce their intake must therefore be encouraged, but the risk is so small that there is no reason to stop eating some of our most nutritious foods. It is important to keep the risk of eating any particular food in perspective. This is often, as in the cases of mercury in fish and acrylamide in prepared foods, exaggerated to such an extent as to become nonsensical and absurd.

It also permits self-styled nutritionists to promote their own interests by taking the germ of truth and distorting it by hyperbole. Once a food-scare rumour has been started, it is extremely difficult to overcome.

---

*The standard Proposition 65 'safe harbour' warning text is as follows: 'Warning: This product contains a chemical known to the State of California to cause cancer.' OEHHA is considering warnings at retail establishments, in restaurants and on food packaging.

Chapter Nineteen

FOOD LABELLING

BY STANLEY FELDMAN

THE MYTH: Food labelling allows us make informed choices about all the food and drink we consume.
THE FACT: Labelling is not applied uniformly and in the case of unpackaged produce is not applied at all.

We used to eat food that we liked and drink water that came straight from the tap. Today, we are told what we should eat and what we should avoid. Unless we follow the instructions, we are threatened with heart attacks, diabetes, sterility, cancer and premature death.

Tap water is out of fashion and a huge industry has appeared to persuade us to drink bottled water, much of which starts out coming from the same source as the tap water that we no longer trust. In fact, water leaches antimony out of its plastic containers. This has led many Germans to give up drinking bottled water. Consumers are now the victims of the very system that was set up to protect them.

I have in front of me a bottle of 'pure water'. It has on its reverse side a list of ten ingredients other than water. On further inspection, none of these is in a concentration that is harmful, and even at 100 times their concentration I doubt it would cause any ill effect if I drank the whole bottle at one go. All are naturally occurring chemicals. I am not influenced by this list of contents. I drink that particular water because it quenches my thirst and I like the taste. If the bottle were filled with tap water, this too would require a list of the minute amounts of harmless chemicals it contains. However, if I take the water straight from the tap, no labelling is necessary, although the concentration of the minute amounts of chemicals will vary according to the region where the water originated.

Labelling of this kind serves no purpose at all. None of the chemicals it contains will harm us in the concentrations present. The one thing I would really like to know is the concentration of the bacterium *Escherichia coli* (usually shortened to *E coli*). Although in itself not dangerous – indeed our bowels are crawling with these bacteria – a high bacterial count does indicate the likelihood of faecal contamination of the water and could lead to illness. All water, whether bottled or not contains *E coli* in concentrations that are harmless to us. In fact, the consumer magazine *Which?* did an investigation that showed the so called 'natural waters' generally had a higher *E coli* count than those made up from tap water. This one potentially important piece of information, which would indicate the purity of the product, is not listed, so why list chemicals that will do us no harm at all? Food labelling has lost its way. It no longer serves to warn the consumer of potential dangers or health risks, but has become a marketing gimmick.

If we were left to our own devices, we would select the food we eat and the fluid we drink because we like the taste; it assuages our hunger and provides the necessary energy and nutriment to sustain life. We would not choose what foods to eat on the basis of its chemical analysis. The purpose of labelling is to make sure we are not misled, our health is not put at risk and we can choose one product in preference to another. Instead, it has become a device that confuses the consumer and can be used to conceal information. It has become customary to display the list of contents on all processed foods regardless of how helpful this list is. We do not label the content of nonprocessed food, such as a lamb chop, a banana or a walnut, although all of these have contents that vary greatly according to how it has been produced and that, in excess, can be harmful to some people. A kipper contains a high concentration of salt but does not require labelling until it is put in a bag, when it becomes 'a processed food'. We expect a kipper to be salty; it does not change when it is put into a bag. We eat it as part of a balanced diet because we like the taste or believe it does us good.

The reasoning behind the consumer pressure for the lists of content to be displayed on processed food is that it allows us to make an informed choice in selecting those foods we are told are good for us and in rejecting those containing substances we are told are bad. The pressure to make us all eat food that experts think is 'healthy' and the resulting consumer anxiety over identifying 'healthy food' have led to the suggestion that foods should be 'traffic-lighted', i.e. colour-coded according to how much salt, sugar or fat they contain. A green mark would indicate food we should 'eat plenty' of, while a red mark would indicate food we should avoid.

It is difficult to see the benefits of such a daft system even if it could be consistently applied. A small packet of sweets would be labelled as bad because it may contain a lot of sugar, which is fattening and bad for developing teeth, while a large bag of the same sweets containing less sugar but with added saccharine would be good. An apple would be good, yet it is possible that it may contain more sugar than some sweets. How would they label a can of Coca-Cola, which contains slightly fewer calories than a similar-sized can of orange juice? Salads would be labelled as a 'good food' but once they are covered in a salad dressing, or salt is added to give them taste, will they become 'bad'?

Experience has taught us that 'expert' opinion on what is and is not nutritionally good for us changes. What is good for us one week can be bad the next. What may be given a green before may suddenly change to 'amber' or 'red'. The system could prove more confusing than helpful.

If we rely on labelling to control the amount of certain elements in our diet it can be fraught with difficulty. Having been warned too much fat in our diet means a heart attack and an early death, we can avoid meat products that are high in fats, but meat from a butcher invariably contains fat and is not labelled. A fat content of much less than 10 per cent would make it too tasteless to eat without some oily sauce or flavouring.

What do we do about cheese? Buy cheese from the counter of the delicatessen and we are blissfully unaware of its fat content. However, shrink-wrapped cheese in the supermarket should have a full chemical analysis on the package. Does this mean we must avoid butchers' shops and cheese from the counter? It is not what we eat but the amount of it that is important in making people fat, and it is the cholesterol we make in our body rather than in the food we eat that predisposes us to heart attacks.

Food manufacturers should be open and declare when preservatives, colouring and water have been added. However, the producers of the farmed fish, recommended as being a 'good' food, often add colouring to the feed of their fish to improve the way the flesh looks. Unless the fish is packaged for supermarkets, it does not have to have a list of contents. Even smoked food such as ham, which may contain added salt, nitrates and water, does not need to be labelled.

Some foods have water deliberately added, a practice used in the processing of some 'chicken pieces', bacon and turkey. This is not harmful in itself – after all, dry food can be unattractive, a limp cucumber is unpalatable and an apple that has dried out lacks the bite of the fresh fruit. In any event, we invariably drink extra fluid with our meals. We don't worry about the water that makes up over 85 per cent of fresh fruit or about the approximately 10 per cent that is sugar. Nevertheless, if water is added, that should be clearly stated and reflected in the price.

Without preservatives, the shelf life of many foods would be short and the extra cost of the subsequent waste would be an unnecessary burden on the consumer and the environment. Nevertheless, it is reasonable to expect the addition of a preservative to be indicated on a list of contents.

If a potential allergen, such as peanut oil or gluten, is present in a product it should be clearly stated so as to warn the unwary. The chaotic state of labelling results in prawns being sold without a warning to the consumer, in spite of the high incidence of shellfish allergy. After all, it is what it purports to be, whereas the packs of Scottish smoked salmon from Sainsbury's have to carry a notice that informs me that it contains – surprise, surprise! – fish.

Go to a health-food shop or a centre of Chinese herbal

remedies and you will find pills and potions on sale, many of which contain toxic substances. These potentially dangerous chemicals are unlicensed, untested and uncontrolled, and their contents can vary alarmingly, yet they are not required to label those contents. So, while we have a list of harmless ingredients listed on a bottle of water, potentially dangerous toxins contained in a bottle herbal remedy will not be listed. We should insist that these products carry a health warning where one is necessary. Instead, because they are promoted as 'healthy' and 'natural', they escape legislation. There is an enormous market in these products. It is estimated that 20 per cent of UK adults take one of these remedies on a regular basis. The result is a paradox: we have strict legislation requiring the labelling of the contents of the harmless chemicals in water, but fight shy of labelling potentially dangerous herbal remedies.

One of the dangers of the way food is packaged and labelled is that it can be used to fool the consumer. Hamburgers or sausages made of '100 per cent beef' may still contain as little as 50 per cent protein (beef is defined as 'the flesh of cattle'). Not all beef is protein: much of it is water!

Products claiming to contain no added sugar may contain high-calorie maple syrup. It requires the reduction of the fat content of a cheese by only 5 per cent for it to be labelled 'a low-fat cheese'. A survey for *Which?* in October 2004 found that some so-called healthy foods contained more saturated fat, sugar or salt than the regular products. It is easy to be seduced by labelling into believing you are eating a healthy diet and forget the dangers of eating too much.

The present system of food labelling is inconsistent. It does not give clear warnings of a potential danger in some fresh foods and as a result it fails to promote the information necessary for a sensible, informed choice. At the end of the day we eat a particular food because it tastes good. No amount of labelling will cajole us into eating food we do not like. Because there is no clear philosophy as to the purpose of listing the contents of food, the system is in a mess. All we should really worry about is that the food we eat is safe, is reasonable value for money and fulfils our nutritional needs, and that our total calorie intake roughly matches our bodily requirement.

How many consumers really know the difference between a picogram and a nanogram? What does a concentration of 1 part per 10^7 mean?* Is there any point in listing these minute concentrations of chemicals? Should the tiny hydrocyanic-acid content of almond be listed? Is it not time to label only those substances that have been added to a food or drink, that can harm you in the concentrations actually present, instead of trying to use labelling to change people's lifestyles? Above all, labelling should be consistent, reliable and accurate and should be restricted to substances that may constitute a risk to the health of the consumer.

* One part in 10 million.

Chapter Twenty

VITAMINS, MINERALS AND OTHER SUPPLEMENTS

BY DAVID A BENDER

THE MYTH: Vitamin supplements promote good health.
THE FACT: Many supplements supply vitamins in what could be dangerously high doses.

Almost half the population of Britain take supplements, spending almost £400 million a year – and the market is growing. Healthy adults use supplements either because they believe that modern foods are nutrient-depleted or to promote 'optimum health'; this may be defined as current wellbeing and maximum resistance to future infectious and degenerative diseases. Some people take high-dose supplements in the belief that they may confer specific health benefits, for example reducing the risk of developing cancer or heart disease.

Many convenience foods are high in fat and sugars, and

relatively poor in vitamins and minerals (i.e. they have a low nutrient density, which is the content of vitamins and minerals expressed per 1,000 calories), but it is not correct to say that the ingredients from which these foods are made are nutrient-depleted. There is no evidence that foods produced by conventional or intensive agriculture are any richer or poorer in nutrients than those produced by traditional or organic farming. Sometimes the varieties grown by organic farmers naturally have a higher nutrient content than some other, possibly higher-yielding, varieties, but the vitamin content of fruits and vegetables varies considerably, depending not only on the variety, but also the growing conditions and stage of ripeness. Apples from one side of the tree may have a very different vitamin content from those on the other side. The mineral content will depend more on that of the soil, and any fertilisers used, than anything else. Nevertheless, people whose diet consists largely of low-nutrient-density foods may well have an inadequate intake of vitamins and minerals, and may benefit from supplements.

Our estimates of vitamin requirements and tables of recommended or reference intakes are amounts that are calculated to ensure that no one suffers from deficiency. Reference or recommended intakes are derived on the basis of the average requirement for a given population group, plus twice the standard deviation around that requirement, so that they are higher than the requirements of almost everyone in the population. Average intakes of most vitamins and minerals in developed countries are above the reference intakes, and certainly deficiency disease is extremely rare among otherwise healthy people. The exception here is iron. Many women have greater losses of iron in menstrual blood loss than can be met from foods, and women generally have very low iron reserves compared with men. Mild iron-deficiency anaemia is not uncommon in premenopausal women, and supplements are needed.

The problem is the definition of the word *requirement*. It is not too difficult to determine a level of intake that will ensure that people do not show any of the subtle biochemical signs of inadequacy, and have adequate body reserves. It is very much more difficult to determine levels of intake that will promote optimum health, which in itself is difficult to define – it is certainly not simply lack of disease. Unfortunately, experiments to determine appropriate levels of intake to maintain optimum health and quality of life into old age will, of necessity, take many years to conduct. There are a number of promising suggestions for metabolic markers of free-radical damage, immune responses and damage to DNA that can be used to determine trace-element and vitamin requirements, but we do not yet know how far these so-called 'biomarkers' reflect the likelihood of developing chronic degenerative diseases such as heart disease, cancer, Parkinsonism or Alzheimer's disease. None of the biomarkers is responsive to only a single nutrient, and all are affected by many non-nutritional factors. To date we do not have any markers that can be used to determine optimum or protective intakes.

The important questions are whether levels of vitamin and mineral intake higher than current reference intakes provide health benefits, and whether high intakes are safe.

Are there benefits from higher levels of intake?

A number of epidemiological studies have produced evidence that people whose intake of specific vitamins and minerals are higher than average, or whose blood levels and body reserves of nutrients are high, are less likely to suffer from heart disease and some cancers. This has led to large-scale trials, in which a group of people are given supplements (commonly for 5–15 years), and their medical history, disease incidence and death are compared with a matched population who do not receive the supplements. In general, these intervention trials have been disappointing. The underlying problem is that a high intake of vitamins and minerals, or a high blood level of a specific nutrient, among people not taking supplements reflects consumption of fruits and vegetables, which contain a wide variety of potentially protective compounds, not only the vitamin or mineral of current interest. Also, a diet that is high in fruit and vegetables is likely to be lower in fat, and especially saturated fat, which in itself is a significant factor in the development of heart disease and some cancers.

Vitamin E and beta-carotene

There is clear epidemiological evidence that people with a high plasma concentration of vitamin E are less at risk from atherosclerosis and heart disease. Intervention studies have not shown any significant benefit from vitamin E supplements. In one large-scale study in UK there was a reduction in nonfatal, but not in fatal, heart attacks. While there are obvious benefits from reducing nonfatal attacks, this is hardly convincing evidence of the benefits of vitamin E supplements. More worryingly, a review of all published trials of vitamin E supplementation showed that people taking relatively high-dose supplements were more likely to die than those not taking the supplements, and only a few trials, other than those in people who were generally nutrient-deficient, showed any beneficial effect of supplements.

There is also clear epidemiological evidence that high intakes, and high blood levels, of beta-carotene are associated with lower incidence of lung, prostate and other cancers. In a study in China, supplements of beta-carotene, vitamin E and selenium to a marginally malnourished population led to a reduction in mortality from a variety of cancers. However, a twelve-year trial of beta-carotene supplements in USA showed no effect on the incidence of heart disease or cancer. The results of two major intervention studies with beta-carotene – one in Finland among smokers and the other in USA among (a) smokers and (b) people who had been exposed to asbestos – both yielded unexpected, and unwanted, results: more people receiving the supposedly protective supplements died from lung (and other) cancer than those receiving placebo. Indeed, the American trials were halted early because of a 46 per cent excess mortality rate from lung cancer among those taking beta-carotene supplements.

Both vitamin E and carotene are antioxidants and might be expected to reduce the free-radical damage that underlies the development of both cancer and cardiovascular disease. However, most compounds that act as antioxidants in the body do so by forming stable radicals that persist long enough to undergo metabolism to non-radical compounds. By definition they therefore form radicals that can penetrate deeper into tissues and plasma lipoproteins, and potentially cause more damage than the oxygen radicals they have replaced.

Vitamin C

Vitamin C is an antioxidant, and also inhibits the formation in the stomach of carcinogenic nitrosamines from dietary amines and nitrites. It might therefore be expected to have protective action against the development of cancer and cardiovascular disease. The epidemiological evidence linking a high intake of vitamin C with reduced cancer incidence is confounded by the fact that the fruits and vegetables that are sources of vitamin C are also rich in a variety of other protective compounds. Studies of biomarkers of oxidative damage to DNA have not provided evidence of a protective effect of vitamin C except in people whose habitual intake was low.

High doses of vitamin C are popularly recommended for the prevention and treatment of the common cold. The evidence from controlled trials is unconvincing, and there is little or no evidence that high intakes of vitamin C reduce the incidence of colds. There is, however, evidence from many studies of a beneficial effect in reducing the severity and duration of symptoms, although this is a notoriously difficult subject to research.

Vitamin C is potentially capable of acting as a pro-oxidant, generating oxygen radicals, but when the intake is greater than about 100–120 milligrams per day the vitamin is excreted unchanged in the urine, so it is unlikely that concentrations in the body will rise high enough for radical formation to occur. However, excretion of vitamin C acidifies the urine, which may increase the risk of forming uric acid and oxalic acid kidney stones (but reduce the risk of forming calcium and magnesium phosphate kidney stones). Relatively high concentrations of vitamin C can react with tissue proteins in the same way as does glucose in people with poorly controlled diabetes, and there is some evidence of increased mortality from cardiovascular disease among postmenopausal women with diabetes who take high dose vitamin C supplements.

Vitamin D and calcium

An intake of vitamin D above what can be obtained from normal diets (possibly in combination with supplementary calcium) delays the loss of bone with increasing age, so supplements may be advisable to prevent, or slow the progression of, osteoporosis and osteomalacia. Certainly, there is good evidence that a high intake of calcium in adolescence and young adulthood leads to greater bone density, and therefore delays the development of osteoporosis and osteomalacia in old age. Normal sunlight exposure may provide the equivalent of 20–50 micrograms per day (considerably above average intakes from foods), so for most people increased sunlight exposure may be more effective than supplements, although we have to balance the beneficial effects on bone against increased risk of skin cancer. There are few dietary sources of vitamin D, and supplements are recommended for the housebound elderly, who have little exposure to sunlight.

Folic acid

The benefits of folic acid supplements taken before and during pregnancy in preventing spina bifida and other neural-tube defects have been demonstrated convincingly, and women planning pregnancy are advised to take supplements of 400 micrograms of folic acid per day – this is more than twice the reference intake, and could not be achieved without the use of supplements. High intakes of folic acid (again, above what could be obtained from normal diets) lower plasma homocysteine, which is a genetically determined risk factor for heart disease and stroke, and low intakes of folic acid are associated with increased risk of colo-rectal cancer.

In USA and a number of other countries, fortification of flour with folic acid has been mandatory for several years, and it is likely that mandatory fortification of flour other than wholemeal will be introduced in UK. In other countries it is not mandatory because of concerns that high intakes of folate may mask the development of anaemia associated with decreased absorption of vitamin B12 in elderly people – a natural consequence of deterioration of gastric function with increasing age – but not prevent the irreversible nerve damage due to vitamin B12 deficiency. In the USA, where folic-acid fortification has been mandatory since 1998, there has been a significant decrease in the incidence of spina bifida and other neural-tube defects, but as yet there is no evidence that folic-acid fortification, or consumption of folic-acid supplements, has any effect on mortality from heart disease and stroke, or the incidence of colo-rectal cancer.

Vitamin B6

Many women take supplements of vitamin B6 of the order of 50–200 milligrams per day (compared with a reference intake of 1.5–2 milligrams) to treat the premenstrual syndrome. There is little evidence from controlled trials that it is effective, and the safety of high intakes of vitamin B6 has been questioned. There is good evidence that intakes in excess of 500 milligrams per day lead to nerve damage, which may be only partly reversed on ceasing the supplementation. However, there is little or no evidence that intakes of up to 200 milligrams per day have any adverse effects.

Vitamin B12

Vitamin B12 is found only in foods of animal origin, or as a result of bacterial contamination of foods, and strict vegetarians (vegans) have a negligible intake, so are indeed well advised to take supplements prepared by bacterial fermentation, which are ethically acceptable to them. Vitamin B12 deficiency can also develop as a result of progressive loss of secretion of gastric juice with increasing age, leading to impaired absorption of the vitamin from foods. Again, supplements are advisable, especially since high intakes of folic acid (from supplements or fortified cereals) can mask the development of anaemia due to vitamin B12 deficiency, but do not protect against the irreversible nerve damage.

There have been reports of vegans who have developed vitamin B12 deficiency because they have eaten plant foods (including algae such as spirulina and seaweed, and fermented soy products such as tofu) believing them to contain vitamin B12, and have not taken supplements. Unfortunately, what is present in these foods is a compound related to vitamin B12, which supports the growth of the micro-organisms that used to be used for measuring vitamin B12 in foods, but is not active as a vitamin in human beings. There have been some reports of algae containing biologically active vitamin B12, but this varies depending on the source of the algae, and it is likely that it is due to contamination of lakes with faecal bacteria that synthesise the vitamin.

Selenium
Selenium is required as part of the body's antioxidant defences, and there is good evidence, from China and other areas of the world where selenium deficiency is common, that supplementation, food fortification or use of selenium-containing fertilisers reduces the incidence of various cancers. There is concern in the UK that average intakes of selenium have fallen by

almost half over the last twenty years, mainly as a result of using wheat grown in Europe, where the soil is relatively poor in selenium, rather than wheat grown in North America and Australia, where soils are richer in selenium. There is, however, little evidence that selenium supplements have any beneficial effect at current average European intakes, and, more worryingly, the margin between an adequate intake of selenium and the level at which signs of toxicity develop is very small.

Fluoride

There is overwhelming evidence that people in areas where the drinking water contains about 1 part per million of fluoride suffer considerably less dental decay than those whose intake of fluoride is lower. This has led to the deliberate fluoridation of water in many areas, with a resultant decrease in dental decay. However, fluoridation of water is an emotive subject, and many people regard it as compulsory 'mass medication'. For people whose water is poor in fluoride, supplements (and the use of fluoride-containing toothpaste and mouthwash) are probably advisable. However, in areas where the fluoride content of water is above about 10 parts per million, there are problems of fluoride toxicity – dark mottling of the teeth may be only a cosmetic problem, but at these high levels of intake there are also problems of changes in bone mineralisation, leading to increased bone fragility and greater susceptibility to fractures. This has led to warnings about the use of fluoride supplements and fluoride-containing toothpaste and mouthwashes.

Safety of high intakes of vitamins and minerals

Vitamins and minerals are considered (correctly) to be foods, and their sale is therefore regulated under food laws. This means that, when high intakes of vitamins are recommended for treatment or prevention of diseases, the consumer has little protection. High-dose supplements are freely available from a variety of outlets – pharmacies, supermarkets and 'health-food' stores. There is an argument that supplement sales should be regulated, with doses of up to (say) three to five times the reference intake freely available, but higher doses to be sold only by pharmacists, who are qualified to give medicinal advice. Some argue that higher does, where there is a possibility of adverse effects, should be available only on prescription, since a qualified medical practitioner is specifically trained to consider the risk–benefit balance of treatments. The counterargument is that there should be no restriction on sales unless there is evidence of a toxic hazard – the consumer should be free to decide.

Vitamins A, D, B6 and niacin are all known to be toxic in excess, as are many minerals. For vitamin A, the intake at which toxic effects occur is about 10–12 times the reference intake for adults, and about three times the reference intake for infants. Some children develop hypercalcaemia and calcinosis as a result of vitamin D intakes as low as 45 micrograms per day, compared with a reference intake of 5–10 micrograms.

Various government reports on reference intakes provide guidance about prudent upper limits of habitual consumption of vitamins and minerals, and the US/Canadian reports have established tolerable upper limits for many. The tolerable upper level is defined as the maximum level of habitual intake that is unlikely to pose any risk of adverse health effects to almost all individuals in the (stated) population group. It is a level of intake that can (with a high degree of probability) be tolerated biologically, but is not a recommended level, and, according to the US Institute of Medicine, there is 'no established benefit' for healthy individuals consuming more than the recommended daily allowance, or RDA.

In the UK, the Food Standards Agency set up the Expert Group on Vitamins and Minerals,

> to establish principles on which controls for ensuring the safety of vitamin and mineral supplements sold under food law can be based; to review the levels of individual vitamins and minerals associated with adverse effects; and to recommend maximum levels of intakes of vitamins and minerals from supplements if appropriate.

The Expert Group has published a series of working documents evaluating the evidence of safety or hazard.

The European Federation of Health Food Manufacturers has published upper limits of vitamins and minerals for use in over-the-counter supplements. Although these are voluntary, responsible manufacturers are likely to abide by them. Problems may arise when people consume supplements made by less responsible manufacturers, who may have poor control over the amount of the vitamins or minerals in their products. Equally, problems may arise when people take a variety of different supplements, each of which contains only the safe upper limit, but in combination may provide an unsafe amount.

Natural versus synthetic vitamins
Some people believe that natural-source vitamins are superior to chemically synthesised vitamins. In most cases this is not true –

the synthetic vitamin is identical to the naturally occurring material, and has exactly the same biological action. There are two exceptions: vitamin E and folic acid.

Naturally occurring vitamin E is a mixture of eight different compounds, with different potency; the most potent is alpha-tocopherol. Alpha-tocopherol has complex stereochemistry, and the different stereo-isomers have different potency. Natural-source alpha-tocopherol consists solely of the most potent isomer, all-*R*-alpha-tocopherol, while the synthetic material is a mixture of the different isomers. This means that natural-source vitamin E is more potent than the synthetic vitamin.

With folic acid the reverse is true. There are various forms of folic acid in foods (collectively called *food folates*), and these are digested and absorbed to different extents. By contrast, synthetic folic acid, as used in supplements and food fortification, consists of a single chemical compound, the most readily absorbed and utilised form, so that synthetic folic acid is some 1.4 times more potent than the mixed folates found in unfortified foods.

Other supplements

There is a bewildering array of other supplements on the market: some are traditional herbal remedies; others are ingredients in so-called functional foods – foods that claim to provide some additional health benefit, or supplements containing nutrients other than vitamins and minerals; others, again, are single amino acids or mixed protein supplements. Some, especially those sold for 'body building', also contain stimulants and potentially harmful anabolic steroids. Increasingly, supplements that contain illegal substances are being sold over the Internet, where there is no regulation, and no redress for the consumer should there be adverse effects. Similarly, Internet advertising may contain misleading claims that might well be illegal if found in more conventional advertising, and could form the basis of prosecution by trading-standards officers, except that no one has jurisdiction over the Internet, and dishonest traders cannot readily be prosecuted.

Fish-oil supplements

There is good evidence from some epidemiological and intervention studies that the fatty acids in fish oil (the omega-3 series of polyunsaturated fatty acids) are protective against atherosclerosis and heart disease, and may also be beneficial in treating osteoarthritis and enhancing immune-system function. The general advice is that people should eat one or two meals of oily fish each week, but some people do not like fish, or are concerned about mercury pollution in wild salmon and tuna, and organic pesticides in farmed salmon and trout. Supplements of cod- and other fish-liver oil are available as a source of omega-3 polyunsaturated fatty acids.

Herbal remedies

A number of modern pharmaceuticals have been derived from naturally occurring compounds in various herbs, many of which have long been used by medical herbalists and in traditional medicine. While some traditional and herbal remedies are effective, there is little evidence of efficacy, or indeed safety, for many. Preparations such as ginseng, gingko biloba and other herbal supplements contain pharmacologically active compounds, many of which interact with prescribed medication, either enhancing or reducing its efficacy. Unfortunately, few people think of such supplements as medication, considering them to be 'natural' and therefore perceiving them as safe, and therefore do not mention them to doctors when they are asked what other medication they are taking. This can have potentially serious effects.

There are two further problems with herbal remedies. The first is that very few have been subjected to rigorous controlled testing for efficacy or safety. Indeed, it is unlikely that many ever will be tested for efficacy, since properly controlled trials are extremely expensive. With prescription medication the costs of development and testing can be recovered from sales while the drug is under patent, but for herbal remedies there is no patent protection, and hence no period of time during which an adequate profit can be made to recoup the costs of testing.

The second problem is one of quality control and standardisation of preparations. Larger and more responsible manufacturers have adequate laboratory facilities to ensure the quality and potency of their products; many smaller companies do not, and the potency (and even safety) of their products may differ widely from one batch to another.

Unfortunately, since supplements are sold under food laws, rather than the laws governing medicines, there is little regulation of the market, and the consumer has little protection against 'snake-oil vendors', quacks and charlatans. In UK, anyone who considers that he or she has been misled by advertising can ask the local trading-standards officer to investigate and bring a prosecution under the Sale of Goods Act. Such prosecutions are difficult, since it can be difficult to counter vague unscientific arguments with precise cautious science.

While a scientist may understand the difference between a properly conducted, randomised, controlled trial and uncontrolled 'trials' and experiments, if the latter have been published (albeit hopefully not in a peer-reviewed medical or scientific journal), it can be difficult to persuade a magistrate who is not a trained scientist. Equally, some of the less reputable manufacturers and suppliers fail to appear in court, then move their business to another county, under the jurisdiction of a different local authority's trading-standards officer, so evading prosecution until another trading-standards officer can be persuaded to take action.

Functional foods

A number of foods are now available that contain ingredients intended and believed to have specific health-promoting effects. Examples include yoghurts containing live cultures of bacteria that are intended to colonise the large intestine with 'friendly' bacteria, and displace potentially pathogenic bacteria – so-called bio-yoghurts. Some foods contain carbohydrates that are not digested in the small intestine, but pass to the colon, where they provide nutrition for desirable intestinal bacteria. There is some evidence that both the probiotics (the live bacterial cultures) and prebiotics (the compounds that nourish 'friendly bacteria') are beneficial, although it is uncertain how long colonisation of the large intestine with probiotics lasts unless you continue to consume the yoghurt.

Two groups of compounds used in (expensive) yoghurt, margarine and other dairy produce – plant sterols and stanol esters – are chemically similar to cholesterol, and inhibit its absorption from the small intestine. Average intakes of cholesterol from the diet are around 0.5 gram per day, but we secrete about 2 grams of cholesterol in the bile each day, and most of this is normally reabsorbed. There is very good evidence that these compounds, together with a prudent diet, reduce serum cholesterol significantly, so avoiding the need for cholesterol-lowering medication in many people.

Sugar is a well-known cause of dental decay, and a number of manufacturers produce sweets and chewing gum containing the five-carbon sugar alcohol xylitol. A number of controlled trials have shown that xylitol specifically inhibits the growth of plaque-forming bacteria in the mouth, and so acts to prevent tooth decay. Such sweets are commonly marketed as 'tooth friendly'.

Chapter Twenty-one

GENETICALLY MODIFIED ORGANISMS

BY PETER LACHMANN

THE MYTH: Genetically modified foods are harmful to human health.
THE FACT: The reported benefits of genetically modified foods are substantial, the health hazards non-existent.

By contrast with BSE, which posed a serious threat to animal health as well as risks to human health, and which required substantial scientific work to evaluate and control, the public furore about health hazards of genetically modified (GM) foods rests on no reliable evidence base and falls little short of mass hysteria. It is a story whose interest lies not in its scientific reality but in the way that a mishandled commercial introduction of two particular GM products allowed an alliance of pressure groups and campaigning media, with a witches' brew of anti-science agendas, to alarm the public and to bring about a situation that is both farcical and alarming.

In this short summary, the scientific background to genetic-modification technology and its application to food crops are discussed, as is the question of what risks, if any, they could conceivably pose either to human health or to the environment.

The scientific background

The 'molecular biological revolution' began with the observation in 1928 by the British bacteriologist, Fred Griffith, that injecting mice with a mixture of heat-killed, virulent pneumococci and living, non-virulent pneumococci killed the mice, from which virulent living organisms could then be recovered. This first observation of genetic modification – the gene for virulence having been picked up by the living bacteria from the dead ones – was a discovery, not an invention. It is a natural process that bacteria use all the time. Professor Oswald Avery and his colleagues in New York showed in 1943-44 – to everyone's great surprise – that it was DNA (deoxyribonucleic acid) that was responsible for producing this transformation, thereby showing that DNA was the genetic material.

In 1953, the American biochemist James Watson and the British biophysicist Francis Crick published their double-helix structure for DNA, from which the mechanism of DNA replication was readily deduced and led on to the sequencing of DNA and eventually of whole genomes. However it was not till the 1970s that a number of new discoveries, in apparently unrelated fields, came together to allow the manipulation of genes – often called *recombinant DNA technology* or *genetic engineering*. These were the discovery of *bacterial plasmids*, the DNA-containing particles that transfer genetic material (for example, genes coding for antibiotic resistance) between bacteria; of *restriction endonucleases*, bacterial enzymes that clip DNA with sequence specificity; and of *reverse transcriptase*, a viral enzyme that copies RNA (ribonucleic acid) back into DNA, which is necessary for the replication of some viruses. By the use of these three discoveries it became possible to clone and manipulate genes. At first the technology was quite difficult and time-consuming, but technical advances, notably a chemical way of reproducing DNA by the *polymerase chain reaction* in the early 1980s allowed its widespread use in biology and medicine.

Many applications of genetic engineering in medicine are well established and not at all controversial. These include the recombinant protein vaccine against hepatitis B, which has been hugely successful in reducing the incidence of this important disease and in preventing many cases of liver cancer. Because the earlier plasma-derived vaccine always carried the danger of contamination with unknown viruses, the recombinant vaccine is much to be preferred on both safety and efficacy grounds. Another example is the use of recombinant growth hormone to treat children with dwarfism. Since the growth hormone extracted from human pituitary glands was able to transmit Creutzfeldt–Jakob disease, or CJD, the new recombinant product was very welcome.

The first application of genetic engineering to food was 'vegetarian cheese'. Strict vegetarians object to eating hard cheese, in which the milk is first curdled with rennet, an enzyme derived from calf stomachs, which involves killing the calf. To avoid using rennet, cheese manufacturers started using chymase, an enzyme made from genetically engineered yeast instead. This was accepted without any opposition. The first genetically modified food plant – the 'flavour savour tomato', which has a genetic modification (antisense pectinase) to delay softening – was introduced to market rather cautiously and was also accepted without obvious controversy.

The present furore has its origins in the introduction of two genetically modified commodity crops by Monsanto and particularly by their (unwise) introduction mixed into unmodified crops so that the consumers would not know whether the product contained genetically modified material.

Two introduced genes (the transgenes) were involved. The first was a gene that makes a plant resistant to the herbicide glyphosphate, which can then be used to kill the weeds in the crop. Oil-seed rape and soya were modified in this way. The second was the *Bacillus thuringiensis* toxin, which confers resistance to stem-boring insects. (This toxin is used in organic agriculture, applied as a spray of whole bacteria.) Maize was modified in this way.

These introductions were not well received! A coalition of those opposed to corporate agriculture and to big business as a whole instituted a campaign to persuade the public that genetically modified organisms (GMOs) were a conspiracy against poor farmers, a fraud on the gullibility of those farmers who grow them and an intrinsic evil and a hazard to human health and to the environment. They were joined by:

- those opposed to science as a whole;
- those worried particularly about genetics and 'playing God';
- those, not least in the media, who saw an opportunity for publicity and gain; and
- a group of those maverick scientists who seem inevitably to be involved in any media controversy about science.

In the United Kingdom the GMO situation was particularly inflamed by the affair of Dr Árpád Pusztai and the GM potatoes, which is therefore worth recording in some detail.

Pusztai worked at the Rowett Institute in Aberdeen, which took part in a research project to study whether introducing lectins (plant proteins that naturally protect against insects) into other plants could improve their insect resistance. Purely for this research (and with no intent to introduce them as a product), potatoes were made transgenic for snowdrop lectin and these transgenic potatoes were tested in a variety of ways. Pusztai, who had worked on lectins as anticancer agents, participated in experiments feeding transgenic potatoes to rats. These experiments had major problems. The worst was that only one line of congenic potato had been made, and this had not been bred further to construct 'congenic' lines of potato that were identical, other than for the presence of the transgene. The single transgenic potato line was compared with ordinary potatoes, and many differences that were unrelated to the transgene, were ignored.

The only meaningful way, short of breeding congenics, of conducting these experiments would have been to make many lines of transgenic potatoes and compare them with many genetically different lines of potatoes that had not been transfected. This was not done, and caused Dr John Gatehouse, who had done the genetic manipulation of the potatoes, subsequently to dissociate himself from the work.

However, the first that the wider world heard of any of this was when Pusztai appeared on a *World in Action* television programme in August 1998 and told the audience that genetically modified potatoes affected organ weights in rats and damaged their immune system. He put the relevant data onto the Web and I was invited by a journalist at that time to take a look at it. It was clear even without knowing that the potato lines were not congenic, that the experiments were poorly designed and showed only small and not clearly interpretable effects, and used a faulty statistical analysis. In view of the public interest the Royal Society issued a statement prepared by a working party and concluded that 'the work was flawed in many aspects of design, execution and analysis and that no conclusion should be drawn from it'. This statement raised the ire of Richard Horton, editor of the *Lancet*, who claimed it to be 'breathtaking impertinence' on the part of the Royal Society to get involved. What is, and what is not, impertinence is clearly very much in the eye of the beholder.

In 1999 the *Lancet* poured more petrol on the flames by publishing a paper by Ewen and Pusztai based on the same experiments (the only ones that had been done at the Rowett) but presenting different results from what had been put on the Web and criticised. They now claimed that there were the reduction in gut mucosal thickness and a small increase in the number of intra-epithelial lymphocytes. This paper was also deeply flawed on the grounds of selection of data, the absence of a proper control group and, again, faulty statistics. In this case the statistics had been cleaned up by the *Lancet* statistician, who had, however, not been informed that these were data 'dredged' from the earlier experiments.

For unknown reasons and from a source that has never been revealed, corrected author proofs of this paper were widely circulated before it was published. This caused considerable protest even before the paper appeared. Most significantly,

Gatehouse wrote to Horton explaining where the work was faulty and dissociating himself from it.

Under the guidelines of the Committee on Publication Ethics (of which Horton was a member), this made the paper unpublishable, since all significant contributors to a work must give their consent to its publication. This letter is said to have reached the *Lancet* after it had gone to press, but there can be no excuse for its not subsequently being published. This Horton declined to do on the grounds that, since the letter had appeared on John Gatehouse's website, it could not be published in the *Lancet*.

This episode demonstrates the extent to which the GM-food debate had abandoned the arena of scientific discourse for that of a media circus. The role of the *Lancet* in this matter – as in the later affair of Dr Andrew Wakefield and the MMR vaccine (see Chapter Twenty-nine, 'The MMR Story') – has hardly enhanced its reputation among the medical and scientific community.

I had telephoned Richard Horton before publication to tell him that I regarded publishing such a flawed paper as immoral and we had a somewhat acrimonious conversation. To my considerable surprise it transpired that someone was listening to this conversation and transmitted an account of it to investigative journalists working for the *Guardian*, where the story subsequently appeared on the front page. To the content of our conversation had been added a picturesque, but entirely fictitious, allegation that I had threatened Horton that his position would be in peril if he published the paper. I imagine that the journalists felt that something of this nature was required to make the story sufficiently newsworthy, and it certainly received a great deal of attention on the anti-GM websites, if not elsewhere.

Not unexpectedly, this article was used by the anti-GMO

campaigners as a vindication of their stance, although it was almost universally repudiated by scientific commentators. Pusztai, now retired, has established himself as a victim of scientific oppression and as a scientific hero for the anti-GMO lobby – a role that he clearly enjoys.

Do GMOs present health hazards?

Pusztai's potatoes apart, are there any reasons to be concerned about the health effects of genetic modification of food? It is essential here to distinguish between the effects of genetic modification as a procedure and the effects of any particular introduced transgene. As far as the procedure itself is concerned, there is absolutely no reason to suppose that it is harmful to human health. The only suggestion that one particular method of introducing transgenes could be harmful comes from Dr Mae-Wan Ho and her colleagues, who have suggested that the uses of a cauliflower mosaic virus promoter can lead to the recombination with viruses such as hepatitis B or HIV to create lethal superviruses. There is however not a scrap of evidence for any such thing. Viruses can recombine only when replicating their genomes inside cells, a situation where the possibility of encountering any cytomegalovirus (CMV) promoter from food is exceedingly remote. Plant promoters in general do not interact with animal viruses and, if they did, we would have known about this since we eat large quantities of CMV in our normal diet. This hazard would appear to be a fantasy.

The possible toxic effects of introducing a new transgene – either because of the properties of the transgene itself or because of secondary effects on the plant – need to be tested, as do all novel foodstuffs, for toxicity and allergenicity. The two major

GMOs on the market at the moment, the *Bacillus thuringiensis* toxin-transfected maize and the oil-seed rape made resistant to glyphosphate, have been eaten for many years by very large numbers of people in the United States and in China, and there is no evidence, even anecdotal, that they do any damage. Indeed, making maize resistant to stem-boring insects reduces the incidence of fungal infection and there is experimental evidence that one mycotoxin (or fungal toxin), fumonisin – which is considered unsafe for horses and pigs – shows a 90 per cent reduction in these cereals compared with the non-transgenic types. The same seems to be true of aflatoxin, which, in patients carrying hepatitis B or hepatitis C virus, is an important cause of liver cancer. For this particular transgene, therefore, the only documented health effects are favourable.

What, then, are the anti-GM arguments?

1. GMOs in reality give no advantage to the farmer and do not have the beneficial properties claimed for them, e.g. reducing insecticide use, giving better yields. This is a curious argument for a lobby group to employ since, if it is true, there is really nothing to lobby about. Farmers are unlikely to grow crops that are of no benefit to them.

2. GM foods are a conspiracy against the public by large agrochemical companies that wish to dominate world agriculture to damage the livelihood of poor farmers and to expose the unsuspecting consumer as well as the environment to unknown risks. Conspiracy theories are notoriously difficult to refute, since the counterarguments are then represented as an example of further conspiracies!

The anti-GMO campaign has overtones of moral fanaticism – GMOs are not just undesirable: they are actually evil – which it shares with the campaigns against genetic intervention in human reproduction. However, while the latter have some religious basis, the major religious groups, including the Vatican, have declined to endorse the anti-GMO campaign.

There is also no doubt that the anti-GM groups have access to considerable sources of finance. One of the British websites devoted entirely to this subject is *GMWatch* (www.gmwatch.org), which publishes profiles of all the many organisations and individuals that it regards as part of the conspiracy to force-feed the public with GMOs. For this it acknowledges financial support from an organisation known as the JMG Foundation. This is described on the Web (www.undueinfluence.com/jmg_foundation.htm) as an 'anti-corporate, anti-capitalist foundation created with part of the fortune of the late billionaire, Sir James Michael Goldsmith. It funds an aggressive campaign to destroy biotech crop production worldwide, is a member of International Forum on Globalization and Funders Network on Trade and Globalization'. Its only reported trustee is Edward Goldsmith, the brother of the late Sir James. This might appear an ironic source of funds for quite such a purpose.

The future of GMOs

There is no question that the selective modification of food plants is possible using techniques of genetic modification and that it is both more precise and more controllable than conventional plant breeding, and also much quicker. Once the media furore has abated or, more probably, has fixed its attention on some different topic, genetic modification of food plants will surely become an entirely routine, uncontroversial and everyday facet of plant breeding. It carries huge potential.

The present products are very much the 'horseless carriage' phase of its development and in the middle future and beyond there are much more important and significant gains to be achieved. The improvement of the nutritional quality of foods – for example, by modifying protein and fatty-acid composition – is certainly possible and one improved food, 'golden rice', which makes beta carotene, is already available. The elimination of known allergens and toxic compounds is also possible, as are food-based vaccines.

One agricultural aim is to breed more salt-tolerant crops and thereby to restore saline-polluted land to agricultural use. This would carry great economic benefits to many poor countries. There is the prospect of engineering cereals to fix nitrogen from the air (as legumes do), thereby reducing the use nitrogenous fertilisers. This is not going to be easy, since this process uses many genes, but it is potentially achievable. The most ambitious project is to increase the efficiency of photosynthesis. The late Lord Porter pointed out that if we could increase the efficiency of photosynthesis from around 1 per cent to around 5 per cent, we could not merely feed all the world from agriculture but also provide all its energy needs. It is not clear that this is possible, but it would be a great triumph.

The future is bright enough, but getting there will need both courage and perseverance.

Chapter Twenty-two

TRANSMISSIBLE SPONGIFORM ENCEPHALOPATHIES – BSE AND vCJD

BY SIR PETER LACHMANN

THE MYTH: BSE resulted from scientific meddling with cattle food.
THE FACT: BSE arose as a rare spontaneous event and spread through the long-established, but probably ill-advised, practice of feeding cattle with 'meat and bone meal'.

The epidemic of bovine spongiform encephalopathy (BSE), or mad-cow disease, which appeared without warning in the UK in the mid-1980s, and its handling by the authorities, is widely held in the media to be the main source of the British public's suspicion both of science and of government. For this reason alone it is well worth exploring what really happened and what lessons should have been learned.

The Background

The original 'transmissible spongiform encephalopathy' (TSE) was *scrapie*, a neurodegenerative disease of sheep that has been recognised since the eighteenth century. Affected animals itch and rub, or *scrape*, themselves against fence posts until they damage their skin, which may be the origin of the name.

In 1937, scrapie was shown to be transmissible from sheep to sheep, and later also to mice, albeit with a long incubation period. It was looked upon as a 'slow-virus' disease, without any virus having been isolated. In the 1950s it was shown that the scrapie agent was extremely resistant to ultraviolet light (UV) and to X-rays, as well as to heat and to chemical fixation. Such properties really exclude any infectious agent with a nucleic-acid genome. John Griffith, a mathematician and theoretical chemist, therefore suggested in 1967 that the scrapie agent might be a protein that can exist in two forms, one of which is infective, and that the infective form catalyses the conversion of the normal to the infectious form. This is essentially what is now regarded as the *prion hypothesis*.

In the 1980s, Stanley Prusiner substantially purified the scrapie agent and found it to be composed wholly of protein. He coined the term *prion* for this protein infectious agent. It was then shown by Charles Weissmann that prions were generated from a normal protein – the *prion-related protein* (PrP), which was coded in the genome by a perfectly conventional gene – and that the formation of the infectious form was indeed a post-translational*

---

*Proteins are made in cells by, first, *transcribing* the DNA of the relevant gene into messenger RNA; and then *translating* the RNA message into protein. Subsequent changes to the protein produced by enzymes or by conformational change are called 'post-translational'.

event. This event involves a change in conformation (shape) involving the conversion of alpha helical structure to beta pleated sheets. The latter form becomes insoluble and very resistant to breakdown by enzymes; this forms the basis of the most commonly used test for prions. Weissmann went on to make the seminal discovery that mice with their PrP gene deleted could neither be infected with scrapie nor transmit it, showing that PrP is absolutely necessary for the disease.

The prion hypothesis is now essentially considered to be established, and its final proof – the generation of infectious prions *in vitro* from genetically engineered PrP – has become available recently. The Nobel Committee was certainly convinced even before this, since it gave the Nobel Prize for Medicine in 1997 to Stanley Prusiner, although, with an eccentricity that is hard to fathom (although not unparalleled), it omitted Charles Weissmann.

Spongiform encephalopathies in man

The sporadic form of spongiform encephalopathy that occurs in man is known as *Creutzfeldt–Jakob disease* (CJD). It affects mainly the elderly and is rapidly progressive, usually causing death in a matter of months. Its incidence is believed to be uniform worldwide at around 1–2 million per year. In the UK the annual number of new cases in the seven years to 2004 has been in the range 50–74. It is significant that CJD incidence is the same in countries where scrapie in sheep is relatively common (for example, the UK) as it is in countries that are scrapie-free (such as Australia and New Zealand). This is powerful evidence against transmission of scrapie from sheep as the cause of sporadic CJD in man.

There are also rare familial forms of spongiform

encephalopathy with dominant inheritance, caused by mutations in the PrP gene. These mutant forms of PrP seem to be much more prone than normal PrP to the spontaneous change in conformation that converts them to infectious prions. When brain tissue from these hereditary spongiform encephalopathies is injected into the brains of normal mice they develop the disease, which is compelling evidence against a viral cause for TSE

There are two other important forms of human TSE. *Kuru* is an epidemic form affecting the Fore people of New Guinea and was recognised in the 1950s. This disease was shown to be due to ritual cannibalism of brains from the dead, particularly by women and children. The epidemic seems to have started around the beginning of the twentieth century, presumably when a brain incubating sporadic CJD was eaten. The Australian authorities then forbade cannibalism and the epidemic subsided – although the last cases occurred some 50 years after the final cannibal feast. These very long incubation times occurred in people who were *heterozygous* (carry both forms) for a particular genetic variation in the PrP gene. All forms of human TSE are influenced by this genetic polymorphism and the heterozygotes are always the most resistant – probably because the conformational change occurs more easily if all the molecules of PrP are truly identical.

The other important form is *iatrogenic* (caused by treatment) CJD. The most frequent cause was the use of human growth hormone, prepared from postmortem human pituitary glands, to treat dwarfism. Transplantation of corneas or of brain membrane (dura mater) were rarer causes. It has been estimated that approximately 1 in 12,000 brains, apparently normal at postmortem, contains prions – and would presumably have given rise to CJD eventually. Since pools of growth hormone were made with upwards of 10,000 pituitaries, it not surprising that the pools were frequently contaminated with prions. Iatrogenic CJD is dying out, as all growth hormone used therapeutically is now genetically engineered.

The mean incubation period of iatrogenic CJD in the genetically most susceptible is in the region of seven years. This incubation period is likely to be shorter than that found when a TSE is transferred to man from another species – such as a cow – by the oral route.

BSE – bovine spongiform encephalopathy

This disease, often called *mad-cow disease*, was first recognised in Britain in 1986 (although with hindsight it probably first arose in the 1970s), and rapidly assumed major epidemic proportions in the UK cattle herd. (Figure 5 shows the number of cases diagnosed from 1986–2004.)

No such cattle TSE had previously been known, and the outbreak was initially confined to the United Kingdom.

The epidemiology of the outbreak was investigated by Dr John Wilesmith at the Veterinary Laboratories Agency. He quickly came to the conclusion that the disease was being spread by feed and that the responsible component of the feed was 'meat and bone meal' – a product of whose existence most people were, at the time, unaware. After the obviously edible parts of an animal carcass have been removed, the rest needs to be disposed of. One of the first processes is to produce 'mechanically recovered meat', which is done by crushing the bones and harvesting the bone marrow and remaining muscle still stuck to bone, which is then processed into a cheap form of meat that can be used in

FIGURE 5

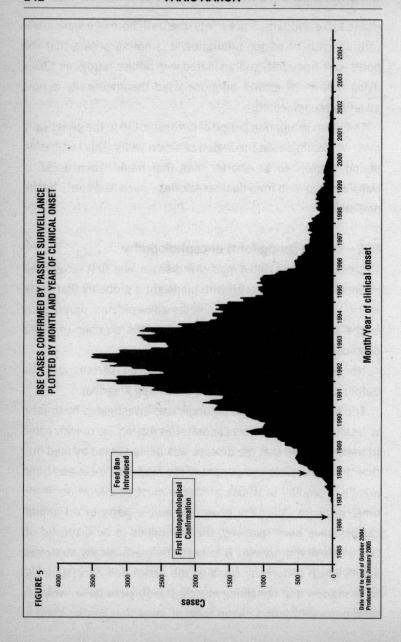

BSE CASES CONFIRMED BY PASSIVE SURVEILLANCE
PLOTTED BY MONTH AND YEAR OF CLINICAL ONSET

Cases

Month/Year of clinical onset

Feed Ban
Introduced

First Histopathological
Confirmation

Date valid to end of October 2004.
Produced 18th January 2005

sausages, pies and burgers. I shall return to this when discussing transmission of BSE to humans. What is then left is 'rendered' by heat treatment and solvent extraction, primarily to produce tallow and, as a side product, the protein-rich residue – meat and bone meal – that is added to animal feed. This has been done for much of the twentieth century all over the industrial world.

In the 1970s, the process of rendering was modified. Demand for tallow was falling and the large oil-price rises of the early 1970s made the rendering process more expensive. For these reasons, the old 'batch' process (analogous to the process by which single-malt whisky is made), was replaced by a 'continuous' process (analogous to that used in blended whiskies). This involved some lowering of the temperature at which rendering was performed. It also involved omitting the final benzene-extraction step.

Wilesmith speculated that these changes may have allowed the scrapie agent in rendered sheep to survive and to infect cattle. This explanation was widely accepted at the time, but is now regarded with some scepticism. The changes in the rendering process originated in the United States and were adopted widely in the industrial world. The UK is by no means the only industrial country that has scrapie in its sheep flock, and it therefore would have been predicted that the outbreak would have occurred more widely. Furthermore, more recent, detailed inactivation studies on the BSE prion indicate that even the original rendering process fails to inactivate it.

It therefore now looks highly probable that the origin of the BSE epidemic lies in the spontaneous generation of this highly unusual and very resistant form of prion in a single animal – possibly a sheep, possibly a cow, or even possibly an exotic animal such as the tigers in Bristol Zoo that died of a TSE and were rendered – which entered the cattle food chain and then rapidly spread in an epidemic fashion. Such a spontaneous event must be extremely rare and the UK was very unlucky. Nevertheless it does emphasise that it may be unwise ever to feed animals on products made from corpses of the same species. The taboo against human cannibalism may be so widespread because communities that did not adhere to it died out from TSEs!

Maverick explanations of BSE

It was probably inevitable that a new disease with such a high economic cost and such intense media exposure should provoke denial and the increasingly familiar rash of maverick alternative theories.

The first on the scene was put forward not by a scientist but by an organic farmer, Mark Purdey, who claimed it was phosmet, an organophosphate insecticide used to prevent warble-fly infestation, that was the real cause of BSE and that, in consequence, the disease was not spread by feed and the precautions that had been put in place were all unnecessary. It was entirely clear right from the outset that phosmet could be neither a necessary nor a sufficient cause of BSE (or any other TSE). The possibility that animals treated with phosmet might be more susceptible to prion infection was not intrinsically impossible, but no persuasive evidence for such an increased sensitivity has come to light in the intervening years. In spite of this, Mark Purdey continues to give his highly eccentric views on the causation not only of BSE but now of a whole variety of other diseases.

A second, and even less reasonable, hypothesis was advanced by Alan Ebringer, a professor of immunology, who proposed that BSE was an autoimmune disease due to antigenic stimulation by cross-reacting gut bacteria, and was also therefore not transmissible. The idea stemmed from a misunderstanding of experiments done by the Weissmann group. They had shown that the immune system is required for the transmission of prions from the gut to the brain but had also shown that injection of prions directly into the brain can cause disease in fully immunodeficient mice, thereby definitively excluding that the disease is autoimmune.

This has not prevented well-known journalists such as William Rees-Mogg and, more recently, Magnus Linklater, from defending the Ebringer view in *The Times*, not on the basis of any scientific argument, but by arguing how nice it would be if the 'scientific establishment' were shown to be wrong and a maverick explanation found to be correct! This is comparable to the campaign run for many years in the *Sunday Times*, defending the views of another maverick, Peter Duesberg, who suggested that AIDS is due not to HIV but to the abuse of recreational drugs.

The government response to the BSE epidemic

Fortunately, there is extensive documentation on this subject from the BSE inquiry, set up by the government in December 1997 under the chairmanship of Lord Phillips. The inquiry reported in December 2000 with the Phillips Report, and is a masterpiece of its kind. The report is, however, sixteen volumes long, and not many people have read it in its entirety. But it is an invaluable source of information about what went on at this time and it is still available at www.bseinquiry.gov.uk.

BSE was originally regarded purely as an animal-health problem, and it was only after some months that the chief medical officer was informed that a risk to human health should be considered. The government then set up a small working party chaired by Richard Southwood, professor of zoology at Oxford. The remit of the Southwood working party was to advise on the implications of BSE and matters relating thereto, and they addressed both human and animal health. They recommended at once that animals with BSE should not be allowed to enter the human food chain after slaughter, and that the carcasses be incinerated. They also recommended that the 'ruminant food ban' (already put in place by the Ministry of Agriculture, Fisheries and Food, as it was then called) that prohibited the feeding of meat and bone meal to cattle and sheep should be made permanent. They were minded to recommend a total ban on the use of meat and bone meal, removing it altogether from the animal food chain. This recommendation was, however, not acceptable to the government on cost grounds, and in consequence it was toned down to the extent that meat and bone meal would continue to be fed to pigs and poultry, and was allowed for export for these purposes.

This turned out to be a very bad decision, and brought to light problems in the government's advisory processes: the government expects an advisory committee to make firm recommendations, but will pressurise the committee to change recommendations if it does not like them. The Phillips Report recognised that both are defects. It is the job of expert committees to examine the scientific facts and to put forward courses of action with the benefits and risks analysed. The final decision then rests with government, which is responsible for making policy and for counting the cost. It is not acceptable for government or its civil servants to put pressure on an advisory committee to reach particular conclusions, since this subverts the advisory process. In principle, the government accepted these conclusions.

In this instance, what happened was certainly very regrettable, because if the complete meat-and-bone-meal ban had been implemented early in 1989, the BSE epidemic would not have taken the extreme course that it did. In practice, the partial ban proved ineffective because it turned out to be impossible adequately to separate pig and poultry food from that given to cows and sheep, and a complete ban was not put into force until 1996.

The Southwood working party favoured the scrapie origin of BSE and, taking comfort from the extensive data that scrapie does not transmit to humans, concluded that the risk to the human population was remote, although it did recommend doing research on transmission from cow to calf. Although these conclusions were justified at the time, the Phillips Report made the cogent point that, after the Southwood working party was dissolved, its recommendations were not reconsidered in the light of new information. When, in 1990, a new BSE-like disease was reported in cats and in certain zoo antelopes (which had probably had access to meat and bone meal), concerns about interspecies transmission should have been reconsidered.

There were voices warning of the dangers of BSE to man in the early 1990s. One of the more prominent was that of Professor Richard Lacey, professor of bacteriology at Leeds, who has a longstanding interest in food safety and infection, and who has a penchant for worst-case scenarios. He predicted that eating any beef at all was a danger and that the whole population was likely to have been contaminated (particularly from those parts of the carcass – the brain, the spinal cord and the intestine – that were known to carry prions), and predicted that there would be 2,000 cases of BSE in humans by the year 2000. This was a greatly overpessimistic prediction, as the actual figure was 84. This and similar predictions were not based on any real data at that time, and it was not clear that they were more than guesses.

The situation was radically transformed in 1996, when the first cases of what is now called *variant CJD* (or vCJD) were described in humans by the CJD Surveillance Unit in Edinburgh. This TSE differed from the usual sporadic CJD in that it affected much younger people, had a more prolonged course and had a distinct, characteristic neuropathology. It was rapidly established that such cases were not being seen elsewhere in the world, and the conclusion was tentatively reached that this was likely to be due to the transmission of BSE to man. This was fairly rapidly confirmed, not only by the similarity of the neuropathology, but by 'strain typing' of the agent in mice. BSE seems to be a single strain of TSE, unlike scrapie, where there are many strains; and the strain (as defined by neuropathology and incubation time in mice) of variant human CJD was identical to that of BSE. A biochemical method of strain typing based on glycosylation patterns of prions was introduced by Collinge, and this also demonstrated that variant CJD was identical to BSE.

At this stage, therefore, it had become clear that transmission to humans had occurred, although the scale of this was, and remains, uncertain. The possibility that a substantial epidemic of this fatal disease might occur in a relatively young population gave rise to alarm among both the public and the regulatory authorities, and much more rigorous precautions began to be taken to exclude prions from the human food chain. The use of meat and bone meal was banned totally.

This ban produced its own problems, since the disposal of meat and bone meal other than by feeding is by no means easy, and it took a considerable time to achieve the necessary incineration. For long periods, meat and bone meal was stored in large amounts with the risk that rats, mice and harvest mites might be spreading it by means outside human control. Nevertheless the complete ban on feeding meat and bone meal did bring about a further steep decline in the BSE epidemic in cattle.

Perhaps surprisingly, a few new cases are still being seen about eight years after the ban was introduced, and this does raise the possibility that there may be vertical transmission from cow to calf in a rare number of instances, perhaps particularly where the cow is in the late stages of incubating the disease when the calf is born. This remains a slight problem in the final eradication of BSE from the UK herd.

There is also little doubt that the epidemic has spread widely, not only to other countries in Europe but also to most, if not all, parts of the world (see Figure 6), not only by the export of British cattle which may have been infected, but also by the export of meat and bone meal in the earlier years of the epidemic. Even in the last year however, the UK still had the largest number of new cases.

Variant CJD
CJD Figures
The figures in Table 2 show the number of suspect cases referred to the CJD surveillance unit in Edinburgh, and the number of deaths of definite and probable cases in the UK, up to 3 February 2006.

FIGURE 6

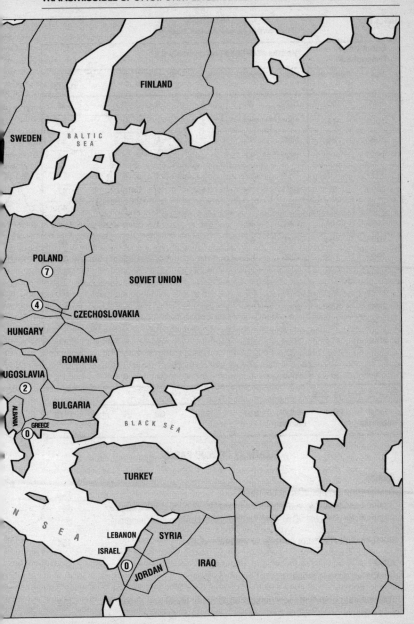

TABLE 2

CJD STATISTICS

From the CJD Surveillance Unit, Edinburgh

Referrals of Suspect CJD		Deaths of definite and probable CJD						
Year	Referrals	Year	Sporadic	Iatrogenic	Familial	GSS	vCJD	Total Deaths
1990	(53)	1990	28	5	0	0	-	33
1991	75	1991	32	1	3	0	-	36
1992	96	1992	45	2	5	1	-	53
1993	78	1993	37	4	5	2	-	46
1994	118	1994	53	1	4	3	-	61
1995	87	1995	35	4	2	3	3	47
1996	134	1996	40	4	2	4	10	60
1997	161	1997	60	6	4	1	10	81
1998	154	1998	63	3	3	2	18	89
1999	170	1999	62	6	2	0	15	85
2000	178	2000	50	1	2	1	28	82
2001	179	2001	58	4	3	2	20	87
2002	163	2002	72	0	4	1	17	94
2003	162	2003	77	5	4	2	18	106
2004	114	2004	52	2	3	1	9	67
2005	119	2005	62	3	6	4	5	80
2006*	10	2006	4	0	0	0	1	5
*As at 3 February 2006								
Total Referrals	2051	Total Deaths	830	51	50	27	154	1112

SUMMARY OF VCJD CASES

Deaths

Deaths from definite vCJD (confirmed):	110
Deaths from probable vCJD (without neuropathological confirmation):	44
Deaths from probable vCJD (neuropathological confirmation pending):	0
Number of deaths from definite or probable vCJD:	**154**

Alive

Number of definite/probable vCJD cases still alive:	5
Total number of definite or probable vCJD cases (dead and alive):	**159**

Table 2 shows a table of all the cases of CJD referred to the surveillance unit in Edinburgh since it was set up in 1990. This shows not only the sporadic disease but also the other forms. It can be seen that by the end of December 2005 the total number of definite or probable vCJD cases was 153. The annual number of cases started at around 10 per year, rose to a maximum (so far) of 28 in 2000, and since then has, if anything, slightly declined.

The interpretation of these figures is not entirely clear because there is no accurate information on the average incubation period and because it is not known when the human population was first exposed to the agent. Those so far showing disease may have genetically determined high susceptibility and short incubation periods, or may have been exposed to unusually large amounts of the agent early in the outbreak. However, the time of maximum exposure to infection from infected beef products was probably between 1990 and 1992. As I write, this is now about fifteen years ago, and it is becoming possible to be reasonably hopeful that the annual number of cases (from this source) will not increase dramatically in the future. However, it is highly likely that new cases will continue to appear for several decades.

How did humans get infected?

The finger of suspicion has been pointed at mechanically recovered meat as the most likely source of prions in the human food chain. This has been used in the manufacture of cheap burgers, sausages and meat pies, and may have been eaten particularly by children. The use of mechanically recovered meat from cattle was banned in 1995 and the use of all 'specified bovine offal' in human food had been forbidden since 1989, so the chance of food-borne infection in the UK must now be remote. One small cluster of cases was attributed to poor slaughter practices by a local butcher.

The extent of human-to-human spread by blood transfusion or tissue transplantation is difficult to predict, although so far there are still only one or two authenticated cases. Precautions have been put in place that include a prohibition of the use of UK plasma for making blood products. Since prions in blood have been found only in some white blood cells, the risk will be much greater from whole-blood transfusion than from plasma, and, with worries about an impending flu epidemic where human antibodies fractionated from plasma may be an important preventive agent, this prohibition may do more harm than good!

What is needed now?

There is now an urgent need to develop tests for prions that are sufficiently sensitive to detect infection in the blood early in the incubation period. Only when this is achieved will it be possible to make accurate estimates of the number of people (and animals) carrying the infection, and to make accurate predictions of the future extent of the epidemic. Such a test would also be invaluable for screening blood and tissue donors.

Furthermore, when treatments are developed – and a number of agents that interfere with the conversion of PrP to prions are under study – one can be fairly confident that they will be effective mainly, or only, in the pre-clinical phase of the disease. By the time that symptoms appear there is already substantial destruction of brain tissue from which recovery will be difficult.

Conclusions

BSE was a disaster for the livestock industry and hugely expensive for the whole country. Variant CJD is a lethal disease of young people, which is a tragedy, but unless there are very unpleasant surprises to come its scale is likely to be limited and not to be compared, even in the UK, to the tragedy of AIDS. It is to be expected that cases will continue to occur for several decades but there is every reason to hope that the number of new cases will not rise appreciably above the current level of approximately 20 per year. The dire predictions made, largely in the lay media, soon after the recognition of vCJD have not come about.

The BSE epidemic arose from a rare spontaneous event and became an epidemic as a result of feeding cattle with products made from cattle carcasses, a practice that had been used throughout the industrialised world for many decades but is now banned. The outbreak was not due, contrary to much media opinion, to any novel science being introduced into animal husbandry. The government response had faults in the early stages, not least in its public utterances, but the cattle epidemic has been brought under control. The mavericks added nothing of value and the media, on the whole, have little to congratulate themselves about. The scientists involved in prion research, on the other hand, have less with which to reproach themselves.

Part Three

HEALTHY LIVING

Chapter Twenty-three

SUN AND THE SKIN: A VIOLATION OF TRUTH

BY SAM SHUSTER

THE MYTH: Exposure to sunlight ages the skin and causes dangerous skin cancer.
THE FACT: Exposure to sunlight has important health benefits and the cancers it causes are functionally benign.

We are constantly regaled about the medical perils of every day life and told that the only sure way to avoid them is death. This chapter is dedicated to those who would prefer to live.

Mankind and the sun have successfully maintained their unequal partnership for some considerable time. We owe our existence to it and Darwinian genetic and social evolution long ago taught us how to cope with the quiddities of that existence and turn them to our advantage. For example, our bodies have developed the ability to use the sun for the production of vitamin D – essential for our bones – and certain immune functions, and that ability is passed on by the safe hand of genetic evolution, which is not subject to the vagaries of its social counterpart.

Unfortunately, our attitude to sun and ultraviolet (UV) light is subject to much perverse and dubious technical 'advice', which society has passively accepted without questioning its provenance. Whatever the subject, there is always a guru. For example, there must be experts on the best way to tie shoelaces. To test this assertion I asked Google, and found 16,500 websites purporting to give the best way to tie shoelaces! The problem is that there are now so many gurus on the dangers of sunshine that their shadow is obliterating the sun and our long-learned understanding of how to live with it.

The sun and the skin

We are told that we must severely limit our exposure to the sun and suntan lamps. If we must take a holiday where there is an opportunity to savour the delights of sunshine, we should avoid it as much as possible. The middle of the day should be considered dead time to be spent in the shade outdoors or indoors reading improving books. We should wear wide-brimmed hats and long-sleeved shirts or blouses and cover our legs, and we must not forget to cover ourselves with expensive, properly ranked, sun-protective creams and lotions. As for the children, on the few precious occasions when the clouds of a British summer evaporate, we must not allow them out of doors before slapping on sticky sunscreens and bullying them into sweaty hats and clothes made with highly sun-protective fabrics. The reasons given for this punitive catalogue of don'ts is that sun exposure ages the skin, and causes cancer. Yet most things we do have risks – what matters is the consequence of that risk, which depends upon the frequency and duration of exposure. Both of these hazards have been grossly exaggerated for UV and its effect on the skin.

The rejuvenation of ageing skin is a money spinner. There is no doubt whatsoever that exposure to UV irradiation, particularly by UVB (the shorter wavelength that causes sunburn, but doesn't travel through window glass), gives skin a weather-beaten look, as does smoking. How long this takes and its severity depends on the dose of sun (or smoking) and your genetically determined response to it. The causal damage is to skin collagen but this is only partly understood. We know that UV promotes molecular cross-links between collagen fibres, making them less elastic, but we do not really know the consequences of this process. While many believe that the weather-beaten, 'Marlboro Man' look justifies giving up smoking, sun exposure is different because, as we shall see later, there are trade-off benefits with other bodily functions. However, this particular sun-and-smoking effect has nothing to do with the ageing process.

The fundamental defect of skin ageing is loss of collagen, the skin's main constituent, which is why ageing skin thins. The loss is 1 per cent a year throughout adult life and is equal in men and women. The reason female skin appears to age faster than male is that women have less skin collagen. This unfair difference is equivalent to fifteen years of ageing! The loss of collagen with age is genetic; it has absolutely nothing to do with UV irradiation and occurs equally in skin that has spent its life covered or exposed. And, contrary to the advertising blurb for anti-ageing creams – which simply irritate the skin, producing inflammation that swells the skin and conceals the wrinkles – nothing is known that reverses this loss of collagen. Ageing of the skin is not due to UV and it cannot be overcome by the products of the cosmetics industry.

Skin cancer is the big scare; it is the main plank of the warnings that have come from government bodies. The case that is made is that skin cancer is the commonest of all cancers and its increasing incidence is causally associated with solar irradiation. These facts are correct but they have been mischievously interpreted to scare us into self-inspection, attendance at special skin clinics and a masochistic, oppressive and totally unnecessary regimen of prophylaxis. Indeed, the very word *cancer* is being deliberately used to create fear and coerce a public acceptance of these measures. Yet the key fact is that about 95 per cent of skin cancers are basal or squamous cell epitheliomas (in a ratio of about 5 to 1), and, although they are called 'cancers', they are functionally benign – they do not spread from the skin and kill. Most are just a centimetre in size; local excision is 95–99 per cent successful; residual microscopic pieces of tumour disappear by themselves and the few recurrences are easily removed. The exceptions are rare and often the consequence of some other diseases. So, while 'skin cancer' is certainly the commonest cancer, the more honest statistic is that skin cancer is the least dangerous cancer; it lies at the very bottom of the mortality table.

So the problem of 'skin cancer' shrivels as soon as you start to examine it, because the vast majority of these lesions are benign. The problem is technical: these benign epitheliomas are classified as cancers from a particular appearance under the microscope, not from their behaviour. The public, for whom the word *cancer* creates fear, do not understand this. While it may be technically correct to say that skin 'cancer' is related to sun exposure, this is meaningless, because these sun-provoked lesions are not really cancers: they are just small, local, slow-growing and, above all, benign. These trivial benign lesions cannot possibly justify the aggressive hue and cry about avoidance of UV exposure. The misunderstanding has been inappropriately talked up by the Australian experience. The high incidence of skin cancer in Australia is the product of high UV exposure in a population whose ancestors included many with pale, freckled skin and red hair. It should not be extrapolated to different populations living in sun-deprived climates.

But if 'skin cancer' is the bait, melanoma is the hook. Melanoma is the least common of the three skin cancers. There is an alleged increase in its incidence and this is blamed on UV. People have been terrified into inspecting their skin regularly, even though it is of doubtful value. Most of us have simple moles and even more have seborrhoeic warts, which enlarge, get darker, itch and bleed in the same way as melanomas. Dermatological clinics are overfilled with patients worried about these totally innocent spots. Malignant melanomas are not found often enough to justify the hoo-ha about early screening, and there is no good evidence that screening saves lives.

We need to have definite answers to two questions:

- Is the increase in melanoma real?
- What is its relationship to UV?

Sadly, the answer to both questions is uncertain.

Certainly, there has been a big increase in reports of melanoma; the problem is that what is now being called melanoma may be nothing of the sort: it seems to be due to a reclassification of what constitutes malignancy. The diagnosis of malignancy in a melanoma is subjective. It's in the eye of the histopathologist looking down a microscope. In the past it was commonplace for histologists to report borderline, minimal or dubiously suspicious histological appearances of moles. Experience of outcomes of these cases taught us that it was not alarming; we did nothing and nothing untoward happened to the patients. Later, as compensation claims began to dictate a more defensive practice, this led the very same lesions to be labelled 'suspicious', without the qualification of 'dubious'. The process moved on, and it didn't take long before brown spots previously labelled benign acquired a new label indicating the possibility of early malignant change. In time this moved on again to probability and finally to certainty. The moles have not changed, but the diagnosis has.

Having seen the process evolve, I have no doubt that relabelling of benign lesions as malignant is a major, if not the main, cause of the increased incidence of reported malignant melanoma. I had confirmation of this from well-known clinicians who had observed the same development in other countries. But an idea is nothing without testing, and, to put it to the test, I proposed to send copies of the histology slides of moles that were labelled benign years ago – and taken from patients found by follow-up not to have had a malignant melanoma – to a panel of histopathologists for their diagnosis by today's criteria. No laboratory would agree to take part in the study. Although they agreed with its design, they appeared fearful of its outcome.

Support for this thesis comes from a variety of sources. The most important is that, while the incidence of melanoma has increased, it has not been accompanied by a corresponding change in mortality. In the UK, the annual number of melanomas in women increased by 250 per cent between 1980 and 2002, but mortality increased by just under 30 per cent and is decreasing. The reason for the apparent improvement is not that we have more effective therapy but that the number of cancers has been swollen by the new-wave melanomas. These have a cure rate of 100 per cent because they were never malignant in the first place; they are paper malignancies, benign moles reclassified! There are other explanations for the diagnostic confusion. For example, it is possible that UV, which is known to increase the number of moles, also induces changes that lead to their being classified as 'atypical', the jargon name for the features on which the histological diagnosis of malignancy may be based.

It has been found that death from melanoma is lower in the higher social classes. Does this mean that the genetic defect that causes the cancer is class-related. This is obvious nonsense; the more likely reason is that the middle classes always turn up first and flock to the clinics with their benign moles, which they have been frightened into having removed, and some of these are labelled malignant when in practice they are really benign. Until we have better diagnostic criteria it is impossible to determine whether the reported increase of malignant melanoma is genuine. The case for an increase in the prevalence of truly malignant melanoma remains unproven.

Even more doubtful is the role of UV as a causal agent. The evidence is fragile and certainly does not justify the present anti-solar terror campaign. What we might expect if UV really caused melanomas is illustrated by the skin epitheliomas. These cancers are caused by UV. They can be easily induced by UV in laboratory animals and in the case of epitheliomas there is an excellent correlation between their prevalence in patients and latitude at which they live, and between the site at which they occur and areas of the body exposed to UV. Even their distribution on the face, head and neck coincides with areas of high UV exposure.

None of this is true of melanomas. Melanomas are difficult to produce experimentally, the correlation with the latitude at which the patients live is marginal, and their site of occurrence does not correspond to the intensity of its UV exposure. They are commonest on the trunk of men, the legs of women, and the soles of the feet of Africans, a phenomenon not to be explained by exposure to the sun's rays. Their reported increase has been much less than the UV-related skin cancers and, unlike the case with epitheliomas, there is no evidence that sun screens prevent them from occurring.

The problem with melanoma, as with many other branches of contemporary clinical research, is that it is based on circumstantial evidence obtained from epidemiological studies rather than an understanding of the pathology. Melanoma is an illustration of the muddle introduced by uncritical acceptance of epidemiology with its almost random generation of unhelpful numbers. A preoccupation with epidemiology has distracted us from the essential biology. We still need to establish the melanoma's cell of origin. Many think it starts in the pigment cell, the melanocyte, but it may start in the 'naevus' cell of the ordinary 'mole'. Establishing this is vital to our understanding, because we know the distribution of moles but not naevus cells over the skin surface. It is well established that UV damage to DNA can produce cancer; but the only sensible conclusion from all the studies to date has to be that, while this effect plays a major role in producing epitheliomas, at worst it can only be marginal for melanomas.

The evidence on the effect of UV on the skin is surprisingly clear: it has no effect on skin's ageing. This is due to thinning of the skin and loss of collagen, although UV does give the same weather-beaten appearance as is caused by smoking. While UV is the main cause of epitheliomatous skin cancers, which are functionally benign, there is no hard evidence that UV is the principal cause of malignant melanomas.

What then should we do about UV exposure and sunscreens? The short answer is that in moderate climates like the UK, apart from avoiding sunburn it doesn't matter, because the risk of exposure is trivial. Of course, children have to learn how much sun they can take without burning and their parents need to ensure they get a gradual UV exposure in order to achieve a protective tan (that is more important in children with ginger hair and freckles, most of whom will need to take care not to burn throughout adult life). In the UK, there is no point in trying to minimise sun exposure to avoid skin cancer because our sun is usually too weak to be a danger.

Although sunscreens will reduce epithelioma formation, they have not been shown to prevent melanomas. The use of a sun blocker, in countries such as the UK, could be harmful, by impairing vitamin D synthesis in the skin, causing a risk of osteoporosis. We still have a lot to learn about what may be the silent benefits of sun exposure. We do not know the significance and purpose of the profound changes in immune mechanisms, the extraordinary improvement in mood and the alleged benefits in bowel and prostatic cancer experienced after sun exposure. We may do more harm avoiding these advantages than anything we might gain from the uncertain benefits of sun avoidance.

But not all of the sun's benefits are uncertain, particularly the protective effect of a suntan. Since there is some epidemiological evidence to suggest that sunburn in children may be more harmful later in life, parents have been told that sun exposure must be avoided in childhood. However, if you take a close look at people who were sunburned as children, you will see areas of white skin that doesn't tan because the pigment cells have been lost by the burning effect of the sun. Such skin will always be oversensitive to sun. It is evident that the original sunburn, and subsequent damage, would have been less had there already been a protective tan. Excessive avoidance and UV screening is a danger because it does not allow a tan, nature's own sunblock, to develop, and as a result exposure is likely to cause sunburn. The dogma, now fossilised in print, is that any tan is a sign of skin damage. This is intuitively improbable. Pigmented melanocytes in the skin are a system that protects it from excessive UV – a system that evolved long before the advent of sunscreens. Even if there was hard evidence that melanoma was UV-induced, it would be all the more important to keep a protective tan.

It must now be evident that the effect of the sun on the skin is in desperate need of illumination, and that the prophylactic message, particularly on melanoma, is unreliable. The problem is, how can we undo the harm being caused by the present anti-UV propaganda and let reason and common sense prevail?

By presenting the fragility of the case against the dangers of UV, I hope I will provoke consideration of real cause of melanoma.

Chapter Twenty-four

COMPLEMENTARY MEDICINE: INTEGRATED WAFFLE?

BY MICHAEL FITZPATRICK

'The worst thing that could happen to the NHS is that we introduce double standards – opinion-based medicine such as complementary therapy and evidence-based medicine for all the rest. Unfortunately, this is precisely what the waffle about "integrated medicine" seems to be all about. Let's not go back to the Dark Ages for the sake of being politically correct.'

PROFESSOR EDZARD ERNST, PROFESSOR OF COMPLEMENTARY MEDICINE, *GUARDIAN*, 2004

THE MYTH: Complementary medicine can be as effective as orthodox medicine.

THE FACT: There is little or no scientific evidence to suggest that complementary medicine is effective.

In the article in the *Guardian* newspaper, Edzard Ernst condemned the government's plans to instruct Britain's GPs to refer patients to practitioners of the various diverse arts of complementary medicine, which were introduced as part of the wider campaign to integrate unproven complementary practices into primary-care medicine within the National Health Service. This campaign has won the enthusiastic sponsorship of Prince Charles and the endorsement of the former radical activist Peter Hain, a former leader of the House of Commons and, at the time of writing, the Secretary of State for both Northern Ireland and Wales.

The advocacy of alternative medicine by the Prince of Wales is consistent with his heritage. The conservative, aristocratic tradition has been reluctant to come to terms with the changes created by the Enlightenment and the French Revolution, which brought great social and political changes in an attempt to organise society according to principles based on reason.

Those who have sought to turn back the wheel of history have upheld the principles of divine and ecclesiastical authority, tradition and social hierarchy. Over the past century these reactionaries and their followers have provided the natural base for conservationist and environmentalist causes. They have also patronised and promoted mystical cults such as theosophy and alternative healing systems such as homeopathy. One of the curiosities of the past 30 years is that many of these views have been taken up by middle-class activists and disillusioned radicals who, like Peter Hain, have played a key role in giving them the legitimacy and mainstream popularity they have recently come to enjoy.

The pursuit of reason and truth is central to the advance of civilisation, and the hostility to science is inherently regressive. It is expressed in the tendencies to suppress all notions of scientific and technological innovation while espousing a mystical conception of nature, the cosmos and personal spirituality. Such views are now commonly embraced by postmodernist cynics as well as by the traditional conservatives. The common feature of this trend is the 'devotion to primality', an emphasis on immediate thoughts, feelings and sensations and the neglect of the import of reflection and new theories in the development of ideas. This antihumanist tendency fuses the interactions between humanity, nature, the individual and society into a single unit: from this perspective, humans and nature are at one and never in conflict. Whatever is natural must therefore be good for man. This approach degrades the importance of the individual and denies rational analysis.

The trend for packaging us as a metaphysical unit results in the abandonment of the historic concept of Cartesian dualism (the radical separation of mind and body declared by the French philosopher René Descartes in the seventeenth century) by the world of complementary health. According to Deepak Chopra, renegade endocrinologist and leading alternative-health guru, 'the body is not a mindless machine; the body and mind are one'. Candace Pert, a neuroscientist who has embraced what she characterises as the 'new paradigm', favours the term *bodymind* to express the way that 'the brain is integrated into the body at a molecular level'. For Pert, the 'bodymind' is part of the 'unity of life' resulting from the ubiquitous chemicals that act as transmitters in all forms of animal life: 'humans share a common heritage, the molecules of emotion, with the most modest of microscopic creatures'.

But what is achieved by replacing Descartes's concept of mind and body with a metaphysically (and terminologically) unified bodymind? The central problem highlighted by Descartes, to discover the relationship between the mind and the body, is replaced by a vacuous holism by these advocates of holistic therapies. Whereas Descartes's approach was a historic innovation that provided the basis for modern medical science, the concept of 'bodymind' is a retreat from science into mysticism. Pert's notion of the 'mobile brain' – what she characterises as 'an apt description of the psychosomatic network through which intelligent information travels from one system to another' – is as unlikely as the nineteenth-century notion of the mobile uterus, which was believed to travel around the female body producing hysterical symptoms. It is no surprise to discover that, having turned her back on science, Pert has become an advocate of New Age mysticism and alternative healing.

The key challenge to scientific medicine is to explain the pathological processes that are the cause of disease states and to deal with the experience of illness.

In dealing with the reality of human disease, reason, despite all its limitations, is the best weapon that we have. Reason tells us that medical science has proved to be dramatically effective in the treatment of a wide range of diseases, from infections to endocrine disorders, in which the pathological processes are fairly well understood. The success of modern scientific medicine is the principle reason why it has prevailed over diverse ancient alternatives (many of which have now re-emerged under the complementary-health umbrella). In other conditions, such as coronary heart disease and cancer, which are major killers of our time and where our medical understanding is less complete and therapy less effective, it is possible to assess the benefits of different treatments and to measure their adverse effects. The judgement of the value of any particular treatment is made with reference to a body of scientific knowledge that is, at least in theory and increasingly in practice, available to the patient as well as to the doctor. By contrast, the client of the alternative practitioner has to rely on faith alone.

In some conditions – such as multiple sclerosis and motor-neurone disease – medical understanding remains limited and treatment virtually nonexistent. In these conditions the patients are in a situation similar to that which prevailed in relation to most diseases a century ago. Just as most patients with multiple sclerosis today opt for conventional rather than alternative medicine, so patients in the past put their trust in scientific medicine. Why they chose orthodox medicine rather than the diverse alternatives on offer before medical science first began to yield effective treatments has long been a matter of controversy among historians. Some have attributed the success of orthodox medicine to the political and organisational skills of the early medical professionals. A more likely explanation is that the commitment of doctors to the advance of medical science persuaded most patients that it was more likely to be beneficial than the alternatives on offer.

Writing in 1859, the German physician Bernard Naunyn observed that doctors' zeal won patients' respect and trust: 'it never occurred to them to inquire whether this zeal was in the interest of treatment or in the interest of science'. At a time when all treatment was experimental, patients and doctors joined in a collective endeavour against disease. Even in these cynical times, most patients still uphold this rational spirit – only to find some doctors retreating from it!

There has been greater criticism of the record of scientific medicine and the medical profession in dealing with the subjective experience of illness. Yet this criticism neglects the major advances that have occurred in recent years.

In the heyday of scientific medicine, from the 1940s to the 1960s, doctors seemed to take little interest in the emotional and psychological aspects of their patients' illnesses. The emergence of scientific medicine as a replacement for the older traditional systems of healing caused the modern practitioners to distance themselves from an evangelical and charismatic style of practice. The quest for rational therapeutic regimes was associated with a conscious drive to eschew the less rational aspects of medical practice. Once doctors were in a position to prescribe effective drugs – and to replace hips and carry out kidney transplants and open-heart surgery – they came to rely less on a good bedside manner. Traditional 'physicianly' skills were allowed to lapse to a point where some doctors, especially in surgical specialties, seemed inclined to dispense even with elementary civilities.

The bureaucratisation of medical practice, whether through systems of insurance or state welfare, helped to make doctors less and less personally involved with the pain and suffering of their patients. The persistence of these trends towards a more mechanistic and algorithmic practice of medicine, conducted through formal – very brief – encounters, has proved a key factor in the growing popularity of alternative practitioners, who offer more empathetic, more personal and lengthy consultations.

Over the past two decades a number of factors have encouraged orthodox doctors to take a greater interest in patients' attitudes towards health and illness. One is a lack of confidence in scientific medicine's capacity to deal with the prevalence of heart disease and cancer in an ageing population. This has encouraged greater medical intervention in the patient's lifestyle, aimed at preventing these diseases. Another is the paradox that, although objective indicators of health register steady improvement, people go to see doctors complaining of a wider range of physical symptoms, which are often inexplicable in terms of any recognised pathological process; they can be categorised as 'doing better, but feeling worse'. The dominant response to the problem of unexplained physical symptoms has been to expand the range of medical diagnosis and the relabelling of collections of symptoms as new diseases, such as ME/chronic fatigue syndrome, repetitive-strain injury, fibromyalgia and numerous psychiatric syndromes and disorders.

Unfortunately, medicine's turn towards the subjective has not been accompanied by a major expansion in the scientific study of what constitutes the experience of 'illness' and the interactions of the mind and the body in the genesis of symptoms. Earlier researches into the links between the nervous, endocrine and immune systems and their role in health and illness – in the new discipline dubbed *psychoneuroimmunology* in the 1980s – have been little developed in mainstream medicine. Instead, they have been given a mystical interpretation and transformed into junk science by the practitioners of complementary therapies.

The shift of medicine away from the treatment of disease to the alleviation of the symptoms of illness in people in whom no disease process can be found has had important consequences. It has reinforced a trend towards the emergence of a society in which the state has sought to provide a range of therapeutic alternatives to orthodox medicine, including those of psychotherapy, counselling and complementary treatments. It legitimises the intrusion of the practice of medicine into the lifestyle of the individual. Instead of these initiatives being 'as well as' proper medicine, they have become 'in place of' it. Today, modern doctors are expected to take on the tasks of social workers, teachers and the police, assuming a coercive role that can only prejudice the doctor–patient relationship.

Just as reason cannot coexist with irrationality, so orthodox medicine cannot be reconciled with an alternative conflicting system. Astronomy and astrology are incompatible ways of studying the stars; alchemy and chemistry are fundamentally different concepts of the elements. Professor Edzard Ernst, who was quoted at the beginning of this chapter, has described alternative medicine as 'a regressive temptation', 'the kind of medicine people took when there was no alternative'.

How can modern medicine begin to overcome its current predicament? It should stick to the rational principles that have made scientific medicine so successful in many spheres, and establish a clear boundary between scientific medicine and that of the non-rational belief systems with their non-scientific approach to healing. Doctors should resist the tendency to extend medical intervention into the wider areas of personal and social lifestyle and confine their efforts to their area of true expertise – the diagnosis and treatment of disease.

Research into the subjective aspects of illness and the effect of mental states on bodily function should be pursued scientifically. As the great nineteenth-century medical scientist Rudolph Virchow argued, 'one must learn and become accustomed to explain the unknown from the known, rather than the reverse'.

Chapter Twenty-five

ALTERNATIVE MEDICINE AND HERBAL REMEDIES

BY STANLEY FELDMAN AND VINCENT MARKS

THE MYTH: Alternative medicine is effective and safe.
THE FACT: They are no better than placebo and may do harm.

Why do so many people flock to shops selling so-called traditional Chinese herbal medicines? Do they never stop to consider that the life expectancy of those Chinese who take these potions is far less than their own? If these remedies were any good, the life expectancy of the Chinese peasant would approach that of his Western counterpart.

What is true for traditional Chinese medicines is equally true for Ayurvedic and other medicines used in developing and undeveloped countries. Some are frankly poisonous, others just ineffective – although a minority do contain useful pharmacologically active ingredients. The story of how an infusion of foxglove became the medicine we now call *digoxin* is well known. It is only one example of the many modern medicines that have had their origins in plants, fungi or bacteria. However, in order for any of these drugs to be used in medicine, the active ingredient has first to be isolated and standardised so that the drug can be administered as pure substances.

When it comes to other forms of treatment such as homeopathy, reflexology, acupuncture, aromatherapy, treatments with magnets and coloured beads, strange rebirthing and voodoo-like rituals, there is scant evidence that they are any better than a placebo. Nevertheless, each year, millions of pounds are wasted, some of it by the NHS, on these patently senseless 'snake oil' cures.

Although presented as alternatives to medicine or as complementary, they are an expensive and potentially dangerous diversion from science-based treatments that have been clinically evaluated. Most have as much credibility as palmistry, astrology and fortune telling.

Acupuncture has been practised in China for thousands of years. It had resurgence in the West during the time of the Cultural Revolution, when millions of Chinese died in a move to abandon science and learning and return to the agrarian culture of former years. All things Western were bad and extravagant claims were made for native cures, such as acupuncture. Its use in today's China is virtually restricted to poor peasants who do not have access to Western medicine. It is very difficult to test its efficacy by acceptable, controlled, double-blind trials because of the placebo effect. This depends as much upon the confidence of the person giving the treatment as the belief of the patient receiving it. It is extremely difficult to assess its success rate in acupuncture trials because the patient always knows when a needle is inserted and will be inclined to react positively.

Those trials that have been carried out suggest that its success rate is slightly higher than that of a placebo. A placebo may produce a significant response rate, depending on the condition being treated. In diseases such as leukaemia, pernicious anaemia, Addison's disease and Type 1 diabetes – where the progress of the condition can be predicted and closely monitored – the placebo response is minimal. The proponents of acupuncture argue that, even though the observed response is little better than placebo, the psychological benefit justifies its use where other measures have failed. As a result, it is frequently used in the treatment of chronic pain when all other measures have failed. Unfortunately, in common with all placebo responses, its effectiveness becomes progressively less each time it is administered.

Homeopathy was the brainchild of a German doctor, Samuel Hahnemann, at the end of the eighteenth century. His idea was diametrically opposite to the Galenic theory that held that illnesses were the result of an excess of one of the hypothetical four basic 'humours' of life. If, according to Galen, you then used a medicine associated with the opposite 'power', it would alleviate the patient's symptoms. These humours were not distinguished from the underlying cause of the disease. The scientific study of the causes of disease, pathology, came into being only in the middle of the nineteenth century.

Hahnemann's treatments were the opposite of Galen. Observing that the bark of the chicona bush caused fever and was also active in combating the ague of malaria, he proposed, without any evidence to support his idea, that, if you suffered from too much of a particular symptom, you could build up resistance to it, by repeatedly taking a dose of a substance that produced the same symptoms. Thus if you were suffering from too much 'bile' in your body, drinking a small amount of a medicine that caused it would cure the effects of the poison. It was sheer witchcraft but had one saving grace: for reasons that have never been explained, Hahnemann believed that the more dilute the poison the more effect it had as a medicine. In effect, so dilute were his medicines that they contained minuscule amounts or none of the original poison.

The treatment came to Britain with the help of Prince Albert. It is said he asked his personal doctor, who practised homeopathy, to advise Prime Minister Disraeli about his indisposition. He thought his present illness was due to his receiving the wrong treatment for his longstanding gout. In Victorian times the treatment for gout was based on medicines containing arsenic. Disraeli gradually got better on the homeopathic regime as a result of abandoning the arsenic treatment given to him by his regular doctors. The patronage of Queen Victoria, who saw the improvement in her prime minister, established homeopathy as a treatment to be used by the royal family in the Britain.

Hahnemann's *law of diminishing similars*, which is the name he gave to the practice of making weaker and weaker doses of so-called allopathic potions until they reached an infinite dilution and contained none of the original material, is still the basis of homeopathy as practised today.

Homeopathy does not make any sense, and it has been described as a way of 'turning water into gold', yet it can be prescribed in the health service. There are still some people who believe that blind clinical trials have established that it is effective. None of these so-called 'random trials' has withstood critical scrutiny. There is absolutely no scientific evidence to support homeopathy. In fact it is impossible to envisage any mechanism by which so few molecules of a medicine, even of a fabulously potent drug, could have any effect on the many billions of cells in the body.

There are a great many other bizarre remedies only a minority of which have been thoroughly investigated. All those that have been investigated thoroughly have been shown to be useless. Sleeping with a magnet under the bed has been shown to have no effect on rheumatism, or on the rate of healing on fractures; administering a coffee enema does not cure cancer; reflexology is entirely without any effect on the body; and no amount of coloured beads changes one's mental powers.

While most of these treatments are just a waste of money they also deceive the public and in some cases defraud them. Other treatment schemes touted by 'snake oil salesmen' may actually cause harm.

Phoney diagnostic tests claim to be able to see what is at the bottom of a patient's ailment by examining the iris of his or her eye, for example. The claim by some alternative practitioners to be able to diagnose nutritional needs by examining faeces is absurd (George III was an enthusiastic copravoyant, but, then, he was mad!). The equally fallacious but less unpleasant vega test, which is said to be able to detect allergies is useless. There is no foundation at present for the belief that one can diagnose cancer by examining any of the body fluids. To date, this is possible only by examining them for cancer cells by means of a microscope. One day it may be possible to use just chemical methods – but not yet.

In this chapter we have illustrated just a few of the phoney claims made by the shady practitioners, many of whom are not graduates from any recognised medical school. Medically qualified homeopaths generally use homeopathy only when the illness they are treating is self-limiting and for which there is no specific treatment. Other homeopaths masquerade as healers, gurus and unlicensed 'alternative medical practitioners'. In former times they would have been called quacks. There is a danger that they may cause harm to patients by preventing someone who is ill from seeking proper advice or taking appropriately prescribed medicine. There is also a potential risk from toxic material unknowingly present in the medicines they prescribe or sell.

Herbal medicines must not be confused with quack medicines, although not all herbal treatments are safe or effective. Many herbs, fungi, bacteria and even some animal products contain some powerful pharmacological agents and there are many reputable drug companies examining them, analysing their ingredients and, in a few cases, finding potentially useful therapeutic compounds. Because many active medicinal compounds undoubtedly do occur in nature or can be made from them (such as the steroid class of medicines), it is difficult to generalise about their safety and usefulness. The problem with herbal medicines, as generally sold, is that they are totally uncontrolled and have rarely been subjected to thorough tests of their safety.

Herbs contain many chemicals, some of which may have a therapeutic effect while others may be poisonous. Many commercial products are a mixture of both types of compound and their contents can differ markedly according to the time of year when they were harvested. The proportions of the various ingredients in the potions may also vary according to who has produced the concoction. The dose regime is haphazard and the ratio of effective dose to the one that is frankly poisonous is never determined. Possible effects on the foetus and the effect of the long-term administration of these drugs are unknown and, in contrast to licensed medicines, there is no post-marketing surveillance. One thing is certain: none of these herbal compounds offers a miraculous cure for any known condition and cases of poisoning by them are seen with regularity in most poison centres around the country.

Why then do people buy phoney cures and patronise alternative practitioners? Why do they spend all that money on treatments known to be useless? In part, it is the failure of modern scientific medicine to cure many of the problems with which it is faced. Where there is a successful, scientific cure available, experience has shown that the demand for alternative forms of treatment rapidly disappears. In the absence of an effective remedy, patients are unwilling to believe that there is nothing that will help them. They clutch at the futile belief that there must be a 'natural' alternative that will cure them and there is no limit to the number of snake-oil salesmen who are willing to provide it.

Chapter Twenty-six
EXERCISE

BY PAUL AICHROTH AND STANLEY FELDMAN

THE MYTH: Fitness and health are synonymous and achievable only by rigorous exercise.
THE FACT: Moderate activity is conducive to good health and overindulgence counterproductive.

There is good evidence of the dangers of a sedentary lifestyle. Statistics suggest the couch potato does not live as long as his active counterpart. American studies have indicated that the reason there are so many more immobile women than men is that they are less inclined to walk to the shops or to engage in any potentially sweaty activity. There is additional, much less persuasive, evidence that exercise can help keep the mind active and help ward off diseases such as obesity, high blood pressure and stroke. It is for these latter reasons that we are encouraged to exercise on a regular basis, especially as we get older.

Against this seemingly commonsense advice there is the less

well-publicised downside of too much exercise and competitive sports. There is a correlation between the incidence of hip and knee arthritis and indulgence in competitive sports, which is reflected in the earlier age at which joint replacement becomes necessary. The development of a thriving specialty of sports medicine, with its own diploma and journals, should be a warning that extreme exercise is not without its dangers. Although good muscle tone and weight reduction may be maintained during the period of aggressive exercise, all too often there is a rebound effect, once the sport has been given up, of flabby bellies and an increase in weight.

The exhortation to play more and more active sports ignores these possible deleterious consequences. There is little evidence that a lot of exercise is better for one's long-term health than a consistent pattern of *moderate* activity. It is fashionable to join a gym and to push the limits of one's exercise ability to demonstrate just how fit one has become, but there is no evidence this is any better than the person who enjoys a brisk walk of 20–30 minutes, or one or two miles a day. Huge muscles built up by weightlifting degenerate more rapidly into flab than those of a person who swims several lengths of a pool regularly.

Proportionately, more people die while out jogging than while walking. Skiing and football have their own list of orthopaedic complications, some of them potentially disabling. Even yoga can produce arthritis of the knee and hip.

The effect of exercise

It is helpful to understand the reasons why exercise is good for you, especially as one gets older, in order to see why *excessive* exercise is unnecessary and may be harmful.

Unless a joint is used it will seize up. This is especially true of the upper limb joints such as the shoulder and elbow. In other joints, inactivity will produce restriction in their range of movement. Blocks of muscles that either bend the joint (the *flexors*) or extend the bent joint (the *extensors*) control our every movement. Weakness in either group will produce instability in the joint. Muscles are maintained by their blood flow, which is enormously increased by exercise. If they are not exercised they degenerate, becoming infiltrated with fat and fibrous tissue. In an extreme, such as a paralysed limb, the fibrous tissue causes rigidity of the muscle and fixation of the joint.

As one gets older there is a tendency for this involutional change to occur unless the muscles are used constantly. It is this that causes the loss of power and the increasing rigidity that occurs with age. The ageing process also affects the sheets of tissue that surround and encapsulate the joints. These tissues become more and more fibrous and contracted unless they are regularly stretched. One of the problems is that these tendonous tissues also become more friable with age and are more readily torn by violent exertion. Anyone who has suffered from tennis elbow will appreciate how painful this type of injury can be. As the blood supply to these tendons is never very good and gets even worse with age, these injuries tend to heal slowly. It seems to make little difference whether they are rested or exercised. An injection of cortisone and local anaesthetic may give some temporary relief.

The ends of the bones of the joints are protected with gristle-like cartilage. This acts like a Teflon lining, preventing the ends of the bones from rubbing against each other. It is the wearing out and loss of this cartilage that causes osteoarthritis.

There is little doubt that osteoarthritis can be caused by

overzealous exercise, which strips the cartilage off the bone. The heavy pounding it takes in contact sports such as rugby football can also cause it to be injured. There is good evidence that it is jeopardised by jogging, although this may be a result of damage to the underlying bone that supports the cartilage. These are all good reasons to suggest that contact sports and violent forms of exercise are not as good for your long-term health as they are often portrayed – however enjoyable they may be. On the positive side, there is no doubt that unless muscle tone is maintained the cartilage at the ends of bones wears out more quickly and arthritic joints become more painful.

Rheumatoid arthritis is different and is caused by an inflammation of the tissues around the joint. This causes painful, swollen joints and it too often destroys the joint. This type of arthritis should be treated with rest and anti-inflammatory drugs. Exercise is indicated only to maintain the alignment of the joint.

The heart is as much a muscle as any others in the body and like them subject to degeneration and infiltration by fat and fibrous tissue. Exercising the heart can slow this process. This is the reason for encouraging people to exercise to a point where they raise their heart rate to about 100–110 beats per minute once or twice a day. There is a danger in overdoing this: increasing the heart rate, especially in older people, may cause angina and it is sensible not to exceed a heart rate of 120 beats per minute.

Exercise is advocated as part of weight-losing programmes. Certainly, the obese person has more need than most to keep his or her muscles in good shape. Indeed obese people are often extremely strong, since they must carry around a lot of extra weight; but, as a means of eliminating excessive fat, exercise is less effective than eating one sandwich fewer or one less slice of cheese each day. After all, migrating birds, who fly about 3,000 miles, lose only 15 per cent of their bodyweight during the course of their journey, but may die of starvation when deprived of food for only a relatively short time before they have laid down the fatty tissue needed on their journey.

There is evidence that regular exercise ratchets up one's metabolism and it is this rather than the actual energy used by the physical work that produces the health benefit. It has long been recognised that patients confined to a wheelchair through muscular weakness from whatever cause have an unusually high incidence of gross obesity that is extremely difficult to treat.

Rigorous exercise increases appetite to such an extent that it may more than compensate for the energy used in doing it!

The message is clear: exercise is good for you. It should include stretching and bending so that as many joints as possible are put through a full range of movements. It is important to maintain muscle tone. However, contact sports, bursts of violent exercise and adopting grossly abnormal postures for any length of time is potentially harmful. It may make you feel better as a result of the secretion of nature's 'happy hormone', endorphin, but there is a price to pay. For most, a good brisk walk of one or two miles a day, accompanied by stretching and bending exercises, is adequate. Swimming once a week is good exercise, but an amble around the shops is not sufficient. Any temptation for the untrained to embark upon a sudden vigorous bout of exercise is potentially harmful. Because a little is good for you, you must not assume that a lot will be better. In exercise, as in all things, it is a matter of moderation; it is getting the dose right that is important.

Chapter Twenty-seven

THE SMOKESCREEN OF PASSIVE SMOKING

BY JAMES LE FANU

THE MYTH: Passive smoking causes lung cancer.
THE FACT: The claim that passive smoking causes lung cancer is statistically improbable and biologically implausible.

The greatest and indeed culminating triumph in the protracted battle against the evils of tobacco in the UK is undoubtedly the government's commitment, on 21 November 2004, to ban smoking in offices, restaurants and most public houses. It is difficult to overestimate the significance of this victory, for until very recently it seemed absurdly utopian to propose that this curtailing of the personal habits of 10 million people might be legally enforceable. Ban people from smoking in pubs? You must be joking!

But now the deed is done and in retrospect the ban, like other public-health triumphs such as the drink-driving law and the compulsory wearing of seatbelts, now seems mere commonsense. Astonishingly, even those who would be expected to oppose the measure as a 'step too far' in curtailing the freedom of the individual seem reconciled – as the erstwhile shadow arts minister Boris Johnson observed in an article in the *Daily Telegraph*:

> 'And I tell you this, gentlemen,' I said and one hundred golfers in black tie boggled drunkenly and hung upon my words, 'you know what this Labour government wants to ban?' I yipped.
>
> 'What?' they chorused, red-faced with anticipatory wrath.
>
> 'They want to stop you – smoking!' I said. 'No more smoking in the workplace, or pubs, or restaurants; no more pint 'n' Castella at the nineteenth hole, and so far as the putting green is a public place, you will probably be forbidden even from having a crafty fag as you steady your nerves!'
>
> 'Outrageous,' they said, and for a while the surf of indignation thundered around me, until a man just to my right piped up in level tones: 'Well, you know, I am all in favour of a ban, actually.'
>
> 'What?' I said, amazed, but before I could get to the bottom of his dissent, two or three others around the room were putting their hands up and demanding a ban on any kind of smoking in public ... the honest truth, they said, was that they used to be smokers themselves, and it was a filthy habit, and they thought the new law would help them to resist any temptation to take it up again.

There can be little doubt that the argument that 'won it' for the ban on smoking in public places was the claim that passive smoking, also known as *environmental tobacco smoke* (ETS), is not merely offensive to others but injurious to health, in the way that active smoking is for the individual, by causing lung cancer and heart disease in innocent bystanders. Following the government's ban on smoking in public places, the merits or otherwise of the relevant scientific evidence are probably now of merely historical interest.

Thus, the sole justification for subjecting it to critical scrutiny would be for it to reveal matters of more general interest – such as the methods by which 'science' is moulded or manipulated to achieve what is presumed to be a legitimate political goal. And here the evidence on passive smoking is a particularly good illustrative example – for, as a public-health specialist confided to the late Professor Alvin Feinstein of Yale University, 'It is rotten science – in a worthy cause. It will help us get rid of cigarettes and become a smoke-free society, and that is all that really matters.'

The US Environmental Protection Agency first began to draw up plans to ban smoking in public in 1988, the preliminary move in its long-term goal to abolish smoking entirely. This required it, however, to move beyond the obvious and self-evident observation that smoking is an antisocial habit, offensive to nonsmokers, to prove that passive smoking was positively harmful to those exposed to it. It was unlikely to be easy to show this, as the scale of exposure of nonsmokers to tobacco is minuscule – estimated at around the equivalent of actively smoking six cigarettes per year. Nonetheless, researchers believed it might be possible to show passive smoking to be a factor in some cases at least of heart disease and lung cancer by the ingenious method of comparing the rates of these diseases in the nonsmoking wives of smoking husbands with those where neither partner smoked. Their findings, as might be expected, were equivocal, with some studies showing a small positive effect, while others, perversely, showed that being married to a smoking husband might even protect against lung cancer. Or even that passive smoking was more dangerous than active smoking – as the nonsmoking wives of heavy smokers seemed to have a higher rate of lung cancer than smoking wives (see Figure 7).

Further, and very interestingly indeed, the types of lung cancer supposedly caused by passive smoking were quite different from those caused by active smoking. This merits a brief elaboration. There are two broad categories of lung cancer, the commoner one being *squamous* and *oat-cell* cancers, which arise from the cells lining the airways (that area obviously maximally exposed to the potential carcinogens in tobacco smoke). The second category of cancer includes what are known as *adenocarcinomas*, and they arise from glandular tissue in the air sacs in the periphery of the lung.

In the early 1950s, when the late Sir Austin Bradford Hill and Sir Richard Doll first produced the devastating evidence implicating smoking in lung cancer, they made the interesting observation that these tobacco-induced cancers were exclusively of the former type – squamous and oat-cell cancers with a powerful dose–response relationship, where the more smoked the greater the risks (see Figure 7). By contrast they found 'no association' between smoking and the adenocarcinomas, and indeed the lung cancers that do occasionally occur in nonsmokers are almost always of this type. This would suggest that whatever their cause might be, it has nothing to do with smoking.

FIGURE 7

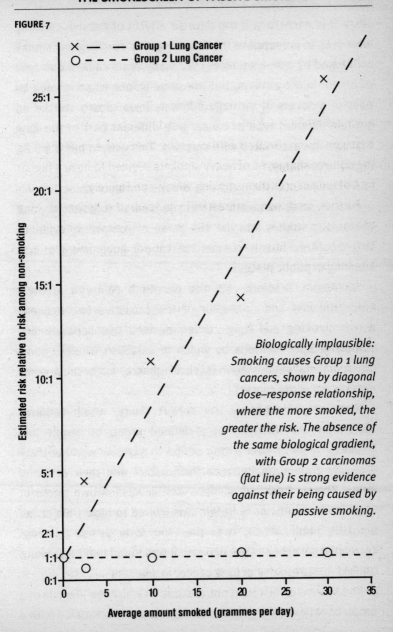

Biologically implausible:
Smoking causes Group 1 lung
cancers, shown by diagonal
dose–response relationship,
where the more smoked, the
greater the risk. The absence of
the same biological gradient,
with Group 2 carcinomas
(flat line) is strong evidence
against their being caused by
passive smoking.

Thus, it is necessary, if the adverse effects of passive smoking were real, to presuppose the following: that carcinogenic smoke as inhaled by active smokers over many years caused one type of cancer in the airways, but the same smoke when inhaled by passive smokers at virtually infinitely lower doses caused an entirely different type of cancer in a different part of the lung that was not associated with smoking. This was, to put it mildly, highly improbable.

So by what statistical alchemy did the protagonists of the evils of passive smoking transform this sow's ear of contradictory and anomalous studies into the silk purse of compelling evidence that would eventually compel the Labour government to ban smoking in public places?

Sir Austin Bradford Hill, the twentieth century's greatest epidemiologist and unraveller of the causative link between active smoking and lung cancer, devised two separate and complementary methods by which to establish whether some environmental phenomenon (such as tobacco) might cause some disease (say lung cancer).

The first of these is the cohort study, which requires monitoring the lifestyles of a defined group of people and following them up over a long period to examine whether there was any correlation between their habits and their cause of death. The most famous of these was Sir Austin's own 'doctors', in which every doctor in Britain was invited to report his or her smoking habit. When, over the next forty years, this was correlated with their cause of death it was found that there was a 25-fold increased risk of lung cancer in smokers.

The second is the case-control study, in which the lifestyle of a group of patients with the disease of interest is compared with a control group and any obvious difference could then be inferred as a putative cause of that disease. Here again, Sir Austin was able to demonstrate a close dose–response relationship, where the more smoked, the greater the subsequent risk of lung cancer.

Self-evidently, the fact that both cohort and case-control types of study came to the same conclusion is clearly very significant, for, where the same question is examined in different ways to produce the same result, this is the most powerful of evidence in favour of the proposition – as here – that active smoking causes lung cancer.

It is thus of interest to know the outcome of these two different methods in investigating the putative link between passive smoking and lung cancer. In 1997 Nicholas Wald, professor of epidemiology at St Bartholomew's Hospital, published a massive synthesis of all the 'accumulated evidence', 37 case-control and cohort studies, and found an impressive 26 per cent increased risk of lung cancer in nonsmokers living with smokers (see Table 3). His personal view that this was 'compelling' evidence was echoed by others, such as Dr David Burns of the University of California, who claimed in the *Journal of the National Cancer Institute* that 'the causal relationship between Environmental Tobacco Smoke and lung cancer is now firmly established'. So how had the sow's ear been transformed into the silk purse?

Few people (other than those with a special interest in the matter) would be bothered to scrutinise Professor Wald's table in any detail – but were they to do so some interesting observations would emerge. Thus starting with the 34 case-controlled studies we note how many of them come from countries such as Japan and China, where the epidemiology of lung cancer is different

Study	Year, country	Women Lung cancer cases	Controls	Relative risk (95% confidence interval)	Men Lung cancer cases	Controls	Relative risk (95% confidence interval)
Case-control studies							
Chan et al	1982, Hong Kong	84	139	0.75 (0.43 to 1.30)			
Correa et a	1983, USA	22	133	2.07 (0.81 to 5.25)	8	180	1.97 (0.38 to 0.32)
Trichopolous et al	1983, Greece	62	190	2.13 (1.19 to 3.83)			
Buffler et al	1984, USA	41	196	0.80 (0.34 to 1.90)	11	90	0.51 (0.14 to 1.79)
Kabat et al	1984, USA	24	25	0.79 (0.25 to 2.45)	12	12	1.00 (0.10 to 5.07)
Lam	1985, Hong Kong	60	144	2.01 (1.09 to 3.72)			
Garfinkel et al	1985, USA	134	402	1.23 (0.81 to 1.87)			
Wu et al	1985, USA	29	62	1.20 (0.50 to 3.30)			
Akiba et al	1986, Japan	94	270	1.52 (0.87 to 2.63)	19	110	2.10 (0.51 to 8.61)
Lee et al	1986, UK	32	66	1.03 (0.41 to 2.55)	15	30	1.31 (0.38 to 4.52)
Koo et al	1987, Hong Kong	86	136	1.55 (0.90 to 2.67)			
Pershagen et al	1987, Sweden	70	294	1.03 (0.61 to 1.74)			
Humble et al	1987, USA	20	162	2.34 (0.81 to 6.75)			
Lam et al	1987, Hong Kong	199	335	1.65 (1.16 to 2.35)			
Gao et al	1987, China	246	375	1.19 (0.82 to 1.73)			
Brownson et al	1987, USA	19	47	1.52 (0.39 to 5.96)			
Geng et al	1988, China	54	93	2.16 (1.08 to 4.29)			
Shimizu et al	1988, Japan	90	163	1.08 (0.64 to 1.82)			
Inoue et al	1988, Japan	22	47	2.55 (0.74 to 8.78)			
Kalandidi et al	1990, Greece	90	116	1.62 (0.90 to 2.91)			
Sobue	1990, Japan	144	731	1.06 (0.74 to 1.52)			
Wu-Williams et al	1990, China	417	602	0.79 (0.62 to 1.02)			
Liu et al	1991, China	54	202	0.74 (0.32 to 1.69)			
Jockel	1991, Germany	23	45	2.27 (0.75 to 6.82)	9	70	2.68 (0.58 to 12.36)
Brownson et al	1992, USA	431	1166	0.97 (0.78 to 1.21)			
Stockwell et al	1992, USA	210	301	1.60 (0.80 to 3.00)			
Du et al	1993, China	75	128	1.19 (0.66 to 2.13)			
Liu et al	1993, China	38	69	1.66 (0.73 to 3.78)			
Fontham et al	1994, USA	651	1253	1.26 (1.04 to 1.54)			
Kabat et al	1995, USA	67	173	1.10 (0.62 to 1.96)	39	98	1.63 (0.69 to 3.85)
Zaridze et al	1995, Russia	162	285	1.66 (1.12 to 2.45)			
Sun et al	1996, China	230	230	1.16 (0.80 to 1.69)			
Wang et al	1996, China	135	135	1.11 (0.67 to 1.84)			
Cohort studies							
Garfinkel	1981, USA	153	176586	1.18 (0.90 to 1.54)			
Hirayama	1984, Japan	200	91340	1.45 (1.02 to 2.08)	64	20225	2.25 (1.06 to 4.76)
Butler	1988, USA	8	9199	2.02 (0.48 to 8.56)			
Cardenas et al	1997, USA	150	192084	1.20 (0.80 to 1.60)	97	96445	1.00 (0.60 to 1.80)
All studies (37 studies of women, 9 studies of men)*							
	1981-97	4626	477924	1.24 (1.13 to 1.36) (P<0.001)	274	117260	1.34 (0.97 to 1.84) (P=0.07)

Statistically implausible: The summary of the 37 studies investigating passive smoking and lung cancer looks very impressive but fails to show the contradictory findings of the Case-Control Studies and the crucial negative findings of the American Cancer Society's massive Cohort Study.

from the West with a particularly high incidence of non-smoking-related adenocarcinoma.

Moving over to the heading 'Relative risk' and scanning downwards, we find the contradictory results already alluded to: some (where the risk is less than one) demonstrate a protective effect for passive smoking; most hover around the non-effects level of one, while a minority show a twofold or more increased risk.

We find a similar pattern when examining the four cohort studies – but look closely at the last and most recent, a massive project conducted by the American Cancer Society with nearly a quarter of a million men and women, where the results hover between the minuscule (1.20) to no effect (1.0) in men and women respectively.

This final cohort study is clearly much the most significant of all in Wald's table, but its very important negative findings have, as it were, been buried by the simple expedient of combining them with the case-control studies, some of whose 'highly significant results' are sufficient to produce the 'overall' effect of an increased risk of 25 per cent.

So how valid is the combined or meta-analysis of those case-control studies? The following year the World Health Organisation concluded the largest such case-control study ever mounted. Its full results, which were never published, found 'there was no association between lung cancer risk and exposure to environmental tobacco smoke'.

Thus the question whether passive smoking causes lung cancer depends on what sort of evidence is the more convincing: the 'positive' results of a Professor Wald's meta-analysis, where the unwarranted inclusion of many small studies from the Far East concealed the outcome of the American Cancer Society's cohort study; or the 'negative' results of two massive studies of different design (the American Cancer Society's cohort study and the WHO case-control study) – the former buried, the second 'repressed'. Clearly commonsense, logic and reasonable judgement would favour the latter, but as we now know it was the former that carried the day. Professor Wald's meta-analysis became the much-sought-after 'proof' that passive smoking was harmful to innocent bystanders, thus providing the scientific rationale for the subsequent criminalisation of smoking in offices, restaurants and most pubs. But the creative statistics involved were all in a good cause – so it doesn't really matter, or does it?

Chapter Twenty-eight
THE AIR WE BREATHE

BY JOHN HENRY

THE MYTH: Pollutants in the air are seriously harmful to health.
THE FACT: The air is cleaner and healthier than it has been for at least 100 years.

Are we being poisoned by the air we breathe? This is a frightening thought – the purity of the air we breathe is one of the aspects of our lives over which, as individuals, we have least control. Because of this, air pollution has been a major concern for many years. However, I hope this chapter will help you to conclude that the overall news is good. Let us start by looking back in time, in order to see if we can find a starting point. History books tell us about the pollution in our cities for millennia. Even ancient Rome used to have an air-pollution problem.

Fifty years ago in Britain, most of the public buildings in our cities used to be black, covered with sooty deposits from atmospheric pollution. However, once the air quality was improved, the buildings were cleaned up. Now, on any sunny day, it can be clearly seen that the glistening white stone remains clean. Older people will still remember, though many younger people may not have heard about, the atmospheric pollution and 'smog' – a combination of smoke and fog – that used to be a frequent occurrence in many cities in Britain. As a boy in southeast London, I well remember the 1950s when the tragic smog outbreaks occurred. I recall my father, a general practitioner, coming home with black soot around his nostrils and giving our family the list of people we knew in the neighbourhood who had died that day. It was incidents like these that led to the improvements in air quality that we now benefit from. Many potential pollutants have been reduced or eliminated. Lead from petrol, asbestos particles, industrial, vehicle and domestic emissions have all been reduced due to the introduction of smokeless fuels and processes that reduce or prevent the escape of particles into the atmosphere. All of this provides us with evidence that air quality has changed markedly for the better in the developed countries over the last half-century or so.

So are we being poisoned by the air we breathe, or are we being scared by the way that stories are being presented? In past years, the press presented us with facts. Today the facts are also presented, but they now have to be stark and unusual enough to produce the sort of headlines that sell a newspaper. For example, we often see news articles about the risks of passive smoking (see Chapter Twenty-seven, 'The Smokescreen of Passive Smoking'), which upsets and concerns many people. But there are very few newspaper articles or television programmes about the dangers of cigarette smoking itself, which is a very much greater hazard. And the strange result is that some people are more concerned about passive smoking than about smoking itself!

Particles in the air are known to be a major cause of long-term respiratory illness. Miners used to suffer from pneumoconiosis due to breathing the particles of coal dust in mines. Overall, fewer than 10 per cent of particles in the air are manmade, so that the vast majority do not come from combustion or from machinery, but the proportion of manmade particles tends to be higher in cities. In recent years, there has been much talk about manmade particles in the atmosphere being linked to death from a number of medical conditions. And it is clear that this is a real effect – it is possible to track all the hospital admissions and deaths occurring in a locality and to compare them with the data about the mass concentrations of PM10 or PM2.5 (milligrams of particulate matter less than 10 micrometres or 2.5 micrometres aerodynamic diameter per cubic metre) in the air day by day. There are more hospital admissions and deaths on the days when there is more PM in the air. But the increase in deaths is small, and they tend to occur in people who are already ill.

The overall effect is that people may be admitted to hospital when PM levels are high, and some may die a few days earlier or later than they would have otherwise done, depending on the amount of PM in the air. At least this was believed until very recently. The latest statistical methods show that the lag between a change in particle levels and increased daily deaths may extend from a day to more than a month. However, it is unlikely that healthy people are much affected by daily fluctuations in levels of air pollution. But long-term exposure to fine particles (PM2.5) is thought to be associated with the risk of dying from cardiovascular disease.

The evidence shows that, after personal factors such as smoking, occupation and diet have been allowed for, there remains an association between long-term levels of these tiny particles and the risk of dying from cardiovascular disease. This was clearly demonstrated some years ago: a distinct drop in the death rate from cardiovascular disease followed banning of all coal sales in Dublin. Clearly, there is a need to reduce further the numbers of particles in the atmosphere, but any effect of reducing peak levels will not be dramatic.

Despite intensive research, there is very little evidence on whether any one type of particle is at fault – it appears that the size of particle is the most important factor. Current thinking suggests that the smallest particles in the air may play an important role. These particles (nanoparticles) occur in large numbers but contribute but little to mass concentrations expressed as PM10 or PM2.5. It has been suggested that these tiny particles set up an inflammatory response in the lung, which, by a complex chain of consequences, causes atherosclerotic lesions in the coronary arteries to become unstable. Evidence in support of this theory is accumulating, and we are likely to hear more about the illnesses caused by nanoparticles in the air.

Another topic that often finds its way into the news is the numbers of people who suffer from, and who die from, asthma. Asthma is increasing in frequency, especially among young people. Asthma-related deaths are on the increase. This is a fact, but it is unlikely to be due to pollution in the air – if anything, it is the reverse! Asthma is now believed to have become more common because people live in much *cleaner* environments, so that they are not exposed to allergens such as house-dust mites when they are very small children. This means that the body does not come to consider these foreign proteins as part of the 'normal' environment, and when children eventually do come into contact with them, at a later stage, the body reacts by developing an allergy to them. So the most developed theory to explain the increase in asthma is that small children are not exposed to pollutants at the point in their development when their body would treat them as normal components of their environment!

However, combustion from domestic fires and motor vehicles produces oxides of nitrogen and other chemical substances that can worsen asthma. There is therefore a clear link between atmospheric pollution by the products of combustion and the severity of asthma, so that asthma can be made worse when there is a lot of combustion taking place, and when the wind and weather conditions are unfavourable.

A question that is frequently asked about asthma is its relationship to thunderstorms. What environmental factor is involved here? There is an increase in severe asthma after thunderstorms. This is because, under normal conditions, pollen particles are not able to reach the small airways and their effect is limited. But, in the very humid air after a thunderstorm, pollen particles break open, releasing the protein particles within. These particles are breathed in and pass much further down the air passages, triggering asthma.

So the conclusion is that there are many factors in the air that are linked with illness, but atmospheric pollution is decreasing due to the concerted efforts of many governments, universities and industrial concerns, and the air is safer to breathe than it has been for many years. This does not mean that we should be complacent, but it is encouraging.

Chapter Twenty-nine
THE MMR STORY
BY MICHAEL FITZPATRICK

THE MYTH: The MMR vaccine causes autism in children.
THE FACT: There is no evidence to suggest that this is the case.

OK, I thought I would be able to write something calm and balanced, drawing on both sides of the arguments for and against childhood vaccinations. But I'm so furious at being LIED to time after time by the government that nothing very calm comes to mind.

Just tell us the truth. Let us make our well-informed minds up. Until then, anyone coming near my children with a new improved vaccination can take a running jump.

– CARMEN REID, 'BE TRUTHFUL ABOUT VACCINES OR KEEP AWAY FROM MY CHILDREN', *SCOTLAND ON SUNDAY*, 15 AUGUST 2004.

T hese are the first and last paragraphs from a diatribe provoked by the announcement by the UK Department of Health in August 2004 of a new 'five-in-one' immunisation for babies against diphtheria, tetanus, pertussis (whooping cough), polio and *Haemophilus influenzae* Type B. The new combination jab includes safer and more effective vaccines against whooping cough and polio, as well as providing additional protection against meningitis. Furthermore, it does not contain the mercury-based preservative thiomersal (known as thimerosal in the US), which has been blamed by some campaigners for developmental disorders in children.

Altogether, one might think, a cause for celebration. Clearly not for Carmen Reid, nor indeed for a growing body of middle-class vaccine refusers. She is almost apoplectic with rage over the introduction of a superior vaccine offering babies wider protection with lower risks of adverse reactions. Why? As with a child having a tantrum, it is not easy to establish exactly what has made her so angry. The ostensible focus of her fury is an implied conspiracy among the government, the drug companies and the doctors to produce propaganda and misinformation, to conceal the grievous dangers that may result from these vaccines. So let's look first at concerns about their possible adverse effects, particularly the alleged link with autism that has provoked much parental anxiety.

The MMR debacle

In the notorious February 1998 *Lancet* paper that launched the MMR (measles, mumps and rubella) scare, Dr Andrew Wakefield and colleagues wrote that 'we did not prove a link between MMR vaccine and this syndrome' ('autistic enterocolitis'). Nor have they proved it in the seven years since. In February 2004, following revelations that Dr Wakefield had failed to declare a conflict of interest arising from his acceptance of £10,000 in legal aid funding from the anti-MMR litigation, ten of his co-authors issued a 'partial retraction' of the paper. This withdrew claims of a link between MMR and autism, but insisted that the identification of a distinctive form of inflammatory bowel disease in children with autism remained valid.

For many critics, the evident bias in the selection of the dozen cases for the *Lancet* study meant that it was also impossible to have any confidence in the concept of 'autistic enterocolitis'. Many of the parents were referred to Wakefield's clinic at the Royal Free Hospital in north London following their earlier exposure to the anti-MMR campaign and to Wakefield's theories of a link with measles. The four links in the proposed chain of causality connecting MMR to autism are speculative – none has been substantiated. I will deal with each in turn.

1. MMR immunisation leads to chronic measles infection (and immune dysfunction).

Though it is well known that MMR may cause minor adverse reactions, it has never been shown to cause measles. Nor has the combination of live (attenuated) viruses in MMR been shown to suppress or otherwise damage the infant immune system.

2. Measles causes 'autistic enterocolitis'.

Apart from the discredited 1998 Lancet *paper and other publications by the same authors, no properly validated research has confirmed the existence of this condition. Claims that studies by Dublin virologist John O'Leary have confirmed an MMR–autism link, mediated by measles-related bowel inflammation, have been repudiated by Professor O'Leary himself.*

3. Leaky bowel allows toxic opioid peptides to enter the bloodstream.

This is obvious nonsense since opioid peptides are produced naturally in the body during acupuncture, exposure to sunlight and sexual activity.

4. 'Opioid excess' in the brain causes autism.

This is based on the fact that autistic children behave like laboratory animals on opiates. There is no evidence to support this theory.

The Medical Research Council considered this proposed causal sequence 'biologically implausible'. Because the MMR vaccine is given after twelve months and the features of autism often become apparent at around eighteen months, it is not surprising that, in cases where behavioural regression appeared soon after vaccination, some parents have blamed the vaccine. However, exhaustive epidemiological researches, conducted with different methods in different countries, have failed to confirm any causal relationship.

In response to the failure of virological and epidemiological research to confirm the MMR–autism hypothesis, its supporters have shifted ground. In the cases reported in the *Lancet* paper, autistic features appeared – on average – within six days of the MMR jab (though an autoimmune process causing bowel inflammation would require several weeks).

One of the most popular claims of the anti-MMR campaign is that MMR is to blame for an 'epidemic of autism'. Since studies have failed to reveal any link between the introduction of MMR and the rise in diagnoses of autism, campaigners now claim that MMR is to blame for only a small subset of autism cases, one too small to measure by epidemiological methods.

As the alleged link between the MMR vaccine and autism has been discredited, anti-immunisation campaigners in Britain have shifted their attention to vaccines containing the mercury-based preservative thiomersal. This has long been the main focus of campaigners in the USA.

Mercury is potentially toxic to the central nervous system and particularly to the developing infant brain, but the total exposure to mercury resulting from the vaccines traditionally administered in the UK over the first six months of life is well below the safety threshold recommended by the World Health Organisation (WHO), which itself incorporates a tenfold safety factor. Babies are likely to receive higher doses of mercury if their mothers consume fish such as shark, marlin and swordfish, which are known to contain relatively high levels of mercury.

Campaigners claim that the symptoms of mercury toxicity are similar to those of autism. On closer inspection, the clinical features of both conditions are quite distinct. Mercury poisoning causes a staggering gait, slurring speech, visual-field disturbances and peripheral neuropathy. In mild cases it produces a nonspecific anxiety and depression; in more severe cases, a toxic psychosis may result. None of these features is characteristic of autism. There have been a number of well-recognised epidemics of mercury poisoning. The most notorious, known as 'pink disease', resulted from the widespread use of proprietary teething powders containing mercury during the first half of the twentieth century. Infants with this condition presented with painful, pink and peeling hands and feet. Though pink disease caused more than a hundred deaths a year in Britain into the 1940s, survivors have never been reported as displaying disorders such as autism.

Vaccines containing mercury have been in use for more than 60 years, during which they have saved countless lives, prevented numerous cases of disability, without causing any more serious problem than an occasional allergic reaction. In February 2003, the UK Committee on Safety of Medicines reviewed two studies, involving more than 100,000 children, and found no association with autism. In February 2004, in response to continuing claims of links between vaccines and autism, the US Institute of Medicine reviewed the evidence and rejected a causal relationship between both mercury-containing vaccines and MMR, and autism. It upheld the current child-immunisation schedule.

The removal of thiomersal-containing vaccines from the child programme has not succeeded in quelling anxieties. While some argued that this merely vindicated earlier claims about the dangers of mercury, others discovered new dangers. According to Carmen Reid's denunciation of the five-in-one vaccine, 'instead of mercury, the new vaccination contains aluminium and formaldehyde, both known neurological toxins, held by some to be responsible for autism'. Aluminium is present in some propriety medicines that are available in chemist shops, it has never caused any toxicity, although exposure to high concentrations of aluminium in the drinking water in Camelford caused some skin irritation.

Combination

A recurrent theme in parental concerns about MMR, one that has been carried over into the response to the new five-in-one jab, is that the combination of vaccines is damaging to the infantile immune system. However, though children receive more vaccines today than in the past, the higher quality of the vaccines means that the number of antigens they receive has declined. For example, the old smallpox vaccine that was used until smallpox was eradicated in the 1970s contained 200 proteins. Now the eleven vaccines routinely administered in the USA contain fewer than 130 proteins (and more than half of these are in the chickenpox vaccine that has recently been introduced in Britain).

According to US vaccine specialist Paul Offit and colleagues, the infant immune system has the theoretical capacity to respond to 'about 10,000 vaccines at any one time'. Putting this point in another way, they reckon that if all eleven vaccines were given at the same time, 'then about 0.1 per cent of the immune system would be "used up" '. They insist that 'young infants have an enormous capacity to respond to multiple vaccines, as well as to the many other challenges present in the environment'. A study in Britain looked specifically at the impact of the MMR combination on the immune system. The authors hypothesised that 'if MMR vaccine does induce clinically significant immunosuppression, susceptibility to infection should be increased in the post-vaccination period'. They found that there was no increased risk of hospitalisation with infections such as pneumonia within three months of vaccination; indeed there was a slight protective effect.

Defaulters and resisters

Following its introduction in the UK in 1988, uptake of MMR rose steadily to reach a peak of 92 per cent in 1995. It began to fall in 1997, before the publication of Dr Wakefield's *Lancet* paper in 1998, after which it fell further. The decline accelerated in the early 2000s, as the anti-MMR campaign gathered momentum. By 2003 uptake had fallen to 80 per cent nationally, and to 70 per cent in London.

Who were the people who were choosing not to give their babies the triple vaccine? Passive defaulters, whose children were not being immunised, were characteristically low-income families experiencing various forms of deprivation and social exclusion. Their failure to have their children immunised was partly attributed to 'parental reluctance' and partly to 'professional apathy', and to the poor provision of primary care and child health services, notably in inner-city areas. Active resisters to immunisation were middle-class, well-educated parents who had chosen not to have their children immunised.

These parents were concerned about the risks of adverse consequences of immunisation, which they felt had been played down in the official information. They often expressed sceptical views towards 'biomedicine' and an openness to alternatives, particularly homeopathy. They were suspicious of the apparent convergence of interests among the medical profession, the government and the vaccine manufacturers. It was the expansion of the numbers of 'active resisters' that reduced uptake of MMR to levels that made outbreaks of measles (and mumps and rubella) a serious possibility, especially in London.

There was a convergence between radical ecological and traditional conservative values in environmentalist and consumerist campaigns. Anti-immunisation sentiment united elements from diverse and often conflicting political traditions.

The rage of suburbia

Carmen Reid's outburst, which was quoted at the beginning of this chapter, cannot be explained solely as a response to changes in the child-immunisation schedule. Her anger can be understood only as an expression of the wider animosities of substantial sections of the middle classes. A closer look at some of the targets of this outrage – the government, the drug companies and science itself – may shed some light on what is bothering the citizens of Middle England. For many commentators, the new protest movements marked a welcome return to mass participation in politics after a period of falling electoral turnouts and a general decline in involvement in political parties.

Another target that has attracted growing middle-class hostility is the corporation. Self-indulgent and backward-looking, the anticapitalists of the 1990s tilted at windmills in the form of McDonald's and Starbucks. Such anticorporate themes are no longer merely the preserve of left-wing weeklies, but can be found across the mass media and in academic publications, not least in medical journals. Like antigovernment feeling, anticorporate sentiment brings together elements from diverse political traditions. It incorporates the suspicion of the small businessman for the big corporation and the prejudice of the Little Englander against global – especially American, even

European – capitalism. A third factor in rising middle-class discontent is a growing scepticism about science, which is often combined with fears about environmental threats to health.

Attitudes towards science and technology are characterised by a high degree of ambivalence. On the one hand, people embrace CAT scans and MRI and other manifestations of technological advance with enthusiasm. On the other hand, visitors to Britain from overseas are bemused by the intensity of public controversy over issues of immunisation. In most other countries, immunisation is widely regarded as an important aspect of public-health policy and is generally uncontroversial – as it was in Britain up to the 1990s. Though in most countries there are small groups that reject immunisation on religious or ideological grounds, they have negligible influence on overall levels of vaccine uptake.

A peculiar combination of factors in Britain in the late 1990s allowed the MMR scare to take off, putting the mass childhood immunisation campaign as a whole in jeopardy. The emergence of a maverick scientist – Dr Andrew Wakefield – was a key factor. Wakefield's success in winning the support of a lawyer pursuing a class action on behalf of a substantial group of parents of autistic children who came to believe strongly in the MMR–autism theory gave the campaign legal-aid funding (up to a total of £15 million) and a strong base of support. Uncritical journalists who promoted Wakefield's theory and his image as champion of families affected by autism (and as a victim of official persecution) provided vital publicity. The feeble and defensive response of the medical establishment, with a few distinguished but beleaguered exceptions, allowed the campaign to gather momentum.

Given the high level of free-floating anxieties and animosities we have identified among the British middle classes, the MMR scare found an immediate resonance. Parents could refuse to have their children immunised or opt for separate vaccines. This assertion of parental rights had the effect of exposing their children to an increased risk of potentially serious infectious diseases. If significant outbreaks of measles occur – which now seems likely, particularly in London – the consequences of this misdirected parental rage could be tragic.

Part Four

MYTH
INTERPRETATION

Chapter Thirty

THE HARM THAT PRESSURE GROUPS CAN CAUSE

BY DICK TAVERNE

When Rachel Carson published *The Silent Spring* in the late 1960s, I fell under her spell. Her picture of a landscape devastated by pesticides, in which birds have vanished from the trees and fish from rivers, where flowers no longer bloom in the fields and people and animals die of mysterious diseases, was both moving and disturbing. She converted tens of thousands of people into passionate environmentalists and could fairly be called the mother of modern environmentalism.

In due course over that decade, I joined Greenpeace and Friends of the Earth and read the works of Barry Commoner and Paul Ehrlich, and *The Limits to Growth* by Donella Meadows and others, which persuaded me at the time not only that the natural world was being damaged almost beyond repair, but that Earth's resources would soon run out unless we abandoned our commitment to economic growth and ever-increasing consumption.

In one sense we are all environmentalists now, in that we regard the beauty of nature around us as one of the blessings of life and accept that we should not deprive our children and grandchildren of the enjoyment it gives us. But I am now a pragmatic environmentalist. I want to be sure that we do not base our actions on false fears and do not apply remedies that are unsupported by evidence and that do more harm than good. Gradually I came to realise that pressure groups that start out with the noblest intentions sometimes allow passion to overrule reason, and sometimes allow ends to corrupt means. They can become casual about evidence and even deliberately mislead. They can become so obsessed with the need for publicity that, in the words of one of the world's best-known climate experts, 'to capture the public's imagination ... we have to offer up scary scenarios, make simplified dramatic statements and make little mention of any doubts we have'. Many passionate environmentalists also fail to balance risk against benefit, with the result that their actions often harm the causes they seek to promote.

Nearly all the forecasts of doom in *Limits to Growth* turned out to be spectacularly wrong. They predicted that we would run out of gold, zinc, mercury and oil before 1992. Paul Ehrlich famously wrote '... the battle to feed humanity is over. In the course of the 1970s hundreds of millions will starve to death.' Had we acted upon these dire prophecies, the consequences would indeed have been disastrous. In Rachel Carson's case, the good she did in alerting us to the dangers of environmental degradation and the need to control the indiscriminate use of insecticides has been outweighed by the harm caused by her apocalyptic visions. Let us look at some examples.

DDT

Great harm was caused by an almost worldwide ban on the use of DDT. Carson had good reason for warning the world about the dangers of this insecticide. Not only was there evidence that DDT caused the thinning of eggshells with consequent damage to bird life, but its long-lasting properties, coupled with its widespread use and its accumulation in the sea, and hence in fish and in the birds and animals that feed on the fish, led to its worldwide dissemination. DDT was even found in the Arctic and Antarctic and can still be detected in the animals that live there some decades after spraying ceased. Today it can still be found in human breast milk, but this is because of the extreme sensitivity of present-day chemical tests that can detect even one molecule in 1,000,000,000,000,000 (one in a million billion).

The evidence of damage to wildlife justified an end to its agricultural use. But Carson also forecast that DDT would be a cause of cancer and hepatitis, and ignored its vital role in controlling the transmission of malaria by killing the mosquitoes that carry the parasite. In fact there is no evidence of any harmful effects of DDT on human health. In World War Two, many people were deliberately exposed to high concentrations of DDT through dusting programmes, or the impregnation of clothes to control lice, without any apparent ill effect. According to the distinguished chemist John Emsley (in *The Consumer's Good Chemical Guide*), 'The chronic toxicity studies on DDT have provided no indication that the insecticide is unsafe for humans.'

On the other side of the balance sheet stands the devastating effect that banning the use of DDT has had in areas afflicted by malaria. The US National Academy of Sciences reported in 1970 that, in little more than two decades, more than 50 million lives were saved by DDT. Similar statements were made by the World Health Organisation in 1999. DDT is the most effective single agent ever developed for saving human life. In Sri Lanka, for example, DDT reduced the number of cases of malaria in 1963 to seventeen; by 1968, after spraying ceased, the number of cases had risen to 2.5 million. Since a virtual ban on the spraying of DDT has become effective in many parts of the world, even on the inside walls of houses where remarkably small concentrations interfere with mosquito behaviour, malaria has come back with a vengeance. Over a million children in Africa alone die from it every year.

Rachel Carson is a warning to us all of the dangers of neglecting the evidence-based approach and the need to weigh risk against benefit.

The campaign for a worldwide ban on DDT continues today, although it aims to phase out its use gradually and is based on a different rationale. The Worldwide Fund for Nature, for example, a generally admirable charity, argues for a ban on the grounds that DDT is a hormone-disrupting chemical and may affect immune, reproductive and nervous systems. No doubt there are grounds for caution. But arguments against retaining DDT for the spraying of the inside walls of houses are mistaken. Such spraying is the cheapest and still the most effective way of preventing malaria. There is no evidence that it presents any risk to humans. Moreover, fears expressed about the effect on hormones fail to separate the effects of DDT from those of other insecticides. Any objective assessment of risks and benefits would come down firmly against a total ban.

Campaigns by Greenpeace

The campaign against the use of DDT is a clear example of harm produced by insufficient concern for evidence, although the motives behind the campaign are laudable. The same cannot be said of some of the campaigns by Greenpeace and its allies. The history of the Brent Spar oil rig is a notorious case of truth and regard for evidence being sacrificed to the concern 'to capture the public's imagination'. In 1995 Shell decided to sink the giant Brent Spar rig in the deep Atlantic. After careful consultation it had concluded that this was the most environmentally friendly method of disposal, among other reasons because the wreck would make an excellent playground for fish. Greenpeace claimed that the rig was full of poisonous residues and that, in any event, sinking a giant rig would pollute the ocean. Day after day brave Greenpeace eco-warriors in their small inflatables were shown on television harassing the giant tugs that towed the rig. Shell petrol stations were boycotted all over Europe, until this apparently all-powerful international oil company was forced to turn back the tugs and agree to dispose of the rig on dry land. It was a triumph for Greenpeace, the environmental David that had humbled the industrial Goliath.

In fact, the losers were not only Shell but the environment. There were no poisonous residues in the rig, and Greenpeace was eventually forced to apologise for its unfounded accusation. Disposal on land was much less environmentally friendly than disposal in the ocean. Indeed, it is hard to see how Greenpeace could have believed its own propaganda, since in 1986 its own ship, the *Rainbow Warrior*, which had been irreparably damaged by French saboteurs, was deliberately sunk off the New Zealand coast by Greenpeace, who then claimed it would make a new reef highly beneficial to marine life.

Other Greenpeace campaigns also damage the environment they claim to protect. Whenever a combined heat and power (CHP) plant is proposed as an efficient means of energy generation, Greenpeace opposes it, because it opposes incinerators. Every incinerator, it claims, increases the amount of dioxins in the air, invariably described as 'the most dangerous chemical known to man'. When Greenpeace wins, industrial and toxic waste is disposed of in landfill sites instead, to which it normally has to be transported over long distances by lorry. Furthermore, the alternative to a CHP plant is invariably a less efficient form of energy generation that releases more greenhouse gases. For both reasons the environment is more, not less, polluted.

As for dioxins, not only do modern incinerators discharge only small amounts into the air, but their demonic properties are hugely exaggerated and largely spurious. As John Emsley has pointed out, only four people, none of them members of the public, have ever been known to have died of dioxin poisoning. The notorious accident at Seveso in 1976, when there was a massive release of dioxins, led to severe cases of skin eruptions, chloracne, a condition that gets better over time, but no deaths. Too often environmentalists ignore the lesson taught by the doctor and chemist Paracelsus in the sixteenth century – that it all depends on the dose. In fact there is evidence that very small doses of dioxins may be beneficial rather than harmful to human health.

GM crops

The issue that has become the crucial battlefield between belief in evidence and belief in dogma is the dispute about genetically modified (GM) crops (see also Chapter Twenty-one, 'Genetically Modified Organisms'). In many ways the campaign against GM technology echoes the campaign against DDT. There is no evidence that GM crops have ever damaged human health, while they have already shown substantial benefits to some of the world's poorest farmers and can potentially make a huge contribution to the reduction of poverty, hunger and disease. More than 5 million small farmers in China, India, South Africa and elsewhere now farm GM cotton. Not only has their income been substantially increased by savings from the reduced use of pesticides, but their health has also benefited. These are actual, proven benefits.

However, the most important feature of genetic modification is its potential. Crops can be genetically modified to grow in arid or saline regions where no crops can grow today; staple crops can be protected against diseases that destroy small farmers' livelihoods; vaccines from plants can offer protection against hepatitis B and childhood diarrhoea, which cause causes millions of deaths. None of these crops are yet in production, but the technology exists and it is very probable that they will be in due course.

There have certainly been plenty of scare stories about GM products. One of the most publicised, which led to fears about 'Frankenstein food', arose from an experiment by Árpád Pusztai a research employee, who claimed that some genetically modified potatoes damaged the immune system of rats. His findings, first broadcast on television (not as a peer-reviewed paper in a scientific journal) were carefully examined by a Royal Society committee and utterly discredited. Generally, there is no reason to regard GM crops as less safe for human consumption than conventional crops, as attested by three other Royal Society reports, one in a combined report from seven international Academies of Sciences, as well as any number of reports by other prestigious committees and notably two reports by the Nuffield Council on Bioethics. Indeed, because they have been extensively tested, GM crops are probably safer than conventional crops. Nor has any evidence emerged that they will create new 'super-weeds' or that they are especially dangerous to biodiversity.

The most notorious misinformation about the damage GM crops cause to the environment concerned the Monarch butterfly. In a laboratory experiment in 1999, heavy sprinkling of pollen from GM corn on milkweed leaves killed the larvae of Monarch butterflies that fed on them. However the experiment was later shown to be deeply flawed. Field tests, as opposed to the laboratory study, showed that the impact on the butterflies of pollen from GM corn was negligible and no different from the effects of conventional corn.

Nevertheless, the literature produced by environmental activists constantly refers to the danger to human health from GM crops 'as proved by Dr Pusztai', the threat that they will give rise to 'super-weeds' by cross-pollination, and the harm they have caused to Monarch butterflies. So effective are campaigns against GM crops by environmental nongovernmental organisations (NGOs) that in 2003 the Zambian government refused food aid from America, some of which had a GM content, because, according to a government spokesman, 'We would rather let our people starve than feed them toxic food'. European hostility to GM food, carefully nurtured by scare stories inspired by green NGOs, now threatens exports with any GM content from China, India and other developing countries. Even China, which leads the world in applying GM technology to crops that are the staple foods of poor countries, is hesitant about granting licences for the commercial cultivation of GM crops because of fears for its exports.

Several well-known aid agencies, widely respected for their dedication to the cause of reducing hunger, poverty and disease, are prominent in the anti-GM campaign. What explains their alliance with green NGOs such as Greenpeace and Friends of the Earth? Partly, it seems, trust in fellow NGOs who are ostensibly devoted, like themselves, to good causes. The motto seems to be, 'If Greenpeace is trying to save the planet, then what it says must be true.' Another explanation of this stance is a shared hostility to multinational companies that have developed GM crops. They suspect them of sinister motives because they believe companies selfishly pursue profits, while they themselves are selflessly dedicated to the service of mankind. Whatever the reasons, lack of respect for evidence and an almost religious belief that GM crops are dangerous leads to paradoxical results.

For example, a document produced by Action Aid, 'Going Against the Grain', ridicules the potential of 'golden rice'. This is rice genetically modified to contain a bacterial gene together with two genes from daffodils that induce it to synthesise a micronutrient, a precursor that is converted into vitamin A in the body. Outside green NGO circles it has been widely hailed as a development of enormous potential for good because it can help to prevent vitamin A deficiency, which is a major cause of blindness and child mortality in developing countries. However, 'Going Against the Grain' quotes a study by Greenpeace, which has not been published in any peer-reviewed journals, that states that a child would have to eat 7 kilograms of rice a day to benefit from it.

In fact the scientists who developed golden rice have demonstrated that this overstates the amount children would have to eat by more than fifteen times. Greenpeace seems unaware that golden rice is designed to act as a *supplement* to vitamin A, and that it is not claimed to supply all the vitamin A children need. But Action Aid and Greenpeace are not, it seems, interested in evidence or balance. None of the weighty studies by the top scientific academies, including those of India, China, Brazil, Mexico and the Third World Academy of Sciences, are quoted in the Action Aid report. Instead it relies almost entirely on papers by green pressure groups or its own branches.

The very anti-GM lobbies that persuaded Zambia to choose starvation rather than food aid from America may well succeed in delaying the introduction of golden rice. As a result, more children will suffer from xerophthalmia (an eye disease) and go blind. Others with vitamin A deficiency will continue to be at risk of contracting infectious diseases such as measles, which will kill many of them. As a study by the Nuffield Council on Bioethics, a mixed committee of scientific experts and lay representatives, observed, we have a moral duty to make the potential benefits of GM technology available to the developing world. But a kind of moral blindness infects NGOs when passion overcomes reason.

Good intentions and good science

The examples I have cited show that good intentions are no guarantee of public benefit. Indeed, it is a common error to assume that what matters is motive, not results. We are told by campaigners that anyone with any association with the corporate world cannot contribute to impartial debate or the welfare of mankind, because association with the profit motive corrupts integrity. Given that, regrettably, public investment in scientific research has declined and that most scientific and technological innovation depends on corporate funds, it follows from this that we should be suspicious of nearly all modern technology and science.

In fact, though scientists have values, science does not. Science itself is objective and in evaluating the importance of scientific findings the motives of the researcher are in the end irrelevant. What matters is the quality of the findings. Are they reproducible? Do they stand up to criticism? Researchers working for a company, even if they are mainly motivated to increase its profits (and most scientists in industry are also concerned to benefit mankind), can produce good science – as can researchers working for Greenpeace, for instance, even if they are chiefly concerned to gain publicity (and no doubt most are mainly motivated to preserve our environment). The most public-spirited, completely independent scientists can produce bad science. In the end the progress of science depends on evidence.

Many NGOs promote many excellent causes, such as campaigns to prevent deforestation and save the whale, when there is no distortion. But, because too many of them do not regard respect for evidence as the golden rule, their actions often severely damage the causes they profess to serve.

Chapter Thirty-one
THE MISUSE OF NUMBERS
BY STANLEY FELDMAN AND VINCENT MARKS

'There are three kinds of lies: lies, damned lies,
and statistics.'
MARK TWAIN

'**T**HIRTY THOUSAND PEOPLE DIE EACH YEAR FROM EATING TOO MUCH FAT',
splashed the headline in a recent newspaper article – but
what would happen if they did stop eating fat? Would they live for
ever or would they succumb to something else within the same
time frame? The answer is of course that they would die of
'something else', possibly even sooner than if they kept on eating
fat. How did anyone come up with this number anyway? Has
anyone – let alone 30,000 – ever had his or her cause of death
certified as due to eating too much fat? The answer is of course
no. The truth is that this figure, like so many, is pure speculation.

The media should carry a health warning: 'Statistics can
damage your life.' Pressure groups, spin doctors and even
Members of Parliament use figures in such a loose way that
numbers, which have an exact meaning, become vague,

imprecise or deliberately misleading. Take for example the headline 'Up to 60 per cent of the population do not understand the proposed EU Constitution'. The statement conveys the impression that the EU Constitution baffles most people. This may be right but it could also mean that as few as 5 per cent or as many as 60 per cent are confused by it. When this careless use of numbers is applied to medical and social problems the result can cause unnecessary alarm, silly therapeutic interventions or large expenditure on an insignificant problem. Let us examine some examples of the misleading use of numbers.

'Up to'

The animal-welfare pressure group, WWF-UK, suggested in June 2004 that global warming would wipe out 'up to one million species of wildlife by 2050'. This conclusion is based on a 'worst-case scenario' occurring at every turn. It can be arrived at only by taking the highest figure for global warming, which is ten times the more realistic ones, an inability of any species to adapt, and the loss of a favourable habit for all species occurring at the same time. Reason tells us that what is bad for one species is likely to be good for another. The only purpose is to produce an absurd figure to frighten the unwary.

The author of the original report, himself an environmental campaigner, complained that the press release was 'a woeful misrepresentation of science' by the pressure group. He had actually suggested in his report that, as few as 5 per cent or as many as 78 per cent of this number of species could be at risk.

Baseline bias

Baseline bias is another way of bamboozling the public and is commonly used by the financial-service industry to convey a misleading impression. Let us say the cost of a barrel of oil has increased from $10 to $70 since 1945. If you want to sell a gas-guzzling aeroplane you might start your survey in 1973, at the time of the Suez crisis, and close it just before the mid-2000s surge in oil prices. You could then draw a graph showing that in the 30-year period covered the price of oil increased by less than inflation.

Baseline bias is a favourite trick of environmental pressure groups. By taking a starting point some 250 years ago you can demonstrate a highly worrying increase in average world temperature. It becomes much less alarming if you start 50 or 100 years ago and minimal if you start in Roman times, when there were vineyards as far north as York. The reason is that 250 years ago saw some of the coldest winters of the millennium. It was the 'little ice age' when the Thames froze over.

Let us say the summer two years ago was particularly warm – and that it was much warmer than last year. What if this year again turns out to be even colder than last? Does this mean that we will have to abandon the 'global warming' scenario – as we did the forecasts of an impending ice age made just 30 or 40 years ago, based on a run of unusually cold years between 1940 and 1970? How long do we wait until we decide the planet is merely emerging, somewhat erratically, from the last ice age and not really getting much warmer?

The secret lies in the starting point or *baseline*. In something as slow to change as global temperature it has to be measured in thousands, not just hundreds, of years if it is to show an incontrovertible trend. The great debate about CO_2 and global warming is a distraction from the real problem of our reliance on fossil fuels and what will happen when we have used them all up.

The one species that won't survive unless alternative supplies of energy are used is mankind – the others seem to get on very well without them.

The decline in atmospheric pollution in London over the past five years, say, is not very impressive, but if one goes back 50 years it's dramatic. The reason for this is that we have succeeded in reducing the major pollutants to such a low level that the rate of improvement has inevitably tailed off, as it always does. Improvements always follow the law of diminishing returns, which says that, as you near perfection, the benefit you obtain from an increased effort becomes less and less. Perfection is never attainable, however nice it might be to think that it is.

Extrapolation

Unless you are aware that figures quoted in an article are an extrapolation beyond the data available you can be fooled into believing that a catastrophe is just around the corner when there is no such thing.

Remember when the number of patients with new-variant Creutzfeldt–Jakob disease was going to reach 100,000 or so within a few years of its discovery? In fact the total number of patients dying from all types of Creutzfeldt–Jakob disease has more or less reached a plateau and is very few more than before the BSE crisis began. (See also Chapter Twenty-two, 'Transmissible Spongiform Encephalopathies – BSE and vCJD'.) A recent revival of the scare predicted that 10,000 UK citizens might die from BSE. It appears to have been based on extrapolating from a sample of about 2,000 tonsils that were examined for the BSE prion. The study revealed one positive and two suspicious tonsils, which, if true for the whole of population of the UK, provides the figure of 10,000 potentially infected people. Extrapolation is always chancy, but when it's based on such a small number of cases it is not only meaningless, but potentially dangerous.

A newspaper article said that 40,000 patients could be dying each year from the side effects of drugs in hospitals (*The Times*, August 2004). The figure was derived by extrapolating from a single hospital study of 28 deaths in patients in whom a side effect of a drug, however unimportant, was recorded at some time during their treatment and who eventually died in the hospital. Included in the deaths were patients who would have died of the disease for which the drugs were being prescribed. No allowance was made for the proportion of the particular hospital's population that was made up of those who were especially vulnerable, such as the very old and sick.

One can see the danger of extrapolation from the results of one small study to the whole country. Patients do undoubtedly die from the side effects of drugs. These are, however, carefully monitored and responsibly reported and do not yield the scary figures quoted in *The Times*.

A 2005 report claimed that cot deaths could be prevented by giving babies dummies to suck in their cots. When one considers how a trial to test this hypothesis might be carried out, one becomes aware of its improbability. About one in 800–1000 babies suffers a cot death. To obtain a statistically valid difference between those babies with dummies and those without would require a study of at least 100,000 babies in each group. Even then, if two babies in the 'with-dummies' group suffered a cot death or fewer than six in the 'without-dummies' group died, the numbers would be likely to be insufficient. Nevertheless, the report was featured in BBC and ITV news programmes and no doubt caused a lot of mothers to rush out and buy dummies.

In recent times, in order to meet this criticism, it has become common to find several separate small studies joined and presented as a large-scale investigation. This is termed *meta-analysis* (which is discussed in Chapter Thirty-two, 'Epidemiology'). Unless all these studies have been conducted on similar populations using the same methods, their results are seldom more reliable than that of the weakest study among them.

The advent of computers with their ability to perform, in a few minutes, complex mathematical calculations that would previously have taken hours, days or even years has encouraged a form of mathematical extrapolation called *modelling*. In biological science, where there are no absolute certainties, modelling can magnify any lack of precision in the subject modelled and amplify the effect of any mistaken assumptions. It is responsible for many of the exaggerated predictions about trends that that are likely to occur in the future, sometimes on the flimsiest of data. It has been described as a pop-art form, since it takes an actual situation and tries to reproduce it artificially on a much larger scale.

Comparing like with like

An environmental pressure group recently claimed that atmospheric pollution in London kills the equivalent number of people each year as would die if two jumbo jets crashed. This scare story originated in a report from the Department of Health, which found that in the very hot summer of 2003 there were 800 more deaths than were expected. It suggested that these deaths were due to ozone pollution. However, the people who would die in an aeroplane crash are, by and large, young and active and would have expected another 20–40 years of life, while the ones who died during the heat wave were elderly, terminally sick patients with breathing problems who had a life expectancy measured in months.

In comparing the numbers who died, in these two situations, the environmentalists were deliberately comparing the wrong things: they should not have been comparing the numbers of deaths but the loss of *years of expected life*. They were comparing apples with oranges. Of course there are other possible causes of death during a heat wave. Most of the deaths that occurred in the elderly in Paris during the hot summer of 2003, where the death toll was much higher than in London, were found to have been due to dehydration.

Significance of 'significance'

Significant means different things to statisticians and laymen. To the layman something significant is usually big and always important. To the statistician and scientist it means only that the difference between two observations is likely to be real rather than one that is due to chance or an error of measurement. Most science involves making measurements, but measurements are never quite as precise or exact as we would like them to be. Two numbers may differ from each other either because of the difficulty of making the measurement or because there is a real difference between them.

It may be comparatively simple to measure the length of a piece of string and compare it with the length of another piece of string, but how do you measure the rainfall in one year and compare it with another or know whether a new drug is better for treating an illness than the one that was formerly available? There was no problem with what used to be called diabetes but is now always referred to Type 1 diabetes (to distinguish it from the much more common Type 2 diabetes, with which it has less in common than their names suggest). Type 1 affects mainly children and before the discovery of insulin in 1921 invariably led to death in coma within a few months or years of onset. An improvement in wellbeing occurred in every patient, sometimes within hours, when they were treated with insulin. The improvement lasted as long as the insulin injections were given and stopped when the insulin was withheld. This left no room for doubt that insulin worked. No one in his right mind would have suggested a randomised, placebo-controlled trial, even if such a trial had been invented by then

The situation is very rarely so clear-cut. Take multiple sclerosis, for example. This slowly progressive illness can last 40 years or more and be punctuated by remarkable spontaneous remissions during which the patient may return, without any outside intervention, to a state indistinguishable from 'normal'. How, in these circumstances, can you be sure that your new treatment is better than a placebo? In order to find out, it is necessary to conduct a randomised, controlled clinical trial in which the benefits of the new treatment are compared with those produced by a placebo, or with the best available treatment, given under exactly the same conditions. But what will you use to judge the success of the drug? Clearly, you cannot rely on just how the patient feels – improvement might be due to either a spontaneous remission or a placebo effect.

Suppose that a remission occurred within one month of starting treatment in 60 out of the 100 patients given the new drug but only 55 of those given the alternative treatment. How can you be sure that the additional benefit was due to the drug and did not reflect a chance occurrence or an unintentional difference between the patients in each group? With appropriate mathematical formulae, the probability that the difference is pure chance can be calculated: if it is less than 1 in 20 the difference is said, by convention, to be 'significant'; if the probability was less than 1 in 100 it would be very described as 'very significant' – and so on, the terminology getting stronger as the probability of the difference being due to chance becomes smaller.

All that the word *significance* means is that the drug did have an effect, though obviously not a very profound one, and certainly not on everyone. It might also happen that after a year the group receiving the supposedly active treatment was no better off than the one receiving the placebo. It may in fact be worse off. Yet such a treatment would undoubtedly be described in the newspapers as a major breakthrough.

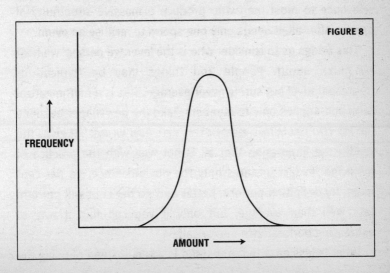

FIGURE 8

FREQUENCY

AMOUNT ⟶

What happens when we want to define 'normal'? To most of us normal means typical and healthy. To the statistician it means something else. It describes a distribution of measurements that, when plotted on graph paper, gives rise to a typical bell-shaped curve (see Figure 8). By convention everything in the tails of the curves, the lowest 2.5 per cent and the highest 2.5 per cent, is called *abnormal*. Using this criterion someone who is 6 foot 6 inches tall is 'abnormally tall' but it is of no clinical consequence.

Just being abnormal does not mean that you are ill or about to become so. A newspaper story in 2004 suggested that wearing a mobile phone might cause sterility. It was based on the tentative findings of a small study in Europe, which found a decrease of up to 30 per cent in the sperm count in people wearing a cell phone compared with a control group who did not. The difference was statistically highly significant. Carrying a mobile phone might possibly be clinically relevant to men on the borderline of fertility who are in their reproductive prime years but would be of no relevance to most men who produce a massive superfluity of sperm. After all, it needs only one sperm to fertilise an ovum.

This brings us to consider who is the 'average person' we hear so much about. People and things may be 'typical' or 'representative' but surely never average. This is a mathematical term and applies only to numbers. Take the newspaper headline '50 PER CENT OF DOCTORS PERFORM LESS WELL THAN AVERAGE'. It gives the reader the impression that all is not well with the practice of medicine. In fact it states only the obvious since, 50 per cent must, by definition perform better and 50 per cent will perform less well than average, but only if you can find a way of expressing performance numerically.

What is less easy to understand is when, instead of using the average, the figure given is something different. It is obviously unlikely that, in spite of what is written in the papers, 60 per cent of UK children weigh more than average unless, to balance the numbers out, there are a lot of extremely underweight children. So when the figure of 60 is given for children who are obese it means something else. Although it is seldom stated, it relates to an artificial level, someone's idea of the ideal size and shape. At the time this was worked out we did not know how many children were above or below this hypothetical ideal. Today it has been found that only 40 per cent of the children fall below it and the other, fatter, 60 per cent are presumed to be overweight.

Few who talk about the supposed 'epidemic of obesity' understand the implication of the figures they use. It is self-evident that those who are just a few pounds over this level are at relatively little risk. It is the few who are *very much* heavier who are the ones at a real disadvantage. One cannot tell from these figures how many people's lives are truly being shortened by their obesity. While it serves to scare people and sell newspapers, unless the way the figure is calculated is given, it is meaningless.

Another potential pitfall is when the figure given is a *median*. A median number tells us that there are as many items on one side of the median number as on the other. Let us consider our student Johnny's examination results. If you were told he scored 60 per cent when the average score in the class of eleven pupils was 50 per cent, you might be well satisfied. However, if three of the eleven boys performed very badly indeed and scored less than 5 per cent, the average for the other eight typical children might reveal Johnny's performance less favourably. If his position in the class was sixth, the median position in the class, you would know that five achieved worse and five achieved better results. In this case his form position might be more revealing. Both figures give valid information, but unless you are told which is being used it can present a misleading impression.

Circumstantial evidence

Many of the scare stories that appear in the media start with an epidemiological study. These compare the rate occurrence or coincidence of two events. Some of these studies are very good, with great care being taken to prevent bias and to limit the effect of outside factors. Nevertheless, they all end up trying to demonstrate an association between a potentially causative factor and an effect.

The problem is that, by itself, evidence of an association between two phenomena is circumstantial and says nothing about their causal relationship to each other, or even if it exists. Take the example given by Darrell Huff in his book *How to Lie with Statistics*: the greatest number of suicides in the UK occur in June. June is also the most popular month for marriages. Does this mean that these two events are related?

Bias

Many studies depend upon the reports of individuals. These can be suspect when they are based on telephone or postal questionnaires. If a study was trying to find out if a particular detergent caused skin irritation and was carried out by post, it is likely that someone not troubled by skin irritation would throw the letter in the bin but one with skin irritation would reply. Unless there was a very high return rate, the results would be subject to bias and be meaningless.

A recent postal questionnaire sent out by the Home Office

reported in 2003 that one in twenty women had been raped. This result is intuitively unlikely. The nature of the questionnaire was bound to give the result it did. It says more about the questioner's bias than the women questioned. One can imagine all those women in an unhappy relationship replying positively to the question, 'Have you ever been sexually assaulted?' whether or not they were actually subject to a physical rape, while most happily married women would laugh while they binned the questionnaire.

The disturbing aspect of this study was not just the waste of taxpayer's money but that the results are likely to be used as the justification for more draconian legislation. Telephone studies are just as likely to be subject to bias, because respondents invariably try to give the answers they think the questioner wants to hear.

Anecdotal evidence

Medicine is not an exact science but a craft based upon the best scientific evidence available: it relies upon the adage that common things occur most often. There will, however, be exceptions to the rule. Some exceptions are predictable, such as the person who lives for ten years after being diagnosed with a condition that carries an average prognosis of a year; some are not only possible but inevitable. The reports of some other unusual events are, however, frankly ridiculous. They start with an anecdotal report and soon become repeated as an accepted fact; they fail to separate a predictable, unusual event from an improbable or impossible one.

Reports appear from time to time of swimmers who have been swept out to sea and are rescued by dolphins who appear and guide them towards the shore. As a result of these anecdotes the story of 'lifesaving' dolphins has gained credence. However, it's likely that it is just a random event and as many dolphins swim out to sea as towards the shore. But we never hear the stories of those swimmers whom dolphins had guided out to sea, because they all drown.

In September 2004, the BBC Radio 4 consumer programme *You and Yours* presented a patient, suffering from a disease whose progress is notoriously difficult to predict, who claimed to have been cured by coffee enemas. The absurdity of this proposition was never questioned. If it was the coffee that saved his life, why did he choose to administer it in such an unpleasant way? Alternatively if it was the enema that cured him, why bother with the coffee? The single anecdotal experience of this patient with his particular fetish was presented as evidence that the orthodox treatment, successfully given to thousands of patients with this disease, was less satisfactory than coffee enemas. In spite of the reported cure, the subject of this report actually died a few months later.

There are many such anecdotal reports, which are given credence by media publicity, like the person whose rheumatism was miraculously cured by sleeping with a magnet under his bed, or the child who went berserk every time he ate a Mars bar. We know of sensible, rational people who believe that wearing a particular-coloured bead can give them vitality and energy.

Tendentious reasoning and the frankly false

Benjamin, aged five, casually remarked, 'God eats a lot of fish.' The background to this improbable assertion was his mother's remark that fish is good for your brain. His tendentious reasoning was that, 'God must be very clever because he can hear what we are saying no matter what language we use.' It follows, therefore, that 'he must eat a lot of fish'.

A report in the *Sunday Times* (August 2004) indicated that salt causes intellectual failure. It appears that an investigation in Boston showed, in a trial of 2,500 people, that high blood pressure was correlated with minor strokes, and minor strokes could cause intellectual degeneration, which is not unreasonable. The author of the report, having read somewhere that salt can cause high blood pressure, twisted the story to implicate salt as the cause of intellectual degeneration. This piece of tendentious reporting ignores the evidence that the Japanese, who eat twice as much salt as an American on average, are no less clever and live longer.

In January 2005 the front page of the *Sunday Times* carried a headline asserting that the tsunami in SE Asia had produced 100,000 orphans. It was based on a report from a children's charity. As the total number of deaths reported at that time was 150,000, assuming each child had to lose two parents to become an orphan and the loss was restricted to only one child per family, then it would have needed 200,000 parents to have been killed to produce the number 100,000 orphans. In fact, since about 80,000 children were included in the total of the dead, the maximum number of orphans that could have been produced was 35,000. The figures are awesome, they did not require the NGO responsible to wave even more shrouds, nor should a responsible paper publish figures that are obviously grossly exaggerated.

Newspapers are often guilty of promoting absurd reports that claim to prevent or cure cancer. A report in *The Times* of 25 January 2005 that 50–65 per cent of all cancers of the kidney can be prevented by eating a banana four to six times a week defies reason, but is virtually impossible to disprove. Should someone who eats four bananas a week develop cancer, then he will automatically fall into the 35–50 per cent of those who, according to the report, do not respond to the prophylactic treatment.

Out of thin air

Then there are numbers apparently picked out of the air but repeated so many times that they develop an authority of their own. Transport for London claims that 20,000 people die each year from atmospheric pollution in London. In fact pollution in London is now lower than it has been for centuries. It is possible that a few severely handicapped people with serious respiratory problems are made worse by diesel fumes from lorries and buses but these are patients on the edge of breathing failure who would not be made better even if they lived in a plastic bubble fed with filtered air.

These figures are frankly false but are constantly repeated by Transport for London in order to justify measures to reduce the use of cars in the city. Because they go unchallenged they become accepted as fact.

With all the numbers that are bandied about to show that this disease or that food is killing us, we should remember that we are living longer, healthier lives and that 'life itself is a fatal disease'. If we do not die of one thing it will increase the death rate from another.

Chapter Thirty-two

EPIDEMIOLOGY

BY STANLEY FELDMAN

'The history of medicine is largely the substitution
of ignorance by fallacies.'
RICHARD GORDON

**THE MYTH: If a particular food is associated with a high death
rate it is dangerous.**
**THE FACT: A casual association is not proof; drinking water is
associated with 100 per cent death rate.**

In the criminal court it is necessary that the case against the
plaintiff should be proven 'beyond reasonable doubt' before
anyone is found guilty. Even in the civil court, where the onus of
proof is reduced, it is necessary to convince the jury that the case
has been established 'on the balance of probabilities'. Even these
rigorous requirements have not stopped occasional prosecutions
from succeeding, only to be shown at a later date that the level of
proof was inadequate or flawed.

When it comes to medicine and healthcare, however,

circumstantial evidence, sometimes of the most tendentious nature, is frequently accepted as sufficient proof for health campaigns that may affect the lifestyle of many, the appointment of health tsars to oversee these changes, and the vilification of anyone who opposes them. The research that generates this circumstantial evidence is called *epidemiology*.

Epidemiology sets out to show a meaningful correlation between a particular circumstance and an event that subsequently occurs. If a positive association is uncovered it is implied that the circumstance studied is the cause of that event. By itself, such an association can only be circumstantial and should never be accepted as sufficient proof of a relationship between the cause and the effect. Only the accumulation of evidence by experimentation can provide proof of such a relationship. A negative association between two events, although seldom published, is however, good evidence that there is no cause-and-effect relationship.

Not all epidemiological research comes up with the wrong answers. It often points the researcher in the right direction. But by itself it cannot prove anything beyond reasonable doubt. It has produced notable successes, suggesting that there is a correlation between a particular disease state and a causative factor, but even the best of these studies produces only evidence that is circumstantial and needs to be subjected to further investigation in order to prove a point. No epidemiological study should be accepted as proof, or its results propagated, until supportive evidence is available. This is particularly true when the results run counter to intuitive reason.

Many years ago, in the mid-nineteenth century, Professor Robert Koch, the discoverer of the bacillus that caused tuberculosis, enumerated the necessary conditions for proof that condition A was caused by B.

The most important of these was that:

- the causative factor B must always be present in condition A
- removing the causative factor B must lessen or cure condition A
- reintroducing B must reproduce A.

Merely demonstrating a statistical relationship between A and B comes nowhere near the standard that Koch required for proof, no matter how carefully the conditions are controlled or what allowance is made in the study to offset any potential source of bias. A casual coincidence between two events remains circumstantial until a causative relationship is proved or Koch's three principal conditions of proof are fulfilled.

Epidemiological successes

In 1854 John Snow removed the handle of the water pump in Broad Street, London, providing evidence to support his theory that cholera was due to drinking contaminated water. This was the first significant adventure in epidemiology and earned him the sobriquet of the 'father of epidemiology'.

It was not a random act but was the result of a truly scientific investigation. Snow had observed that, in his Soho parish, those who drew their water from the Broad Street pump suffered a very high incidence of cholera, while neighbours who used a nearby pump, with water coming from another source, did not. He removed the pump handle to stop people using water from the suspect pump. The incidence of new cases of cholera fell to one, and that patient had used old contaminated water. This provided Snow with proof that the source of the cholera was in the water coming from the pump.

His idea was not predicated on the removal of the pump handle, nor was it proof of the cause of cholera. He did not know that it was caused by a microbe. His study had shown that cholera occurred in those drinking water from the Broad Street pump, and that removing this source stopped the disease. He had demonstrated two of Koch's postulates. Epidemiological research of this sort, used to support or disprove a theory, is valuable and its results constitute legitimate proof.

In 1956 Richard Doll and Bradford Hill published his epoch-making epidemiological study on smoking and cancer of the lung. This alerted us to the very real dangers of smoking. By comparing two very large groups of reasonably matched adults, Doll was able to demonstrate a dramatically increased risk of cancer of the lungs in smokers. What gave this study credence, raising it above the level of circumstantial evidence, was that he showed that the risk increased with the number of cigarettes smoked and the duration of smoking. It was dose-related. His results fitted in with scientific and intuitive reasoning. However, it remained only a casual association until it was demonstrated that those who stopped smoking dramatically reduced the risk of developing cancer of the lung. This later study fulfilled Koch's second postulate. No doubt if it had been ethical to reintroduce smoking in those who had given it up, the third postulate could also have been demonstrated.

Compare these studies with more recent ones, which have been used to justify attempts to coerce behavioural changes or social changes, and one begins to see the weakness of epidemiological evidence.

Too many variables

Several epidemiological studies have demonstrated an association between income and longevity of life. It has been deduced from these that poverty causes disease. This conclusion is intuitively suspect, as the actual causes of many of the common diseases are known and only casually related to the income of those who suffer them. The definition of poverty keeps changing; it varies from place to place and is not necessarily a reflection of income but rather of a way of life. There are many different causes of poverty and its effects are far from uniform.

Poverty may be caused by the disease itself, which may limit the patient's ability to work. A low income in one group may be associated with insanitary housing, while in another it may be reflected in the diet. It is impossible to separate any one cause or to produce evidence of any particular element, such as bad housing, poor level of knowledge, unhealthy lifestyle, depression, bad diet or an ethnic genetic susceptibility, because of the lack of specificity in the study. As a result, these studies are impossible to interpret in a scientifically meaningful manner.

There is little evidence that removing these people from poverty reverses the reduced life expectancy, at least in the short term. The association between poverty and health shown in these studies is undoubtedly valid, but they cannot be taken as proven evidence that it is the poverty itself, the low income, that is the cause of a shortened life expectancy.

If one takes a blunderbuss approach to a disease and casts one's net too wide by studying all the possible circumstances with which it could be associated, one of them is likely to show a positive correlation with something – but this does not constitute evidence that it alone is the cause of the problem. One such study suggested that there was an association between pesticide in food and brain tumours. The view was then promulgated that pesticides caused tumours of the brain. However it ignored the absence of brain tumours in crop sprayers – the group of people exposed to the greatest dose of pesticides for the longest period.

Those advocating a ban on smoking in public places often quote an epidemiological study indicating a link between parental smoking habits and childhood asthma. Smoking, for all its ill effects on health, has never been implicated as a cause of asthma; indeed before 1960, when cigarette smoking was widespread, the incidence of childhood asthma was much lower than at present. Another study found that passive smoking was more dangerous than actually inhaling the smoke directly. The laws of physics dictate that the concentration of any noxious substance contained in the smoke would decrease by the square of the distance it travelled. It would be four times less when the distance was doubled and sixteen times more dilute when the range was increased fourfold. Common sense suggests that the conclusions drawn from these studies are wrong. While one can sympathise with the objectives of those trying to dissuade people from smoking, this should not involve bad science

Meta-analysis

This important-sounding technique hides a statistical trick that is commonly used to support tendentious epidemiological results. It combines the results of several studies so as to boost the numbers, the so-called 'power' of the investigation. It is a technique that is open to abuse. By combining the results of ten bad studies, it is suggested, we end up with one good one.

The methods used in the various studies often differ significantly, as do the methods used for the collection of data, the criteria for inclusion in the investigation, and the numbers involved. The end result is then rehashed as additional new evidence, which can now be said to 'be supported by the work of many scientists'. It is frequently used to lump studies together so as to disguise their individual weaknesses. (See also Chapter Thirty-one, 'The Misuse of Numbers'.)

Bad science

Another example of the failure to encompass the complexity of the problem being studied and, as a result, coming to the wrong conclusion occurred in 1954 in the USA. Two eminent doctors from the Massachusetts General Hospital, Henry Beecher and Professor D.A. Todd, investigated the effect of the introduction of curare, a muscle-relaxant drug, on anaesthetic mortality. Their large study was carried out in ten US teaching institutions. Beecher and Todd found that the mortality rate associated with the use of curare was four times higher in the patients receiving the drug than in patients who did not receive curare. As a result, they concluded that the use of curare was lethal. The use of curare fell dramatically in the USA and it was many years before its use was re-established in America.

The results ran counter to the experience in the UK, where it was used in far bigger doses than in America and in a greater variety of cases. Beecher and Todd came to the wrong conclusion – they had ignored the effect on anaesthetic mortality of the way the drug was being used. The students and nurses who used the drug most frequently in America were not properly trained, and they did not appreciate the need for artificial ventilation or the need to reverse any residual effect of the drug at the end of an operation. It was not the drug that killed patients – it was the way it was used.

Unlikely results

Too small a study or a freak sample group can reveal coincidences that defy reason. The extrapolation of the results obtained from a specific study to a wider, general population can produce unjustified conclusions. A study carried out in 2005 came to the conclusion that cot deaths were due to the practice of parents' sleeping with their baby in the same bed. Some babies may have died from this cause, which can be described as accidental smothering, but they are not cot deaths. Because of the rarity of cot deaths, the numbers studied are unlikely to be sufficient. A study would need to follow at least a million babies before it produced meaningful results.

Darrel Huff suggested that there is a direct correlation between the number of storks nesting in Denmark each year and the number of live births in the country. However, to deduce from this that the babies' arrival was due to the storks would be unlikely to be accepted by most people! Yet people seem ready to believe the improbable when some epidemiological questionnaire carried out for someone's PhD thesis comes up with comparable nonsense

A recent study found that the people of the island of Okinawa lived longer than those in the USA or Europe. This was attributed to eating a diet based on yams. It was concluded that if we eat more yams we would live longer. Apart from the fact that it is impossible to prove (or disprove) without a study that lasted longer than a lifetime, it ignored the fact that ethnically similar Japanese also had a similar long life expectancy. The effect is probably genetic rather than food- or environment-related.

Another study suggested that the use of antiperspirants could cause cancer of the breast. This is intuitive nonsense. Even if antiperspirants did influence the incidence of the disease, it would require an enormous study over twenty years to determine any contributory effect. The extrapolation of the results of the well-designed study on long-term hormone-replacement therapy (HRT) with a combination of drugs hardly ever used today, to the risk associated with current medication, caused a panic in all users of HRT.

Just as misleading are the generalisations made from studies of an effect in an artificially restricted area, or with a particular causative factor. One of the most influential of these studies was the demonstration of clusters of children with leukaemia in certain areas near the Sellafield nuclear reprocessing plant. This has been extrapolated to suggest that 'nuclear anything' causes leukaemia. It has fuelled the totally irrational fear of nuclear energy. There is plenty of good scientific evidence that there is no correlation between a low background of radioactive emissions, such as occur naturally in Cornwall and Scotland, and leukaemia. It is also known that clusters of leukaemia occur where there is no possible source of radioactivity.

Unfortunately, the more bizarre the coincidence revealed in an epidemiological survey, the more publicity it receives and the more likely it becomes that people will take it as factual evidence.

Let us assume we have carried out a survey on the relationship between obesity and cancer. In the control group of a thousand people, ten were found to have developed cancer during the five years of the study, while twelve out of the thousand developed the disease in the obese group. One can see the headlines claiming that there is a 20 per cent greater risk of cancer if you are overweight. However, there is also evidence that fat people who develop cancer live longer than thin ones. As a result there will inevitably be more fat people alive with cancer than thin ones at any time, and this could account for these figures. To base government advice on this type of epidemiological evidence is dangerous. There are plenty of possible reasons why fat people have a slightly higher incidence of cancer than thin people, while the evidence that obesity causes cancer is poor.

It is an unfortunate product of information technology that it is increasingly easy to collect numbers. Numbers are used to determine policy, to reward effort and to condemn those not reaching targets. Nearly all of these numbers demonstrate a crude correlation between two events; they are in fact epidemiological studies. The government uses these fallible epidemiological statistics as though they were proven evidence. They are used to assess the achievement of education, policing, health policies and social behaviour. These raw statistics are meaningless unless and until they have been subject to corroboration by other means. To show that drinking red wine or eating vegetables is associated with a reduced incidence of cancer does not by itself prove that red wine and vegetables prevent cancer. It could be that those drinking the wine or eating the vegetables do not live long enough to suffer from the cancer! It is only whole-life survival studies that prove that this explanation is nonsense.

A casual association of two events does not constitute proof. It is, at best, circumstantial evidence. It should not be used to infer that some schools achieve worse results than others, or some police forces arrest more criminals than others, or some food fads are healthy, unless there is other supporting evidence.

In this world of instant information, the accuracy and validity of circumstantial evidence and the casual association of two events is too readily accepted as proof. Every day the news media regale us with 'proof', nearly always based upon some epidemiological study, that this or that effect causes ill health. Often there is insufficient analysis of the way the information is collected and of the influence of factors that cannot be controlled when the significance of the data is evaluated. We must recognise epidemiological surveys for what they are and treat their results with caution – they merely constitute circumstantial evidence that would not stand up in any court of law although the results may be the reason for undertaking further investigation.

FURTHER READING

A list of references to articles in the text is held by the publisher

Action Aid, 'Going Against the Grain' (May 2003).

Alderman, M H et al, 'Dietary Sodium Intake and Mortality: the National Health and Nutrition Examination Survey (NHANES I)', *Lancet*, 351 (1998), pp. 781-5

Alderman, M H, 'Salt, blood pressure and human health', *Hypertension* (2000), pp. 368-90.

Andres R, 'Mortality and Obesity: the rationale for age-specific height-weight tables,' *Principles of Geriatric Medicine:* editors Andres R, Bierman, EL and Hazzard W R (New York: McGraw-Hill Books, 1985).

Atkins, R, *Diet Revolution* (London: Vermillion, 2003).

'Bamboozled, Baffled and Bombarded', Report of National Consumer Council, 2002.

Bender, D A, 'Non-nutritional uses of vitamin B6', *British Journal of Nutrition*, 81 (1999), pp. 7–20.

Bennett, W, and Gurin, J, *The Dieter's Dilemma* (1982).

Blot, W J, et al, 'Nutrition intervention trials in Linxian, China: supplementation with specific vitamin/mineral combinations, cancer incidence, and disease-specific mortality in the general population', *Journal of the National Cancer Institute*, 85 (1993), pp. 1483–92.

Bookchain, M, *Re-enchanting Humanity: A defence of the human spirit against antihumanism, misanthropy and primitivism* (1995).

Bowry, V W, et al, 'Vitamin E in human low-density lipoprotein.

When and how this antioxidant becomes a pro-oxidant', *Biochemical Journal*, 288 (1992), pp. 341–4.

Brignall, John, 'Complete list of things that can give you cancer', www.spiked-online.co.uk

'Clear Labelling Task Force', Food Standards Agency, 2002
Degregori, T R, *Origins of the Organic Agriculture Debate*
(Blackwell Publishing, 2003)

Department of Health, 'Dietary Reference Values for Food Energy
and Nutrients for the United Kingdom' (London: HMSO, 1991)
Department of Health, 'Folic Acid and the Prevention of Disease'
(London: HMSO, 2000).

Department of Health: Committee on the Medical Effects of
Air Pollutants, 'Non-biological particles and health' (London:
HMSO, 1995).

Dickerson, W T, and Lee, H A, *Nutrition in the Clinical
Management of Disease* (Arnold, 1978).

'Dietary Reference Values for Food Energy and Nutrients for the
United Kingdom: Report of the Panel on Dietary Reference
Values of the Committee on Medical Aspects of Food Policy',
Report on Health and Social Subjects, 41 (London: HMSO, 1991).

'Diet, Nutrition and Preventing Chronic Disease', WHO, 2002
Dixon-Woods, M, 'Writing wrongs? An analysis of published
discourses about the use of patient information leaflets',
Soc Sci Med 52 (2001), pp. 1417-32

Doll, R, and Bradford Hill, A, 'Smoking and Carcinoma of the
Lung', *BMJ* (September 1950), pp. 740-9.

Doll, R, and Bradford Hill, A, 'Lung cancer and other causes of death in relation to smoking', *BMJ* (1956), pp. 1071-81.

Doll, R, and Bradford Hill, A, 'Mortality of doctors in relation to their smoking habits', *BMJ* (June 1954), pp. 1451-5.

Douglas, R M, et al, 'Vitamin C for preventing and treating the common cold', *Cochrane Database Systematic Review*, 2, CD001980.

Emsley, J, *The Consumers' Good Chemical Guide* (1994).

Examination Survey (NHANES I), *Lancet,* 351 (1998), pp. 781-5.

Expert Group on Vitamins and Minerals, www.foodstandards.gov.uk/science/ouradvisors/vitamind.

FAO/WHO, 'Human Vitamin and Mineral Requirements: Report of a joint FAO/WHO expert consultation' (2001).

Fairfield, K M, and Fletcher, R H, 'Vitamins for chronic disease prevention in adults: scientific review', *Journal of the American Medical Association*, 287 (2002), pp. 3116–26.

Fitzpatrick, Dr M, 'A Sickening White Paper', www.spiked-online.co.uk

Fitzpatrick, Dr M, *MMR and Autism: What Parents Need to Know* (London: Routledge, 2004).

Flechsig, E, and Weissmann, C, 'The Role of PrP in Health and Disease', *Curr Mol Med* 4(4), pp. 337-53.

Furedi, F, 'The Politics of Fear', *spiked*, 28 October 2004, http://www.spiked-online.com/Printable/00000000CA760.htm
Gennari, C, 'Calcium and vitamin D nutrition and bone disease of the elderly', *Public Health Nutrition*, 4 (2001), pp. 547–59.

Gey, K F, 'Cardiovascular disease and vitamins. Concurrent correction of "suboptimal" plasma antioxidant levels may, as important part of "optimal" nutrition, help to prevent early stages of cardiovascular disease and cancer, respectively', *Biblio Nutritio et Dieta*, 52 (1995), pp. 75–91.

Glinsmann W, Irausquin H, Park YK, 'Report from FDA's Sugars Task Force 1986: evaluation of health aspects of sugars contained in carbohydrate sweetners', *Journal of Nutrition*, 116 (November 1986), Supplement 118.

Hackshaw, AK, Law, MR, Wald, NJ, 'The accumulated evidence on lung cancer and environmental tobacco smoke', *BMJ*, 315 (1997), pp 980-8.

Hawker, R W, 'Renal and Body Fluids', *Notebook of Medical Physiology* (1982).

Heath, C W, 'Passive smoking', *Lancet*, 1 (1993), p. 526.

Hennekens, C. H., et al, 'Lack of effect of long-term supplementation with beta carotene on the incidence of malignant neoplasms and cardiovascular disease', *New England Journal of Medicine*, 334 (1996), pp. 1145–9.

Higginbotham, A R et al, *Aspects of Applied Biology*, 62 (2000), pp. 15-20.

Holick, M F, 'The use and interpretation of assays for vitamin D and its metabolites', *Journal of Nutrition*, 120, Suppl. 11 (1990), pp. 1464–9.

Homocysteine-Lowering Trialists' Collaboration, 'Lowering blood homocysteine with folic acid based supplements: meta-analysis of randomized trials', *BMJ*, 316 (1998), pp. 894-8.

Hooper, L et al, 'Systemic review of long term effects of advice to reduce dietary salt in adults', *British Medical Journal*, 325 (2002), pp. 628-36.

House of Lords Select Committee, 'Organic Fanning and the European Union', 1999.

Huff, D, *How to Live with Statistics* (Pelican Books, 1979).
'Improving Children's Diet', Parliamentary Office of Science and Technology, (London: HMSO, 2003).

Institute of Medicine, *Dietary Reference Intakes for Calcium, Phosphorus, Magnesium, Vitamin D and Fluoride* (Washington, DC: National Academy Press, 1997).

Institute of Medicine, *Dietary Reference Values for Thiamin, Riboflavin, Niacin, Vitamin B6, Folate, Vitamin B12, Pantothenic Acid, Biotin and Choline* (Washington, DC: National Academy Press, 1998).

Institute of Medicine, *Dietary Reference Intakes for Vitamin A, Vitamin K, Arsenic, Boron, Chromium, Copper, Iodine, Iron, Manganese, Molybdenum, Nickel, Silicon, Vanadium and Zinc* (Washington, DC: National Academy Press, 2001).

Institute of Medicine, *Dietary Reference Values for Vitamin C, Vitamin E, Selenium and Carotenoids* (Washington DC: National Academy Press, 2000).

International Co-Operative Salt Research Group, 'An international study of electrolyte excretion and blood pressure', *British Medical Journal*, 297 (1988), pp. 319-28.

Klatsky, A L, 'Drink to your Health', *Scientific American*, 283 (Feb 2003), p. 62-9

Lachmann, P J, 'Diet and Diseases: Facts and Fantasies', 1999, http://www.acmedsci.ac.uk/f_pubs.htm

Lomborg, B, *The Skeptical Environmentalist* (Cambridge University Press, 2001).

Macdonald, V, 'Passive smoking doesn't cause cancer – official', *Sunday Telegraph* (March 1998).

Maddox, J, 'The Doomsday Syndrome', *Lancet* (1972).

Mason, T J, 'The descriptive epidemiology of lung cancer', in Samet, J (ed), *Epidemiology of Lung Cancer* (Marcel Dekker, 1994), pp. 52–5.

Meadows, D, et al, *Limits to Growth* (Potomac, 1972).

Meleady, R, and Graham, I, 'Plasma homocysteine as a cardiovascular risk factor: causal, consequential, or of no consequence?', *Nutrition Reviews*, 57 (1999), pp. 299–305.

Moore, P, 'Environmentalism for the 21st century', www.greenspirit.com

'New Approaches to define Nutrient Requirements', *American Journal of Clinical Nutrition*, 63 (1996), pp. 983s–1001s.

NHS Centre for Reviews and Dissemination, 'Report 18: A Systematic Review of Water Fluoridation' (September 2000), http://www.york.ac.uk/inst/crd/pdf/fluorid.pdf

Nuffield Council on Bio-ethics, *GM Crops in Developing Countries* (2004), p. 53.

Nuffield Council on Bio-ethics, 'GM crops: ethical and social issues' (1999),

http://www.nuffieldbioethics.org/go/ourwork/gmcrops/publication_301.html

Omenn, G S, 'Effects of a combination of beta carotene and vitamin A on lung cancer and cardiovascular disease', *New England Journal of Medicine*, 334 (1996), pp. 1150–5.

Parliamentary Office of Science and Technology, 'Improving Children's Diet', report (September 2003).

Pastana, C, *Fluids and Electrolytes* (Baltimore: Williams & Wilkins, 1980).

Rayman, M, 'The importance of selenium to human health', *Lancet*, 356 (2000), pp. 233-41.

Reichman, W J, *Use and Abuse of Statistics* (Penguin Books, 1952).

Roitt, I, *Essential Immunology* (Blackwell Scientific, 1979).

Royal Society, 'GMOs and Pusztai' (1999).

Royal Society, 'Transgenic Plants and World Agriculture' (July 2000), http://www.agbios.com/docroot/articles/2000192-A.pdf

Ruxton, C H S, et al, 'The impact of long-chain n-3 polyunsaturated fatty acids on human health', *Nutrition Research Reviews*, 18 (2005).

Schlosser, Eric, *Fast Food Nation* (Penguin Books, 2002).

Shimizu, T, 'Health claims on functional foods: the Japanese regulations and an international comparison', *Nutrition Research Reviews*, 16, pp. 241–52.

Shrimpton, D, 'Vitamins and Minerals: A Scientific Evaluation of the Range of Safe Intakes', European Federation of Health Product Manufacturers (Brussels, 1997).

Starr, Sandy, 'Science, risk and the price of precaution', www.spiked-online.co.uk

Stephens, N G, et al, 'Randomised controlled trial of vitamin E in patients with coronary disease: Cambridge Heart Antioxidant Study (CHAOS)', *Lancet*, 347 (1996), pp. 781–6.

Sullivan, L P, and Grantham, J J, *Physiology of the Kidney* (Philadelphia, 1982).

'Symposium on Optimum Nutrition', *Proceedings of the Nutrition Society*, 58 (1999), pp. 395–512.

Tallis, R, *Hippocratic Oaths: medicine and discontents* (2004).

Taubes, G, 'The political science of salt', *Science*, 281 (1998), pp. 898-907.

The GM Science Review, 2003/2004, http://www.gmsciencedebate.org.uk/

Thomas, M J, and Giblin, V, 'Cure of cutaneous melanoma', *British Medical Journal*, 332, (2006), pp. 987-88.

Timio, M, et al, 'Age and blood pressure changes: a 20-year follow up of nuns in a secluded order', *Hypertension*, 12 (1988), pp. 457-61.

Trewavas, A J, 'Urban Myths of Organic Farming', *Nature*, 409 (2001).

Upston, J, 'Tocopherol-mediated peroxidation of lipoproteins: implications for vitamin E as a potential antiatherogenic supplement', *FASEB Journal*, 13 (1999), pp. 977–94.

Verney, E B, 'Renal Excretion of Water and Salt', *Lancet*, 1237 (1957).

Vieth, R, 'Vitamin D supplementation, 25-hydroxyvitamin D concentrations, and safety', *American Journal of Clinical Nutrition*, 69 (1999), pp. 842–56.

Wang, X-D, and Russell, R, 'Procarcinogenic and anticarcinogenic effects of ß-carotene', *Nutrition Reviews*, 57 (1999), pp. 263–72.

Will, R, 'Variant Creutzfeldt-Jakob disease' *Folia Neuropathol*, 42, Suppl. A (2004), pp. 77–83.

Willett W C, and Stampfer, M J, 'Rebuilding the Food Pyramid', *Scientific American*, 298 (Jan 2003), pp. 52-59.

Williams, R T, *Detoxication Mechanisms*
(London: Chapman Hall, 1947).

Young, A J, and Lowe, G M, 'Antioxidant and pro-oxidant
properties of carotenoids', *Archives of Biochemistry and
Biophysics*, 385 (2001), pp. 20–7.